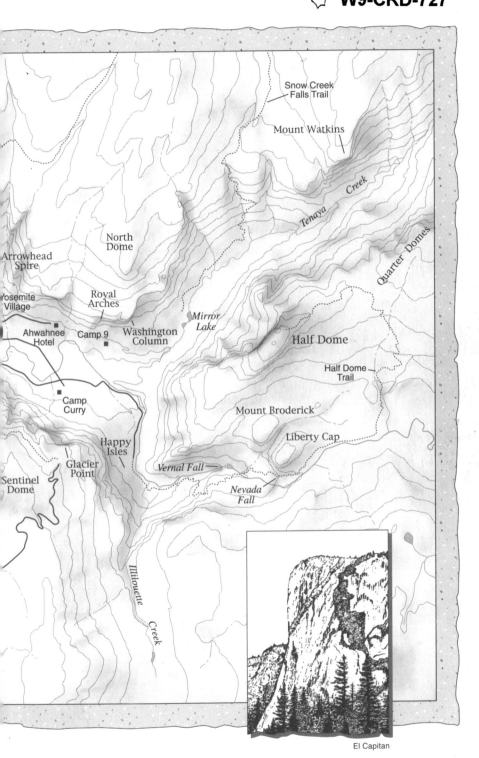

Snow Creek
Falls Trail

Mount Watkins

Tenaya Creek

Quarter Domes

North
Dome

Arrowhead
Spire

Yosemite
Village

Royal
Arches

Mirror
Lake

Ahwahnee
Hotel

Camp 9

Washington
Column

Half Dome

Half Dome
Trail

Camp
Curry

Mount Broderick

Liberty Cap

Happy
Isles

Glacier
Point

Vernal Fall

Sentinel
Dome

Nevada
Fall

Illilouette Creek

El Capitan

CAMP 4

Recollections of a Yosemite Rockclimber

CAMP 4

Recollections of a Yosemite Rockclimber

Steve Roper

THE
MOUNTAINEERS

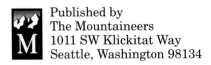 Published by
The Mountaineers
1011 SW Klickitat Way
Seattle, Washington 98134

8 7 6 5 4
5 4 3 2 1

Published simultaneously in Great Britain by Bâton Wicks Publications, London. All trade inquiries to: Cordee, 3a DeMontfort Street, Leicester, England, LE1 7HD

Published simultaneously in Canada by Douglas & McIntyre, Ltd., 1615 Venables Street, Vancouver, B.C. V5L 2H1

Manufactured in the United States of America

Edited by Linda Gunnarson
Cover design by Watson Graphics
Book typesetting and design by The Mountaineers Books
Book layout by Virginia Hand

Cover photograph: Climber and Upper Yosemite Fall (Photo: Galen Rowell/ Mountain Light)
Frontispiece: Stemming up the Meat Grinder, a 5.10 crack route (Photo: Roger Breedlove/Ascent Collection)
Endpaper map: Matt Kania

Library of Congress Cataloging in Publication Data
Roper, Steve.
    Camp 4 : recollections of a Yosemite rockclimber / Steve Roper.
    p.   cm.
    Includes bibliographical references (p.   ) and index.
    ISBN 0-89886-381-3
    1. Rock climbing--California--Yosemite Valley--History.
    2. Mountaineers--United States--Biography. I. Title. II. Title:
    Camp four.
GV199.42.C22Y6763 1994
796.5'223'0979447--dc20   94-3505
                                                            CIP

Contents

The seasons still exert their magic, rejuvenating influence on the earth, and the earth is herself, and the Cathedral Rocks and El Capitan still remind you that life is a significant experience, and the smell of bay mixed with pine on an isolated ledge carries nostalgia from another world, yours, one which blacktops and glittering restaurants have failed to invade. Things are unchanged. There is calm.

—Mike Borghoff, 1962

Just why is Yosemite climbing so different? Why does it have techniques, ethics and equipment all of its own? The basic reason lies in the nature of the rock itself. Nowhere else in the world is the rock so exfoliated, so glacier-polished, and so devoid of handholds. All of the climbing lines follow vertical crack systems. Every piton crack, every handhold is a vertical one. Special techniques and equipment have evolved through absolute necessity.

—Yvon Chouinard, 1963

Preface

I avoided writing this book for many years, thirty to be exact. In my possession is a copy of a wildly enthusiastic letter written to Yosemite pioneer Allen Steck in June 1964: "You and I must write the history of Valley climbing!" it begins. "You'll take the old guys; I'll do the modern stuff." Steck replied cautiously, thinking of the work involved, and our project died after another exchange of letters. Now, of course, I'm glad this happened, for Yosemite climbing was still in its infancy in 1964. What if we had written a book when only four routes existed on El Capitan? When Frank Sacherer and Chuck Pratt had not yet begun their mad scramble to eliminate artificial aid from walls big and small? When we had never heard the names Madsen, Schmitz, Hennek, Lauria, Davis, or Kroger?

During the last few years, whenever I told stories about the old days in Camp 4, listeners would beg me to "get it down on paper," as if a wine-induced campfire rave could simply be translated word for word into a coherent story. Steck was right: writing a climbing history is a lot of work. This was why I waited, always thinking someone else would do it. No one did. Then, in May 1990, my friend Hugh Swift insisted that I "write it down before it's too late." Eight months later Hugh died suddenly, on a shockingly ordinary day; he would never write about his beloved Himalaya again. I saw his point; we are mortal, and when we die, a vast storehouse of unique information goes with us.

Other friends pressed me hard also, including Royal Robbins and Jim Sims. But the catalyst was Steck, who, in 1992, casually mentioned to The Mountaineers Books that I was the ideal person to write about the halcyon days of Valley climbing. Donna DeShazo, director of that publishing house, responded within days, catching me off guard with her flattery. Who could resist? To all these people, I owe my thanks: I couldn't have even begun the project without your support.

To put into print the recollections of a bygone era is like traversing unroped along a frightfully exposed ridge. On one side lies the void ruled by the Knave of Embellishment, that devil who whispers, "Your story's not that powerful; make it juicier." On the other side of the ridge resides

7

the Champion of Truth, imploring always, "Write only what's provable, what's on the record." No writer can deal with personal events without becoming aware of treading this narrow arête. Present beliefs about the past can significantly alter our perceptions of long-ago events. For instance, as a reasonably mature adult, I now find some of my youthful escapades embarrassing. Could I really have been all *that* crude? And, writing about the old days from a more mature perspective, have I toned down events or overjustified my behavior? All I can say is that I've tried to tell it like it was.

Many climbers helped me along the path, though any flaws that remain, of course, are mine. The following people dredged their brains for memories, writing extensive letters, chatting at length on the phone, or loaning me diaries or other historical material: Eric Beck, Rich Calderwood, Yvon Chouinard, Nick Clinch, Dave Cook, Mike Corbett, Scott Davis, Bill Dunmire, John Evans, Tom Frost, Morgan Harris, Mort Hempel, Tom Higgins, Al Macdonald, Elaine Matthews, Wayne Merry, Bruce Meyer, John Morton, Royal Robbins, Jan Sacherer, George Sessions, John Shonle, Bill Stall, Allen Steck, Bob Swift, and Frank Tarver.

Others who helped in various ways with information or advice were Jerry Anderson, Eric Brand, Floyd Burnette, Ad Carter, R. D. Caughron, Gerry Czamanske, Jeff Dozier, Jules Eichorn, Joe Fitschen, Jeff Foott, Warren Harding, John Harlin III, Marilyn Harlin, Richard Hechtel, Steve Jervis, Ellen Searby Joli, Chris Jones, Tom Jukes, Bob Kamps, Joe Kelsey, Chuck Kroger, Doris Leonard, Dick Long, Norma Limp, George Meyers, Jim Needham, Wally Reed, Galen Rowell, Lowell Skoog, Claude Suhl, John Thackray, Walt Vennum, Ken Wilson, and Les Wilson.

In addition to sifting through all the information supplied by the above-mentioned people, I obtained contemporary material from the hundreds of letters I received from climbers during the 1950s and 1960s. Somehow I knew these would one day be valuable, and they accompanied me on many a move. Many of the quotes in this book come from these torn and stained letters; some come from interviews; and the majority from those three indispensable journals of the time: *Summit,* the *American Alpine Journal,* and the *Sierra Club Bulletin.* Detailed source information will be found at the end of the book.

Most climbers in the old days didn't own cameras, so it was fortunate that Glen Denny roamed the Valley during the 1960s, taking thousands of black-and-white shots of climbing and climbers. Glen graciously allowed me to sift through his vast collection of negatives, and his splendid portraits of the major Camp 4 players enrich this book in ways that words cannot. Although many of these portraits were taken in the mid- to late sixties, I have often used them to illustrate earlier times.

Librarians are the most unheralded members of our society, I sometimes feel. Unfailingly polite and knowledgeable, they possess a gene that won't let them rest until they've solved a problem. My thanks to two such people, Linda Eade of the Yosemite National Park Library and Phoebe Adams of the Sierra Club Library.

Several people read various versions of the manuscript along the way and steered me in the right direction when I wanted to go elsewhere. Allen Steck looked over the first few chapters; Royal Robbins read them all and offered cogent suggestions and acerbic marginal comments such as "Foul language seems unnecessary here, Steve." Margaret Foster and Donna DeShazo, of The Mountaineers Books, helped keep the project moving along with calmness and professionalism. Freelance editor Linda Gunnarson, a woman I've worked with for sixteen years, knows more about rock climbing and mountaineering than any nonclimber I know. She tactfully offered hundreds of comments, often beginning marginal notes with "Maybe explain here what you mean by...." Finally, my wife, Kathy, endured many nights of "bedtime stories," staving off sleep long enough to catch inconsistencies of logic and forcing me to analyze, more deeply than I had, some of the controversies and philosophical differences of this fascinating group of Camp 4 residents. To all of you, many thanks.

The original Camp 4 entrance sign, now in private hands, 1994 (Photo: Steve Roper)

Introduction

By purest happenstance, unless one believes in divine intervention, I lived in Yosemite Valley's Camp 4 during the 1960s, when a unique American rock-climbing movement was in full swing. The Golden Age of Yosemite climbing—the quarter-century period from 1947 to 1971—began with the first ascent of the Lost Arrow Chimney, at the time the most difficult rock climb ever done. Other remarkable climbs followed shortly, and in Camp 4, and on the great granite cliffs, I witnessed events that in later years took on mythic qualities. I strode among giants, friends tell me now, though at the time I felt more like a misfit associating with oddballs.

The huge walls of Yosemite Valley were virtually untouched as World War II drew to a close. The place was ripe for a climbing transformation: the United States lagged far behind Europe. During the 1930s, in the Alps, the world's best climbers had accomplished dozens of fine routes up fearful mountain faces and steep rock walls. Yosemite, however, presented unique challenges, and it's easy to see why its big walls remained unclimbed. The granite was not only extraordinarily monolithic, but the relatively few crack systems shot straight up—and often ended in the middle of nowhere. This caused problems, for the Valley has few horizontal traverse possibilities, which so often can make a route easier. Yosemite also featured holdless, water-polished jamcracks—and jamming technique was the hardest style of climbing to master. The Valley was also known for its hot weather; even in springtime the temperatures often hovered in the nineties. This meant that lots of water would have to be hauled along on a multiday route. And water is heavy.

Such obstacles presented brand-new challenges with little precedent; Yosemite would obviously require a new style of climbing. Anyone who wanted to get up a huge Valley wall would have to master smooth jamcracks, invent specialized equipment for less-than-perfect piton cracks, and figure out a way to haul big loads up the hot, near-vertical faces. During the 1950s and 1960s a small group of climbers overcame all these difficulties. The rest of the mountain world watched in awe for a decade, then joined in, later spreading out to the stupendous cliffs of Patagonia

11

and Baffin Island, using the techniques developed by Valley climbers.

The climbers who came to the Valley in the 1930s had done some marvelous routes, especially considering they were outfitted with soft pitons, hemp ropes, and floppy tennis shoes. They were the true pioneers of Yosemite climbing. Nevertheless, it was the post–World War II generations who took the word "impossible" out of the American rock-climbing vocabulary. Swiss-born John Salathé was the first to see that artificial climbing would open up vast new possibilities, and his Arrow Chimney climb proved him right. The 1950s opened with the bold climb of Sentinel's north face, done by Salathé and Allen Steck. The two other great climbs of the decade—the northwest face of Half Dome and the Nose of El Capitan—showed that the biggest walls were possible, and the names Royal Robbins and Warren Harding, the respective leaders of these two epics, will forever stand for vision and courage. Later came an incredible free-climbing renaissance, led by talented climbers such as Mark Powell, Chuck Pratt, Bob Kamps, and Frank Sacherer, men who flowed smoothly up the jamcracks and vertical faces that had appalled earlier climbers.

Seeing that the equipment of the day wasn't adequate for Valley climbing, a few visionaries invented some remarkable tools. Salathé hand-forged hard steel pitons; Dick Long and Tom Frost independently developed the wide-angle piton known as a bong-bong; and Yvon Chouinard came up with a tough "postage-stamp piton," the rurp. All three of these innovative devices enabled climbers to nail their way up cracks earlier thought unusable. Robbins devised a splendid new hauling technique, one that allowed longer climbs to be done. Finally, late in the Golden Age, Chouinard and Frost developed a huge variety of nuts, those magical devices brought over from England in the mid-1960s. The cracks of Yosemite, already becoming scarred by pitons, were thus spared further damage.

This twenty-five-year period, with its breathtaking climbing feats and radical equipment innovations, was one of the most significant periods in American climbing history. Little has been written about the period, though bits and pieces of the story are well known. I decided to tell the whole story; this book is both a history of early Valley climbing and a personal reminiscence. I was fortunate enough to meet many of the old-timers when I began climbing as a teenager on the Berkeley, California, practice rocks in the mid-1950s. They taught me a great deal, and by drilling safety techniques into my head probably saved my life a dozen times in the years to come. Later, I met and climbed with virtually every participant of the Golden Age. I am lucky to have come into contact with so many talented and interesting people: not many climbers can say they learned rappelling from Dave Brower, off-width jamming from Chuck Pratt, and hand-crack techniques from Royal Robbins.

Because the 1960s was the formative time in establishing Valley climbing as a world-renowned phenomenon, I concentrate heavily on this decade. In those brief years Camp 4 underwent a massive change. Once the home of about a half-dozen climbing bums—people scorned by most tourists and nonclimbers—the campground sported ten times that number by 1970, and rock climbing had became a respectable activity, one that increasing numbers of park visitors paid money to do.

The reader expecting a blow-by-blow account of every climb done in the Valley from 1933 through 1971 will be disappointed. Several hundred different climbers created 507 routes (including first free ascents) during this period, but most of those ascents added little to the ongoing evolution of Valley climbing. I concentrate on those breakthrough routes that stand out even today as bold or innovative. Neither do I spend much time on the minor players of Valley climbing, though they enjoyed themselves every bit as much as the main stars. Only a few men (women hadn't yet made their mark, though they would) pushed the limits of the possible, and this is their story.

I focus on the most significant climbs, the most visionary climbers, the most far-reaching equipment advances, the most riveting controversies, and the most revealing anecdotes. My choices are subjective, of course. By significant climbs I usually—but not always—mean first ascents of either big walls or fierce jamcracks, climbs that, by their very boldness, upped the ante. By visionary climbers I mean those who saw that the big walls could be climbed using no fixed ropes, or with few bolts, or in a more efficient style, or perhaps with a new kind of equipment. Such people, and there were but a few, thought long and hard about rock climbing and then *acted* on their ideas. By describing the various controversies and showing how certain climbers reacted, I hope to evoke the feisty spirit of the times, when talking about climbing was secondary only to the real thing. By relating anecdotes, usually of the nonclimbing variety, I hope to reveal something of the personalities of these most fascinating people. To keep focused on the subject of Yosemite climbing, however, I include only a few tantalizing details of the participants' "outside" lives. Although a great part of our lives revolved around the good outdoor life, we were not *solely* one-track Yosemite rockclimbers—which this book may seem to imply. We had winter jobs, girlfriends or wives, and nonclimbing friends. We attended concerts and gymnastic meets. We hitchhiked and rode freight trains; we visited the magnificent sandstone towers of the Southwest; we climbed high summits in the Tetons; we skied and backpacked in the High Sierra.

We couldn't keep up this pace forever, and by the early 1970s the most famous Camp 4 cragrats—Pratt, Chouinard, Frost, and Robbins—had given up serious climbing and moved on to other activities. I close my story in 1971, a time when Valley climbing was undergoing a massive upheaval. The 1970 El Cap climb known as the Dawn Wall created a maelstrom of ill feeling, as did the partial "erasure" of the route a few months later. Standing in line to do the standard routes didn't seem much fun, either: climbing was becoming a mainstream activity. The relative solitude of Camp 4 had given way to the crowded conditions of Sunnyside, the renamed camp.

Thus, the early 1970s, to my mind, signal the end of a special era of Valley climbing.

Later climbers, of course, managed astonishing feats, some of which are mentioned in the epilogue of this book. Big walls were done free and superfast; the crack-climbing techniques invented by Pratt and Sacherer were refined to the point where even cracks running under ceilings could be jammed. The story of these later generations, those who inhabited Sunnyside Campground in the seventies and eighties, must be told—and soon will be, I'm sure.

Climbing in the Valley during the 1960s was an intense experience, and few stayed long. Although a small cadre of climbers, including myself, spent about ten springs, ten summers, and ten autumns in the Valley, many others departed after only a few years. This is a thorny problem for a climbing historian, even for one who was there: it is sometimes impossible to recall the specific participants in any given situation. When I use "we" and "us," I am often referring to a revolving group of climbers who came and went through Camp 4.

When writing about documented climbs and well-remembered controversial issues, however, I attempt to assign the credit or blame to those directly responsible. On some subjects, Camp 4 climbers had diametrically opposed views, and one of the major themes of this book concerns the methods by which the big climbs were established. I am unabashedly on the side of the "Valley Christians," as Warren Harding called those who tried to impose a set of ethics to contain the proliferation of fixed ropes and bolts. Some, like Harding, thought climbers shouldn't have to obey such "rules." Others, like Robbins, thought climbers should agree to rely largely on their honed skills and inner strength. If we subdued the big walls with technology, he felt, then the adventurous spirit of climbing would be lost. Both men, of course, were giants in Valley climbing, and we needed both: Harding demonstrated that huge walls were possible in the first place; Robbins demonstrated how *well* such big walls could be done.

I have often wondered how a group of unorthodox young people, mostly in their early twenties, came to spend so much time in the Valley during the 1960s. First of all, of course, we all loved the outdoors, and we loved challenges. It is difficult to explain to a nonclimber the intense physical and mental pleasure that climbing offers. When the muscles work well, when a potentially dangerous problem is solved in a calm and thoughtful manner, when a lazy lunch on a narrow, sunlit ledge high up a cliff seems infinitely better than lying on a Waikiki beach—then one knows Nirvana. Climbing is usually great fun, and if in this book I don't emphasize this aspect often enough, it's because I concentrate on the more serious climbs, the ones where fear was palpable and laughter rare. Yet for every big climb we struggled up, dreading the unknown—and sometimes wishing we were elsewhere, perhaps on the beach at Waikiki—we accomplished dozens of lesser routes that offered pure kinesthetic joy.

Still, why did we spend so much time in the Valley?

Perhaps the key word is "rebellion." Many of us regarded the 1950s and 1960s as a time when the world—and especially our country—had lost its way. We saw materialism and complacence during the Eisenhower years. John Kennedy gave youth hope, but the events at Dallas made youth despair. An outpost called Vietnam forced its way into an unwilling national psyche. It was a hard time to be proud of our country. Perhaps we stayed close to the cliffs because we didn't want to join mainstream society. We Valley cragrats of the sixties were mostly college dropouts going nowhere, fast. Intellects inhabited the campground—and so did an equal number of pseudo-intellects. We were gentle folk but quietly assertive, even boisterous at times.

Few among our group could be called neurotic, but there's no doubt we were socially backward. "Who here has ever been to a dance?" someone once asked at a campfire. A dozen climbers—fit, not particularly ugly, mostly virginal young males—pondered the question. One of us finally ventured: "I went to a high-school prom once, but I didn't dance." These same rebellious eccentrics, however, were the most gifted rockclimbers in the world, and I hope I evoke their spirit and their times.

CHAPTER 1

The Profound Abyss: 1933–1946

Looking back upon the climb, we find our greatest satisfaction in having demonstrated, at least to ourselves, that by the proper application of climbing technique extremely difficult ascents can be made in safety.... If any member of the party had fallen, his injuries would, at the worst, have been a few scratches and bruises.

—Bestor Robinson, ruminating on the 1934 climb of the Higher Cathedral Spire

Yosemite Valley had hardly been first encountered by whites before the accolades poured in. Horace Greeley, heeding his own famous advice, went west, visiting the site in 1859 and calling it "the profound abyss." He went on to say that he knew "no single wonder of nature on earth which can claim superiority over the Yosemite." John Muir later called the Valley "the grandest, most divine of all earthly dwelling places." Ralph Waldo Emerson offered a more folksy compliment: "This valley is the only place that comes up to the brag about it, and exceeds it."

Yosemite Valley defies easy description. As Muir put it, "every attempt to appreciate any one feature is beaten down by the overwhelming influence of all the others...." Located high up the western slope of California's Sierra Nevada, the Valley, on the most rudimentary level, is simply a deep granite slot in the earth's surface. A mile wide, seven miles long, and about 3,000 feet deep, the walls of this U-shaped trench are huge, white, and exceptionally clean and steep. Waterfalls plunge over the rim; noble forests and acres of meadowlands line the 4,000-foot-high Valley floor. One of the most serene rivers anywhere, the Merced, snakes through this paradise powerfully but with hardly a single ripple, so level is the Valley floor. This small Shangri-la, one of the most beautiful spots of our planet, is by far the most striking feature of 1,200-square-mile Yosemite National Park, a wilderness of rugged mountains and remote canyons.

J. Smeaton Chase, an English traveler, described Yosemite Valley in 1911 as "a great cleft, or chasm, which one might imagine to have been the work of some exasperated Titan who, standing with feet placed fifty miles apart...raised his hands palm to palm over his head, and struck upon the earth with such fury as to cleave a gap nearly a mile in depth...." Vivid though this image is, the story of Yosemite's creation is equally dramatic— even though it happened a little more slowly. As the Sierra was uplifted during millions of years in the Tertiary Period, a river began cutting a trench, eventually forming a significant V-shaped canyon. The greatest period of uplift came two million years ago, and the raging river plucked away the weaker rock and deepened the canyon even further. Then, about a million years ago, came the first of several ice ages, the principal agents that formed the Valley we see today. The Valley was utterly buried by the largest of these ice sheets; only the top 700 feet of Half Dome and the last few hundred feet of El Capitan rose above the glacial expanse. For hundreds of centuries at a time the future site of Camp 4 lay frozen beneath

Yosemite Valley from the west. El Capitan rises on the left; Half Dome and Sentinel Rock are visible left and right, respectively, of the spindly treetop in the center. (Photo: Glen Denny)

the ice. The walls of the Valley were smoothed and polished constantly by the inexorable movement of the glaciers, the last of which retreated only about 10,000 years ago; the nearest remnants—pocket glaciers at high elevation—lie some twenty miles to the east.

Many people savor every aspect of this splendid geological wonder, paying more attention to the polished cliffs and the glacial erratics than to the commercialism that pervades the Valley floor. For other present-day visitors, the Valley is absolutely ruined, its sanctity gone forever; the original inhabitants, if any remained, would undoubtedly agree. Rockclimbers might side with Muir: "the tide of visitors will float slowly about the *bottom* of the valley as harmless scum collecting in hotel and saloon eddies, leaving the rocks and falls eloquent as ever...." Muir, wondering about the future of this hallowed place, wrote this in 1870 while lamenting the fact that "there are about fifty visitors in the valley at present."

Muir was prophetic: overcrowded as Yosemite now is (four million people visit the park each year), the Valley's cliffs remain essentially unchanged, and the waterfalls pour over the rim just as they have since the glaciers departed. Few visitors take the time to explore the quiet regions of the Valley, but one group does little else: rockclimbers daily shun the crowds to seek out the beauty up close, touching the rock itself, and gazing at the sights from high ledges. Climbers have been flocking to the Yosemite for sixty years now, for, with excellent weather, near-perfect rock, and demanding problems—both big and small—the place is a climbers' mecca. Hundreds of people now swarm over the rocks each spring and summer day, finding challenges at every turn. But it wasn't always this crowded.

John Muir was the first Yosemite rockclimber we know about; in 1869 he somehow wriggled his way to the top of Cathedral Peak, a gracefully sculpted horn south of Tuolumne Meadows, that splendid locale in Yosemite's highcountry. Rated Class 4 nowadays—meaning most people wish a rope and a belay—the summit block was soloed, unroped, by the thirty-one-year-old Scot. Later, when he worked at a sawmill down in the Valley, Muir scrambled around ledges and gullies whenever he had the time, though he left few records.

The first climber of note in the Valley itself was a Scottish sailor and carpenter, George Anderson, and he garnered a true prize: Half Dome, the most incredibly shaped piece of rock in America. In 1875 he spent a week drilling holes for eyebolts and establishing a skein of fixed ropes up the forty-five-degree east slope, the side hidden from the Valley floor. This slope isn't particularly steep, but smooth, featureless granite can be intimidating, and Anderson deserves credit for being Yosemite's first technical climber. No one climbed Half Dome unaided by Anderson's pegs and ropes (cables were erected later) until 1931.

After Anderson's climb, no rock climbing of any sort took place for decades. Then, during the 1920s, several local residents began exploring the Valley's out-of-the-way places. William Kat, an accomplished woodworker, visited numerous Class 4 ledges and outcrops; two minor Valley features bear his name today. Two other well-known scramblers of the time were Yosemite postmaster Charles Michael and his wife, Enid, the Valley's preeminent birder—and first woman climber.

The exploits of these early pioneers, admirable though they are, cannot be considered important rock climbs. Basically, these people, with the exception of Anderson, simply scampered around on exposed ledges. And one can argue that even Anderson used more technology than he had to: if he had found a daring young partner to scramble up the slope, dragging a light line up to the top, he would have saved himself a lot of drilling.

Serious climbing, as practiced in Europe since the 1850s, required specialized equipment and techniques. Before 1930 both were unknown entities in California. That year, however, brought the winds of change. During the summer of 1930, forty-two-year-old Francis Farquhar, editor of the *Sierra Club Bulletin*—the esteemed journal of the San Francisco–based climbing and conservation organization called the Sierra Club—climbed in British Columbia with some of his former Harvard classmates. A Harvard mathematician named Robert Underhill also attended the outing, and he had exciting stories to convey. For the past few summers the professor had climbed in the Alps, and now he was full of information about roped climbing, something barely heard of in North America. He had recently put this new knowledge to the test in the Tetons, establishing the most challenging rock climbs in the country. Farquhar, intrigued, solicited an article from Underhill for the *Bulletin,* and "On the Use and Management of the Rope in Rock Work," a twenty-page treatise, appeared in the February 1931 issue. This immediately piqued the interest of the San Francisco Bay Area's Sierra Club members—and others—who at this time were competent mountaineers. (This meant they could, and often did, climb glaciated peaks and rugged rock summits. Skilled at maneuvering through mountain terrain, they still could not be called rockclimbers, people skilled at roped climbing on high and exposed cliffs.)

Farquhar had also invited Underhill to California to meet the Bay Area climbers, but the professor couldn't come west until August 1931. In July an impatient Farquhar taught the simple belay and rappel techniques he had learned in Canada to a small group on Unicorn Peak, above Tuolumne Meadows. Their July 12 climb of its north face soon entered into legend as the first Club-organized roped climb in the Sierra.

When Underhill arrived a few weeks later, he grabbed two promising teenaged climbers, Jules Eichorn and Glen Dawson, as well as the grand old man (he was forty-six) of Sierra mountaineering, Norman Clyde, and off they went into the mountains. In a five-day whirlwind tour, the foursome—along with others on occasion—climbed three new technical rock routes, including the east face of 14,494-foot Mount Whitney, the country's highest summit.

Underhill soon returned east, never again to climb in California, and Clyde returned to his private haunts on the east side of the Sierra. It was left to the two youths to carry on, and Dawson and Eichorn began to impart their new knowledge to friends back home. Dawson, a UCLA student, stuck fairly close to Los Angeles, though his name is forever linked to the Whitney region, where he made several more outstanding ascents. Eichorn, a nineteen-year-old studying the piano with Ansel Adams in San Francisco, was to use his new knowledge to make several matchless first ascents in the Valley during the years to come.

During the winter of 1931–32 Eichorn began experimenting with ropes on three small Berkeley practice rocks with law student Dick Leonard, lawyer Bestor Robinson, and a handful of others. On March 13, 1932, the small band formed the Cragmont Climbing Club, named after one of the Berkeley rocks. In November this informal club merged with the Sierra Club's new Rock Climbing Section, always referred to as simply the RCS. Some climbers weren't happy with this merger, feeling there should be a special category called "Cragmont Climbers" for the CCC founders who hadn't joined the Sierra Club. But cliques were unacceptable to the new RCS leaders, so the idea was abandoned.

Since safety was uppermost in everyone's mind, the RCS climbers, now numbering fifty-two, spent much of 1932 and 1933 learning to belay and rappel properly. They quickly discovered that the European shoulder belay—or its variant, the under-the-armpits belay—wasn't for them: it was a crude and even dangerous technique. So they invented the hip belay, in which the rope was placed around the lower waist, thus affording a more stable center of gravity. The belayers also experimented with letting the rope slip slightly around the waist when bringing a falling leader to a stop. This "dynamic" belay eased the strain on the two humans and the rope itself, the weak link in the equipment chain. Over and over again, for hours at a time, the neophytes jumped off overhangs to be caught by ropes tended by well-anchored and well-padded belayers. It was fun—and it was instructive.

Those California mountaineers who had seen Yosemite Valley knew that its cliffs were orders of magnitude above lowly Cragmont Rock. Leonard, by 1933 the prime mover of the group (one could, without much argument, call him the father of California rock climbing), insisted that no one was going to climb in Yosemite until he or she had mastered the proper techniques. That this took a few years may seem strange, but these folks were either serious students or young professionals; neither group had the time or money, especially at the height of the Depression, to go climbing often. In fact, they thought it a good season if they went to the local rocks eight times a year and to the High Sierra once.

At the start of Labor Day weekend in 1933, seven vehicles independently puttered up the winding roads of the Sierra foothills, encountering other cars only occasionally, even though it was Friday night. The caravan, containing the most overtrained rockclimbers in America, was at last approaching the granite of Yosemite Valley. No one had ever done a roped climb in this place—and seventeen people now hoped to change this.

The gorge they entered was by no means as pristine as it had been when members of the Mariposa Battalion rode into it in 1851. Those soldiers, pursuing Indians who had been harassing white settlers in the foothills below, discovered a paradise, one not to last long. The whites quickly moved in, bringing "civilization" with them. Stage roads appeared gradually; so did rustic hotels. Then, in 1913, automobiles were allowed into the Valley—and the stampede began.

But the Valley was still relatively unspoiled in September 1933; a few lodges stood near the Merced River or serene side creeks, blending beautifully into the forest. A small store sold cans of beans and not much else. Rangers didn't carry guns, and they actually waved to you as they passed. The Yosemite "jail"—a room in the post office—saw perhaps three drunks a year. The trails were paths, not paved thoroughfares.

The drive from the Bay Area took six hours or so, and the climbers who left late Friday didn't get much sleep that night. Around midnight they finally pulled into Camp 9, one of about six Valley campgrounds. Located directly beneath the mighty curves of the Royal Arches, this pleasant forested site, known familiarly as the Organization Campground, was to be home to virtually every Sierra Club rock-climbing outing during the 1930s.

September 2, 1933, marks the true beginning of serious roped Valley climbing. On this Saturday most members of the RCS spread out into the nearby mountains or onto easy gully climbs; even though they had received rigid training, these climbers remained scramblers at heart, interested in rope management mainly to get them out of trouble when needed.

Four determined men, however, set out to attempt the Valley's first roped climb. Leonard, Eichorn, and Robinson teamed up with chemist Hervey Voge for an attempt on the jutting prow called the Washington Column, located across the Valley from the Half Dome massif. (The formation, named around 1865, supposedly resembles our first president from some angles; the likeness escapes me entirely.) Why the Column instead of some other cliff? The answer: trees. Many of the Valley's cliffs were treeless and steep, and therefore terrifying. The Column, steep though it was, blossomed with trees. This meant safe belay stances and ready-made rappel points if things went bad.

Having spent the morning on a reconnaissance of the Valley, the foursome didn't rope up until midafternoon. But soon they were climbing efficiently up the broken, slightly decomposed rock, in three hours reaching what became known as Lunch Ledge. This inconspicuous spot, some 1,000 feet above the talus, lay only halfway up the Column. The hour was late and the climbing looked hard above—too hard to rush and too steep to do safely. In fact, safety was uppermost in everyone's mind, especially Eichorn's, for just four days earlier he had buried, high on a remote High Sierra spire, the shattered body of mountaineer Walter Starr, Jr., who had fallen while solo climbing.

Down they rappelled on their hemp ropes, using the newly acquired Dülfer method, a German technique that required wrapping the rope around the body. This "body rappel" could be painful if proper padding wasn't used, but if all went well, it was exhilarating. "Possibly the greatest sport in rock-climbing," wrote Leonard about a later descent, "is the thrill of roping down in long bounds through space, of dropping almost freely with something of the acceleration of gravity, then stopping smoothly under full control."

On Monday the same quartet climbed back to Lunch Ledge, intent on finishing the route. They managed to get only fifty feet higher before a steep, decomposed chimney stopped them, so down they went once again, this time to pile into their cars and start the long drive home: the holiday weekend was over. Incomplete though the Lunch Ledge climb was, it was a huge step upward from Cragmont Rock.

If you gaze up at the Washington Column today, you will be hard-pressed to locate Lunch Ledge, a nondescript platform. The first time I did the route, in 1957, I was sorely disappointed. "But where's the ledge?" I asked my experienced companion as he began setting up a rappel. "You're standing on it, dumbo," he said.

As a cheeky sixteen-year-old, I thought little of the significance of this first Yosemite climb; I was out for difficulty and summits and glory. Later, when I had read more about the old-timers, I would sometimes climb to the ledge alone and try to imagine what they had felt as they climbed with their half-inch hemp ropes and their crepe-rubber-soled tennis shoes. Thinking about doing a body rappel on five-sixteenth-inch hemp, I could almost feel its bristly texture sawing my body in half.

Lunch Ledge was simply an exploratory climb, a flexing of the muscles. Bigger challenges lay everywhere, and the RCS members well knew it. "When are you people going to climb the Cathedral Spires?" asked everyone who heard of the new RCS activities. Named in 1862, the two Cathedral Spires rise boldly out of the forested talus on the south side of the Valley, opposite El Capitan. Easily the biggest free-standing formations in California, they impressed all who viewed them, tourists and climbers alike. Both shafts looked impregnable—and therefore challenging—but the climbers of the thirties naturally wanted to reach the higher and more impressive one first. Its downhill side, the 1,000-foot-high northwest face visible from the Valley floor, was obviously "impossible," and twenty-six years would go by before anyone even attempted it. But the uphill side of the Higher Cathedral Spire, where it merged into the steep slope, was but 400 feet high. Was there a route on this hidden south face?

On the Sunday of the historic Labor Day trip of 1933, Eichorn, Robinson, and Leonard had hiked up to the southern base of the Higher Spire (climbers have always referred to the two pinnacles as simply the Higher Spire and the Lower Spire, omitting "Cathedral"). Leonard wrote about his first impression: "After four hours of ineffectual climbing on the southwest face, and three hours more upon the southeast and east faces, we were turned away by the sheer difficulty of the climbing." It's no wonder they failed: their "pitons" on this reconnaissance were ten-inch-long nails!

On November 5, armed with pitons and carabiners obtained by mail from Sporthaus Schuster, a large sporting-goods store in Munich, the trio returned to the southern face and managed to climb two pitches before darkness forced a retreat. "By means of pitons as a direct aid," Leonard wrote, "we were able to overcome two holdless, vertical, ten-foot pitches...." This attempt is historic, for it signified the first use of artificial aid in Yosemite—and one of the first times in the country. The technique of driving pitons into the rock in order to grab them, or to stand on them, or to attach slings to them—in other words, to use them to gain elevation—was common in the Alps. Underhill, trained in Europe, might have been expected to embrace this technique, but he was unyielding on the use of artificial aid: "Every pitch," he wrote, "must be surmounted by one's own unaided abilities...." The pioneer Yosemite climbers respected Underhill, of course, but confronting firsthand the smoothness and sheerness of the Valley's cliffs, they realized they would not get far unless they used, occasionally at least, some form of "artificial" techniques. The trick, as they saw it, was to use as little direct aid as possible: the game was *climbing*, after all, not engineering. This adventurous attitude was to be emulated by most of the better climbers in the years to come.

The three men took their Higher Spire project so seriously that during the winter of 1933–34 they examined photographs of the pinnacle with a microscope and a protractor, trying to determine the lowest-angled terrain—still some seventy-five degrees in most places. After ordering more pitons from Sporthaus Schuster (they now possessed fifty-five), the trio was set to go as soon as the snow melted.

The Valley's first climbing spectators accompanied Leonard, Eichorn, and Robinson to the base of the Higher Spire on April 15, 1934, and present were two high-powered ones: Farquhar, by now the president of the Sierra Club, and Bert Harwell, the park's chief naturalist, on hand to witness history. In a few hours the trio had reached their previous high point, a ledge at the base of a steep orange trough later known as the Rotten Chimney. Here, Eichorn and Leonard alternated pounding in the crude spikes, hanging on to them to inch upward. Where the crack ended, Leonard made a clever traverse out to the left to reach easier ground. Finally, as the sun turned the Valley golden, the men nailed a last pitch to the spacious summit and planted an American flag—surely the only time such a practice ever took place in Yosemite.

The Lower Spire, just down the talus slope from its neighbor, was almost as imposing, though not as perfectly shaped. On November 4, 1933, Leonard, Eichorn, and Robinson had tried the pinnacle, failing halfway up when faced with a sheer wall. Flushed by their success on the Higher Spire, however, the same trio managed to make the Lower Spire, after one more failure, on August 25, 1934. Overall, the climb was easier than its

John Evans leads the first hard pitch of the Higher Cathedral Spire. (Photo: Glen Denny)

bigger neighbor, but one pitch presented special difficulties. From a huge platform halfway up the spire, a fairly blank eighty-five-degree wall barred progress. Using a shoulder stand and aid pitons, and changing the lead six times, the team finally approached a fantastic piece of granite, the Flake. Leonard described it as "a very thin sheet of granite, thirty feet high and twenty feet broad, standing out about ten inches from the main cliff. At the outer edge it is not more than a quarter of an inch thick." To reach this formation the leader had to first lasso a sharp projection on it, then climb hand over hand, and finally swing a leg over the projection. The difficulties, however, were hardly over. Traditional lieback technique was out of the question because of the Flake's fragility, so a new procedure came into play: Leonard, by now the leader, used his piton hammer to knock "a series of nicks" on the knife edge. These manmade footholds allowed him to move upward about twenty feet without placing much outward strain on the Flake, and soon Leonard waved to his companions from the top of the pitch. The trio reached the top a few hours later.

The three men thought nothing of altering the rock to suit their needs. "Safety first" was their motto, and one can hardly blame them for not wishing to pull straight out on the monstrous blade of granite. They simply regarded manufacturing holds as necessary. Luckily, this technique was not to be emulated (with rare exceptions) for many decades, when altering the rock became highly controversial.

By and large, the two Cathedral Spire climbs of 1934 set a marvelous standard for future climbers. An ethic had unconsciously evolved, one that seems to me to speak volumes about the character of the three climbers involved. Train hard for a climb and know what you're getting into. Be bold—but practice proper safety measures. Don't be afraid to turn back. Most of all, don't subdue the rock with technology: use sophisticated gear—but use it wisely. Except for the hold-cutting on the Lower Spire, these three men did a splendid job. They are the first modern-day climbing heroes of Yosemite.

During the mid- to late 1930s, Bay Area climbers put up routes on many Yosemite cliffs, but these climbs generally skirted the formations' steepest faces in favor of gullies, ramps, or corners off to the sides. For instance, Glacier Point was climbed by means of an obscure chimney system far around the corner from the main cliff. Minor pinnacles such as Arrowhead Spire and Church Tower also felt the boots of rockclimbers.

The most active person during this period was Dave Brower, a graceful, lanky climber who began climbing on the Berkeley rocks in 1934, at age twenty-two. A few months after he first touched rock, a confidential report prepared by the RCS's Technical Climbing Committee rated Brower's "climbing technique" a fourteen on a scale of fifteen; the only ones to get the top rating were Leonard and Eichorn. No one else was close. On the same chart, neophyte Brower scored two out of a possible ten for "experience" and sixteen out of thirty for "judgment."

Brower was a master of delicate climbing, and, since the climbers of the 1930s sought out the lower-angled cliffs and avoided strenuous jamcracks, the Valley was the perfect place for him. A person with great strength had no real advantage; delicacy and finesse counted for much more. In fact, looking at photos of the climbers of this period, one is struck by how unprepossessing their physiques are: no bulging muscles or massive torsos are visible. One of Brower's climbing partners, Bruce Meyer, later described him as "always fast, efficient, and graceful. He would bound over the talus blocks on the approach, not unlike a mountain goat. Climbing with him in those years was an emotional experience, and I can readily see where he gained his fervor in taking on environmental issues and challenges."

Brower wasn't the only active climber of the mid-thirties, of course, and, because he was elsewhere, he didn't take part in one of the finest adventures of the 1930s, the first ascent of the Royal Arches. These enormous, layered arcs just to the left of the Washington Column spring directly out of the forest and curve upward until they fade out horizontally close to the Valley rim. So prominent are these onionskin-like features that the Indians had several names for the formation. "Scho-ko-ni" referred to the arched shade of an infant's cradle; and "Hunto" meant an eye. This cliff was the bailiwick of Morgan Harris, a zoology junior at the University of California at Berkeley. Harris had lounged in meadows below the recently built Ahwahnee Hotel for hours, studying the precipice with binoculars. He knew that the main arches couldn't be climbed; clearly, that was far too intimidating. But off to the left lay nonoverhanging terrain, studded with trees and blessed with cracks. One attempt, in torrid weather, failed—Harris spent a week in the UC Berkeley hospital recovering from sunstroke. After yet another attempt, Harris, Ken Adam, and Kenneth Davis succeeded on October 9, 1936, during the autumn Sierra Club outing.

The climbing on the route wasn't too tough, but the routefinding and rope techniques proved daunting. One new procedure, called by Harris a "swinging rope traverse," overcame an otherwise unclimbable blank section. (Later this technique became known as a "pendulum traverse," or, more simply, a "pendulum.") Harris, wishing to cross a blank slab in order to reach a narrow ledge some twenty feet to his left, climbed straight upward about twenty-five feet, placed a piton, and had his belayer lower him from it. Then, held tight by the rope from above, Harris began running back and forth across the wall, straining to reach the narrow ledge and finally succeeding.

Later, after yet another pendulum, the trio reached "an old tree-trunk," a feature soon to become famous as the Rotten Log. This twenty-five-foot-long, foot-thick dead log bridged a chasm, affording a unique method of

The Royal Arches. The 1936 route goes up the tree-studded section of cliff to the left of the most prominent arch. (Photo: Steve Roper)

reaching the other side. Harris had spotted this golden trunk from the meadow and hoped it would be strong enough to hold his weight. It was, though it vibrated crazily as he led across it. (Many thousands of climbers shuffled along this tilted and shaky pole in the decades to come; it finally parted company with the rock in the spring of 1984.) The three men reached the rim a few hours later, having completed the most complex route since the ascents of the two Cathedral Spires.

Harris was on a roll. On the following day, October 10, he and two others tried to reach the top of Sentinel Rock from the north, but failed. On the eleventh, beginning a long and fruitful climbing partnership, he teamed up with Brower to make the first ascent of Cathedral Chimney, the huge gash separating the Higher and Middle Cathedral Rocks. The next day the pair were first up Panorama Cliff, the dark-gray wall rising above Vernal Fall. Thus, in the space of four days, Harris made first ascents of three major Valley features and attempted one more—a remarkable effort.

Brower and Harris utterly dominated Yosemite climbing in the mid-to late 1930s; they went on to establish nine more routes together, including long and involved climbs such as the Yosemite Point Couloir and the Circular Staircase on Sentinel Rock. Harris ended up with fourteen Valley first ascents; Brower garnered sixteen, a total not surpassed until 1957.

By the end of the 1930s only twenty-three routes had been established in the Valley. Why so few? There are several reasons. Rock climbing was not a particularly popular sport in the 1930s; most Sierra Clubbers still thought of themselves primarily as mountaineers and spent their vacations at higher elevations, often outside California. For instance, fearsome Mount Waddington, in British Columbia, was nearly climbed in 1935 by Leonard, Eichorn, Brower, Robinson, and other Club climbers. Moreover, the RCS members seemed content to repeat established climbs, taking neophytes up them and basically just having a good time. No one was yet obsessed by Yosemite rock climbing. Finally, few people could afford to buy equipment and travel in California during the Depression Era—even the Sierra Club scheduled only two trips each year, one on Memorial Day weekend and the other in mid-October.

Still, a small but steady stream of climbers made their way to Yosemite each year during the thirties. The most popular climb of the decade turned out to be the Washington Column via the Piton Traverse, a 1935 route that continued to the rim from Lunch Ledge. This rather nondescript route, pioneered by Leonard, Harris, and Jack Riegelhuth, marked the first time the Column had been climbed from bottom to top. Fourteen ascents of this route had been logged by the end of 1939. The two Cathedral Spires didn't lag far behind; both had seen nine ascents by decade's end.

The Sierra Club trips were always memorable, according to the participants. One archetypal outing took place during sparkling weather on Memorial Day weekend in 1939. Thirty-seven members of the RCS showed up, and most of the participants went off daily to easy routes, such as Grizzly Peak, the Gunsight Gully, and Mount Starr King. Lunch Ledge accommodated several parties, as did the easy back side of the Leaning Tower. One party accomplished the fourth ascent of Arrowhead Spire; another bagged the second ascent of the Church Tower. Brower, Leonard, and newcomer Raffi Bedayan made the first ground-to-top roped ascent of Glacier Point. The prize of that weekend, however, was Pulpit Rock, a striking pinnacle at the far west end of the Valley. This rock, attempted several times, finally fell on Monday to Raffi Bedayan, Carl Jensen, and Randolph May.

Women came along on all of these Sierra Club trips, but their unspoken avoidance of the major routes established a precedent that would endure until the late 1960s. Mountaineer G. R. Bunn once wrote, with laughable logic, that the ascent of a moderate Sierra peak was "too dangerous to be undertaken by the ladies of the party, no matter how good mountaineers they might be." Raffi Bedayan wrote of a decision reached before a strenuous day: "It was heartily agreed (by the boys) that the girls should be left behind to rest...." Despite such views, women did accomplish prominent climbs in the Valley. The first to do so was the remarkable Marjory Bridge, a feisty young woman from San Francisco. In 1933 she made an early ascent of the east face of Mount Whitney, one of the most demanding high-mountain routes in the country. Her first Valley route was the west side of Illilouette Fall, a minor climb but significant because she was the first woman ever to participate in a roped Valley first ascent. Bridge's career peaked in October 1934 when she climbed, with two men, the Higher Spire, a feat that, according to Leonard, placed her "in the front rank of the women climbers of America." Two months later, Bridge married Francis Farquhar and settled down to a more traditional life. Her place in the Valley was soon taken, however, by women such as Ethel Mae Hill, Virginia Greever, and Olive Dyer; all three participated in minor first ascents.

Every person born before 1930 remembers where he or she was when the news of Pearl Harbor burst over the airwaves. Yosemite newcomer Fritz Lippmann certainly didn't hear the news early. As the bombs were falling, the twenty-year-old student (soon to be a B-17 pilot) was otherwise engaged: the last Valley ascent before the United States declared war was in progress, and it was the most harrowing one yet. Lippmann and Torcom Bedayan, brother of Raffi, were determined to get up a sinister-looking slash in the wall just to the left of Arrowhead Spire. Lippmann had failed twice already on the West Arrowhead Chimney, for room-size boulders choked the dark slot, causing untold problems. On this quiet and chilly Sunday, December 7, 1941, at the base of the final and biggest chockstone, Lippmann began working his way up what he later called "a suicide route." Using "poor direct-aid pitons," and tackling a "horror pitch" where "retreat was impossible," Lippmann finally pulled over the top of the chockstone.

The above quotes, used by Lippmann in his *Sierra Club Bulletin* account of the climb, upset the established climbers, for his tactics seemed irresponsible, if not dangerous. Dave Brower, by this time associate editor of the *Bulletin,* appended a note to Lippmann's account. While praising the pair's boldness and sense of adventure, he added, "But the aging climbers among us—those nearly or over thirty—cannot help but wish that, with their technique, they had carried with them the mental factor of safety that Richard M. Leonard...has taken with him." Bill Shand, a Cal Tech grad student in chemistry and an experienced Yosemite climber, wrote in 1944 that the West Arrowhead Chimney achievement was "a route which borders on the suicide climbs of the Wetterstein and the Kaisergebirge," prewar feats done in the Alps by Germans and Austrians.

The climbs of the next generation would make the West Arrowhead Chimney route look like a picnic. But the attack on Pearl Harbor, which Lippmann and Bedayan quickly heard about upon their return, and its tumultuous aftermath put an almost complete halt to Yosemite climbing for four long years: only three minor first ascents were recorded between 1942 and April 1946. Sierra Club trips totally ceased, and a quietness settled over the Valley.

About 1,000 Sierra Clubbers served in the military during World War II, an extraordinary one-quarter of the membership. Many of the organization's rockclimbers served as instructors in the famous 10th Mountain Division, a unit that saw much action (of the nonclimbing variety) in northern Italy. Fifteen Sierra Clubbers never returned, though all the climbers mentioned above survived.

During all the years I spent in Camp 4, I assumed that the climbers of the 1930s had stayed there on their holiday weekends. I was disabused of this notion only recently: Camp 4 didn't even exist in the thirties, at least as an official numbered campground. The site had been used informally by Sierra Club skiers as a winter campsite since 1930, and by 1939 the official park brochure listed the site as a picnic ground. The 1941 edition of the same brochure showed its new status: Camp 4. (This number was chosen because the same number had been assigned to a campsite several hundred yards away at the turn of the century; it had been dismantled around World War I.)

Located under the wide massif of the Three Brothers, and a quarter-mile west of Lower Yosemite Fall, Camp 4 in the late 1940s contained about forty to fifty tables scattered across some two acres of gently sloping forested terrain. The lower, flatter section of the campground was a fairly organized place, with well-spaced tables and a network of dirt roads. But the upper part, closest to the talus slopes, had no official roads; one could drive just about anywhere through the forest. No chains moored the tables to the earth, so sometimes several tables would be grouped together. Since there were no numbered sites, one simply drove up and threw down a sleeping bag in any vacant patch of forest duff.

Enormous incense cedars dominated the site, though oaks and ponderosa pines rose here and there. Boulders dotted the entire upper camp, where the climbers usually stayed, and some of these were gargantuan, perfect for practice climbing.

Into this soon-to-be-famous campground came the postwar climbers, especially when they weren't part of a major Sierra Club group, which still reserved Camp 9 for their big outings. Camp 4 was nearly empty, even on weekends, for tourism was down after the war and climbing still the province of the few. Indeed, the climbing action picked up very slowly as people got their lives back in order. Many of the older climbers had settled down with families and jobs. Leonard, Brower, and Harris, for instance, never again made a first ascent in the Valley, though they went out often to local Bay Area boulders and helped train newcomers.

The new Camp 4 generation—among them Jack Arnold, Robin Hansen, Dick Houston, and Fritz Lippmann—were more worldly wise than their predecessors. Following the war, foreign journals, replete with tales of heroism and new techniques in the Alps, became increasingly available in this country. Californians also began to realize that prewar Europeans had done multiday routes on the enormous limestone walls of the Dolomites, climbs far bolder than those so far accomplished in the United States. (These were hardly "suicide" climbs done by Nazis, as thought by many pundits; they were first-rate routes done by first-rate rockclimbers.)

Oddly enough, a European-born climber now helped raise the climbing standards of the Valley, though he had never even touched rock in his native Switzerland. John Salathé was no young upstart, like Fritz Lippmann; he was forty-six when he took up the sport. He was no Dave Brower either, for his free-climbing talents were suspect. Rarely did Salathé shine on a free pitch, but one exception is still legendary among California climbers. In February 1947 he led Dick Houston and Robin Hansen up the first ascent of the Hand, a scary and treacherous climb in Pinnacles National Monument, a volcanic region in west-central California. Placing three worthless protection pitons on this loose and exposed pitch, Salathé so frightened his partners that they traded off the belay chores constantly, not wanting to be the belayer of record when the old fellow took his last fall.

Nor was Salathé a gatherer of first ascents, like Brower: he had but seven in his six-year Yosemite career. No, Salathé is remembered for other things: his pitons; his tenacity; his eccentricity; and, most of all, his big-wall vision.

Born in Niederschöntal, a peasant village some twelve miles southeast of Basel, on June 14, 1899, Salathé left home in his early twenties, apprenticed as a blacksmith, and then, at age twenty-three, made his way westward, working as a merchant seaman in the Atlantic for four years. He ended up in Montreal, where he married in 1929, emigrating to the United States shortly thereafter. In 1932 he founded a one-man blacksmithing firm, the Peninsula Wrought Iron Works, on Highway 101 (the old highway, now called El Camino Real), in San Mateo, a pleasant town twenty miles south of San Francisco.

After thirteen years of making wrought-iron gates and ornamental fireplace screens for affluent Bay Area patrons, Salathé became ill, an event that radically changed his life. I heard about this event from Salathé himself, at his campsite at Bridalveil Creek Campground in June 1963.

One morning in 1945, feeling wretched, he looked out the back window of his San Mateo shop and saw a cow and a calf grazing peacefully. A voice suddenly said, "John, look at those healthy animals. They eat grass, not meat. You eat meat and you are always feeling sick." Salathé conversed with this "angel" for a while and suddenly saw the light. He not only became a lifelong vegetarian that very day, he had many further conversations with angels.

Doctors told Salathé that the fresh air of the Sierra would be beneficial, so up he went to Tuolumne Meadows. When, by pure chance, he happened across the Sierra Club's lodge, the caretaker told him about the organization and its outings; Salathé listened attentively. Back in the Bay Area, sometime in the fall of 1945, Salathé showed up at a scheduled Sierra Club climb at Hunters' Hill, a 150-foot-high formation near Vallejo. Robin Hansen led a complex and highly exposed pitch that went around a corner to a hidden ledge. He got into his belay mode and then yelled loudly for Salathé to "climb freely," meaning not to grab the rope or the pitons. "I felt no activity on the rope for two or three minutes," Hansen reported later, "and suddenly John appeared around the corner unroped! He thought I meant to climb free of the rope!"

Whether it was the new sport, the new diet, the solicitude of the angels, or simply the passage of time, Salathé got well. Physically well, that is. Mentally, he later became eccentric and paranoid, finally slipping into a fantasy world where religious matters dominated every thought.

Salathé quickly picked up the rudiments of rock climbing, though, at his age, he wasn't agile. Realizing this, he became obsessed with the technical aspects of the sport, especially the relatively new concept of artificial climbing. The climbers of the thirties had used direct aid, of course, but only for extremely short stretches—and only to reach easier rock. No one of the previous generation had done aid climbing for its own sake. Leonard, for instance, had written in 1936 about why his team had retreated from a big route: "It could not be climbed without excessive use of pitons as artificial aid. The undefined borderline between justifiable and unjustifiable use of direct aid would have to be crossed."

Salathé, who didn't worry about such philosophical minutiae, realized that direct-aid techniques would dominate Valley climbing in the years to come. Yet he knew that the pitons of the day, either imported from Europe or bought from army surplus stores, were not really suitable for use in the Valley. In ideal cracks these malleable steel pitons worked fine, but many cracks tended to deteriorate just below the surface: they were either bottomed—that is, they stopped or tapered to a hairline not far beneath the surface—or they didn't go straight back, but jigged and jagged. When hammered into a crack, a relatively soft piton would balk at either of these conditions. In a bottomed crack it would simply stop, with most of its length protruding from the crack. In a badly twisted crack it would begin to buckle once it hit an obstruction. In a moderately deformed crack, the piton could

John Salathé holds forth in Yosemite, 1963. (Photo: Allen Steck)

be forced in—and would be excellent—but often it couldn't be removed. If it was, it would likely be so battered as to be worthless for further use: not often could a piton stand up to twenty placements. And, of course, the thinner the piton, the more likely that it would deform.

Salathé saw the need for tougher pitons—thin, reusable ones that could be forced farther into bottomed cracks and pounded into contorted cracks without buckling. He wanted a piton that would dominate the granite, not the other way around. He decided to fashion his own, an event that led to an enduring legend—one never substantiated. As Salathé looked around his shop for something tough, the story goes, his eyes fixed on an old Model-A Ford axle. Axles, he knew, had to be tough, so he got out his torches, hammers, and tongs, and carved several crude pitons out of it. This story probably originated with a 1948 *Sierra Club Bulletin* article by Anton ("Ax") Nelson, who mentioned that Salathé had made pitons from "40/60 carbon steel with vanadium in it—the alloy from which Model-A Ford axles are made." Axles being difficult to work with, it would seem more plausible that Salathé simply used bars of the 40/60 alloy, which he could have obtained easily and cheaply. In any case, the resulting hand-forged and heat-treated pitons, beautifully fashioned into the standard horizontal shape, were far tougher than the European pitons of the day. Most of these handsome objects bore an imprint, a tiny "P" inside a diamond, the logo of the Peninsula Wrought Iron Works.

Salathé gave away some of these pitons and sold a few others, but most Bay Area climbers had to make do with the old, soft pitons for another decade until imitations appeared. Luckily, a few new styles of commercial pitons became available in the mid-1940s, such as the "ring wafer," a tiny but soft blade, and two sizes of angle pitons. All three, developed by the military, were readily available in surplus stores after the war. Another valuable byproduct of the war effort was the aluminum carabiner, weighing in at 45 percent of the weight of the prewar steel models. This may sound trivial until one considers that an early party on El Capitan's Nose calculated that they'd saved slightly more than ten pounds on the leader's hardware sling by using aluminum carabiners instead of steel.

Another major equipment advance took place right after the war. Nylon, a synthetic polymer invented in 1930 by DuPont chemists (but not commercially produced until 1938), quickly became a "miracle" material. During the war Leonard and others, while serving in the Quartermaster Corps in Washington, D.C., developed nylon ropes for the army's mountain troops. Two million feet were manufactured, and much of this ended up in surplus stores. Durable, elastic, and extremely strong, nylon ropes were well suited for mountaineering. Climbers were quick to sense that falls, once greatly feared, no longer mattered as much: a nylon rope could not break. If certain conditions were met (no sharp edges to cut the rope, for instance), a human could free-fall 200 feet and live. Hemp, or manila, ropes soon went out of fashion, though thinner sizes, for rappelling, persisted until 1957.

The first major new postwar route symbolized the direction the new generation would take: the rockclimber as a skilled direct-aid technician. Salathé's pitons helped him get to within a few feet of the Lost Arrow's summit, but that wasn't all: he was the first Yosemite climber ever to spend hours in slings, aiding up cracks that couldn't be climbed free.

The Lost Arrow Spire, an awesome piece of rock architecture, is a finger of smooth granite attached to the Valley's north rim, several hundred yards east of Upper Yosemite Fall. Prominent enough to be noted by both Indians and pioneers, the Arrow had captivated the climbers of the 1930s. Rising close to 200 feet above the Arrow Notch, the rubble-filled gap separating it from the main cliff, the Lost Arrow Spire (also known as the Arrow Tip and the Last Error—a rather nice pun) looked impossible. Only half the size of the Higher Spire, the Arrow's height above the notch wasn't the problem. Rather, it was the smoothness and the exposure that deterred climbers. After a reconnaissance from the rim in 1935, Dick Leonard had stated: "It was unanimously agreed that we would never attempt it." That same year, Dave Brower and others investigated the Arrow Chimney, the ominous 1,200-foot slot that shoots up to the Arrow Notch from below; they didn't get far. Two years later, Brower and Leonard made a more serious attempt from the bottom, reaching a point 350 feet above the ground. Leonard, prophetic about the realities of climbing, later wrote: "The route to the [notch] from below is perfectly possible, but would require experts capable of ascending a very long chimney at a very high angle."

Salathé, a practical man, decided in August 1946 to rappel to the Arrow Notch and see what lay on the *outside* face of the spire: maybe perfect cracks shot up to the top. Incredibly, no one had ever rappelled into the notch to look, though Brower had once tried. Salathé was supposed to meet two other climbers, but they failed to show up. A more balanced man would have come back another time, but Salathé was not a normal person. Alone, he rappelled 200 feet down dead-vertical granite into the Arrow Notch, a dark and lonely place never before touched by humans. Wisely, he left the two ropes in place for his retreat.

A narrow ledge ran out from the notch onto the Arrow and then tapered to nothing at a sickeningly exposed dropoff. Salathé figured he might as well take a look, so he set up a crude self-belay system and went traipsing out. From the end of the shelf he looked up toward a spacious ledge, forty feet above. Could he reach it? A short crack led upward, so out came his special pitons. Although Salathé could hammer them but an inch into the incipient crack, they were firmly lodged, thanks to the last few hammer blows. Soft-steel pitons would have buckled during these last hits, but the hard steel didn't: the pitons, in fact, penetrated just enough farther to wedge tightly.

Soon Salathé was stumped. "I looked around once," he told a climber years later, "but no piton crack. I looked around twice, but no piton crack. I was going to have to climb down, but I looked around again and saw a tiny crack. I got in a wafer piton and then I could free both hands to drill an expansion bolt."

Salathé had several "firsts" during his career in the Valley, and this was one: he was the first ever to use a bolt for upward progress. Bolts for climbing had been invented in about 1920 in Europe, but the first use of them in the United States had been in 1939, on New Mexico's Shiprock, where four were placed for safety reasons, not aid. A protection bolt appeared prior to 1940 on the Higher Spire—this was probably Yosemite's first.

Placing a bolt takes time, and so does managing solo rope techniques. In midafternoon, after finishing a second pitch, the blacksmith pulled up onto what is now called Salathé Ledge, a hideously exposed platform on the Arrow's outer face. Having made only seventy feet, down he rappelled to the Arrow Notch, knowing he had no chance that day.

But how to get back to the rim? The rope shot up the dead-vertical wall for some 200 feet; going hand-over-hand was clearly impossible.

Salathé wasn't in the least worried: he would prusik up the rope, a technique that all Sierra Clubbers had learned. The procedure, typically used on glaciers or for rescues, was not yet a Yosemite climbing custom, though it soon was to become routine on big walls. Salathé's long prusik that day marks another first in Yosemite. The technique was simple in theory. Three prusik knots—a simple hitch developed by Austrian Karl Prusik in the 1920s—were fastened to the fixed rope. The upper one was then affixed to a chest loop, the others to foot slings. Each knot could be slid up the fixed rope with a bit of effort, but when body weight was applied, the knot would tighten and jam tightly onto the rope. One progressed slowly upward, moving the unweighted knots up one by one, with the weight mostly on one foot sling. Prusiking wasn't easy. Fashioned from nonslippery five-sixteenth-inch manila rope, the knots had to be loosened slightly each time after body weight was applied in order to get them to slide a foot or two farther up the rope. More often than not, the knots twisted into iron-hard puzzles and had to be straightened out. Salathé dealt with these problems calmly, taking about ninety minutes to reach the rim. Soon this courageous, visionary man was trudging down the trail to Camp 4.

Salathé had seen disconnected cracks shooting higher, so during the next week, back in the Bay Area, he called a new climbing friend, John Thune, telling him, "I have found a rock in Yosemite that has never been climbed. It is an easy one." Thune fell for this line, and a few days later, in late August, they were both standing in the Arrow Notch. Thune, even more inexperienced than Salathé, was to be the belayer, and his skills were tested instantly: the blacksmith's first piton popped and he plunged over the abyss. Thune later described the scene: "Slowly John worked his way back to the notch and said with a smile, 'Well, we start over again.' He had little fear of high places. I did the shaking for him."

Higher, on the third pitch, Salathé led off into new territory up the eighty-five-degree rock, patiently pounding in his pitons and moving upward, literally inch by inch. The cracks, slightly better than they had been below, led upward about eighty feet and then stopped altogether. Ax Nelson, some months later, described the scene: "...in the last light of day [Salathé] looked up onto the smoothly polished angle of the monolithic tip of the Arrow, a surface which tapered to the summit 30 feet away. The remaining interval could not be covered without some drastic kind of artificial aid. It was high time to retreat. They did."

Nelson, Lippmann, Arnold, and Hansen, hearing of this magnificent effort, were impressed: Salathé would soon stand atop the coveted spire. They decided to act, Nelson later writing, "It must be admitted that competition is the essence of sport and the spur to thought." What followed, although a fascinating chapter in the Lost Arrow's history, was hardly in the spirit of the new age. The Arrow was "conquered"; it was not "climbed." In one of the greatest rope stunts ever pulled off in climbing history, the

Arrow fell to tricksters on Labor Day, 1946, just days after the Salathé-Thune attempt.

In the 1930s some unknown technocrat had suggested lassoing the Arrow's summit, but after one attempt this was seen to be folly: the summit was about eighty feet out from the rim—and rounded. Still, if a rope could be thrown all the way over the top, climbers repeating Salathé's route might be able to reach it and use it to bypass what Nelson called the "flint-hard and flawless" summit region. The foursome took turns all day Saturday casting a rope across the void. Finally, Hansen made a perfect toss, and the weighted light line soared over the top and slithered down the outer face to land on Salathé Ledge.

On Sunday, Nelson and Arnold rappelled to the Arrow Notch and began working their way upward. Without having the advantage of Salathé's pitons, the pair's progress was painfully slow; incredibly, they made only forty feet that day, half of what Salathé had done alone. "As we further diminish the crack's possibilities," Nelson wrote later, "it becomes doubtful that many others will ever climb the Lost Arrow." The pair ignominiously retreated the forty feet to the notch and bivouacked.

On Monday they resorted to yet another clever rope maneuver: they lassoed a protruding flake twenty-five feet above them and prusiked up onto Salathé Ledge. Although their respect for the middle-aged Swiss had grown as the day went on, Nelson wrote that "it seems as though Salathé and Thune used the last poor piton cracks for the last time." His opinion about the state of the cracks was far off base: hundreds of parties were to use these same cracks in the decades ahead.

The light line that Hansen had hurled over the summit lay curled on Salathé Ledge; their troubles were over. Or were they? After hauling across two thicker ropes from the rim, the duo had a taut line anchored to Salathé Ledge and the rim. The fear now, of course, was that the rope might slip off the rounded summit. Although the leader was to be belayed from above and below, the consequences of a rope slippage would be awful. Nelson, a big man, turned to his friend Arnold and pointed upward. (Of a pitch earlier on the climb, Nelson had written: "The stern code of the climber decrees that the lightest man shall lead doubtful pitches.") Thus, Jack Arnold, by virtue of his diminutive size, was fated to become the first person to stand atop the Arrow. After quickly puffing three cigarettes, he attached his prusik knots to the rope and moved upward. All went well, and at 4:30 P.M. on September 2, 1946, Arnold gingerly crept onto the Arrow's summit. He had spent several years in a German POW camp during the war, often thinking about the Arrow, which he had first attempted in 1940. Now, at last, he stood on its summit.

Reaction was swift—and not all favorable. Salathé, according to an unpublished manuscript by Nelson, "contemptuously dismissed the climb as a 'rope trick.'" Much later, Salathé told me, in all seriousness, that the team had enjoyed "the help of the devil." Brower, by this time editor of the *Sierra Club Bulletin,* wrote a short note in the December 1946 issue: "Those of us who used to use an occasional piton or two for direct aid are already speaking of the Golden Age of Mechanized Climbing." Brower, though joking, proved prophetic: the Lost Arrow climb marked the beginning of a new era, one in which innovative equipment and bold direct-aid climbing would play a huge role. The Golden Age was about to begin.

Two climbers near the top of the Lost Arrow Spire (Photo: Glen Denny)

CHAPTER 2

A Technical Age:
1947–1957

Many have questioned the quality of this sort of achievement, deploring the use of pitons, tension traverses, and expansion bolts, but the record speaks for itself. This is a technical age and climbers will continue in the future to look for new routes. There is nothing more satisfying than being a pioneer.

—Allen Steck, justifying the first ascent of Sentinel's north face, 1950

Even Ax Nelson was contrite about the Lost Arrow rope trick, calling it "an admission of the Arrow's unclimbability." The last crackless section, everyone knew, could be overcome using bolts; the rope trick hadn't really been necessary. Aside from this, the major players knew that the real challenge was to climb from the base to the top via the Arrow Chimney, the 1,200-foot-long gash attempted before World War II by Dick Leonard and Dave Brower. Salathé and Nelson talked about doing this, but another climb beckoned first: the rounded southwest face of Half Dome.

John Muir had noted the dome's "noble dimensions," implying that the sheer northwest face was not the only feature worth looking at. He was right, for the dome is spectacular from all sides. The huge southwest face—best appreciated from Glacier Point—had caught the eye of Dick Leonard, Bestor Robinson, and Henry Beers as early as June 1933. They had thought it might be possible to scramble up the face, for it didn't look terribly steep. Ill-equipped, the trio badly underestimated the route: they wandered up easy slabs to the beginning of the much steeper section above, then retreated. Leonard and Jules Eichorn came back two years later, with Brower, the master friction climber, along to help out. This time, even with a full complement of iron, they were able to get only seventy-five feet higher. The next attempt, a few months later, was made by Leonard, Brower, and Robinson; as they approached the face they reconsidered the whole project. Far too much artificial aid would be needed, the trio felt, so they didn't even bother to rope up.

Such thoughts never entered the mind of the next climbers to approach the face, Salathé and Nelson. In October 1946 they approached the face with enough gear for several days. Another Sierra Club team from the Rock Climbing Section, a foursome, was on the scene, but Salathé and Nelson went off first and soon were forging new ground up what Nelson later called "The" crack. This solitary feature shot upward for hundreds of feet; no chance of getting lost here! The crack was badly bottomed, but Salathé's iron—and his tenacity—again worked its magic. Aid pitch after aid pitch led upward. Few ledges appeared; the pair often belayed from sloping footholds.

Intimidated, the four men on the ground soon gave up all plans to join the upper team, a wise idea, for six people simply wouldn't fit on this ledgeless climb. The October day was short, and sunset caught the pair high on the route. So Salathé and Nelson simply stopped in their tracks and bivouacked on a small stance, Yosemite's first climbing bivouac.

The climb was over early the next day, and the pair rappelled to the ground to greet their friends. Their 150 piton placements was by far a Yosemite record, and during the next year the southwest face of Half Dome stood as America's hardest route. True, it was not a steep wall, nor was it especially high—only about 900 feet of roped climbing. Yet the aid climbing was extremely difficult and continuous—as hard as had ever been done. Still, the route never entered into the realm of legend, probably because it was so soon eclipsed by the Lost Arrow Chimney climb.

The Arrow Chimney, like Half Dome, presented few routefinding problems—Leonard and Brower had called the route "terrifyingly clear" in 1937—but the steepness and continuity meant that special direct-aid skills would be required. Anyone who did the route would need stamina, for it was obviously a multiday climb. This meant logistical problems: how much weight could climbers haul along with them?

Salathé and Nelson pondered this question, but as they did, competitors arrived. The Valley's climbing history before World War II had been totally dominated by Northern Californians, but the north-south balance had changed with the arrival, in 1944, of Chuck Wilts and Spencer Austin, two climbers from the Los Angeles area. In that year the pair made the first free ascent of the Higher Spire, proving they were excellent climbers. In October 1946 the pair attempted the Arrow Chimney but retreated after reaching a point 100 feet higher than the Leonard-Brower effort of 1937. Salathé and Nelson, spurred by this "success," went into action, making two serious attempts in the summer of 1947. A subtle rivalry ensued as Wilts and Austin, knowing time was running out, made an all-out effort in August, spending two and a half days and pioneering a few hundred feet of new terrain. They met their match at a steep and rotten headwall, turning back only 400 feet below the Arrow Notch. The race was on; somebody would make it soon, Southern Californians or Northern.

The concept of "big-wall climbing"—which can be defined as a multiday effort involving direct aid on a large and steep rock wall—was well established during the 1947 attempts on this route. But we note the successes, not the failures; and so the five-day Arrow Chimney adventure of September 1947 by Ax Nelson and John Salathé was a true Valley milestone: the first big-wall climb ever done in the United States—and without a doubt the beginning of the Golden Age of Yosemite climbing.

For a big-wall climb the pair took remarkably little equipment. Eighteen pitons, varying from thin horizontals to one-inch angles, plus twelve carabiners, made up the gear rack. Eighteen expansion bolts were carried, along with several carbide-tipped drills and drill holders. Such a huge bolt kit had never before been assembled, but, as Nelson wrote later, "Their use is fair, it seems, when one [is heading] to a place where pitons or holds can again be used." The Star Dryvin bolts, with a length of one inch and a diameter of three-eighths of an inch, took at least forty-five minutes to place. Rotating the drill after each blow of the hammer, the bolter would have to hit the holder with great force perhaps a thousand times before the proper depth was reached. Then the bolt itself, with a hanger attached, would be inserted. A sturdy nail would then be driven in, expanding the device tightly against the interior of the hole.

Only one climbing rope, a 120-foot nylon one, was carried; at twenty-two dollars per rope, this was an expensive item. For hauling and other needs, the pair took two thinner manila ropes, one 150 feet long and the other 300 feet. For the long aid pitches they expected, the duo brought along specially made slings, each with several aluminum "stirrups" attached horizontally for greater foot comfort.

To keep the weight down, the pair took very little water: just six quarts total. (As one who craves water while climbing, I still shudder when I think of this.) This meant about one quart per man per day for the three days plus a few hours that it took to reach the Arrow Notch, where plenty of liquid lay in wait, lowered by friends on the rim. The pair also kept food to a minimum. "That we should lose a great deal of weight on the climb was assumed," Nelson wrote later. Salathé must have convinced Nelson of the benefits of vegetarianism, for among the nine pounds of food carried, no meat was included. Instead, they took what Nelson called "ideal food": raisins, dates, walnuts, and gelatin candy.

The headwall that had defeated Wilts and Austin proved to be the crux: Salathé took eight full hours to climb 150 feet, placing three bolts and doing a masterful job of pitoning. Soft pitons, like the ones Wilts and Austin had carried, would have been virtually worthless, and here was where Salathé's tough pitons worked their magic, for the cracks were rotten and bottomed. He pounded these pitons mercilessly, forcing them to penetrate to the end of the crack. The rock was so decomposed in this section that, at one point, according to Nelson, Salathé "mined a great flake of detached granite to knock window holes in it."

Early on the morning of their fifth day, Salathé and Nelson began bolting the "flint-hard" summit section, the only possible way to reach the top without another rope trick. The pair took many hours to place nine bolts on this crackless section, but finally both men stood yodeling on the tiny summit. By an order of magnitude, the Arrow Chimney route was America's most difficult climb. Was it the world's hardest pure rock climb? Only the big routes in the Dolomites were in the same league, but if the time taken is an indicator of difficulty—which it might not be—the longest first-ascent time for a Dolomite route was only three days.

Ax Nelson's long, eloquent account of the route, "Five Days and Nights on the Lost Arrow," published in the 1948 *Sierra Club Bulletin,* was a watershed piece—and certainly a welcome addition to the climbing literature. Long articles about individual American rock-climbing routes were extremely rare at this time. Articles on technique were common, as were back-of-the-journal notes concerning individual climbs. Yet the vast majority of early climbers wrote nothing at all, leaving the reporting job to people such as Leonard or Brower, who had close ties to the prestigious *Bulletin.*

Nelson was one of the first American writers to consider the reasons why people climb. For instance, he wrote that "one cannot climb at all unless he has sufficient urge to do so. Danger must be met—indeed, it must be *used*—to an extent beyond that incurred in normal life. That is one reason men climb; for only in response to challenge does a man become his best." Nelson also spoke of "discipline" and training regimens involving "brisk calisthenics" and "long marches with little or no water." One gets the impression from Nelson's article that climbers will always prevail if they train like soldiers and exercise phenomenal self-control. This stern tone, bordering on the fanatical, was also a first in American climbing writing.

Although twenty-six new Valley routes were done during the 1940s, none matched Salathé and Nelson's Half Dome adventure and their various Arrow sagas. Yet it was obvious to all that the Valley was full of climbs the caliber of those routes. The next generation, which included virtually no climbers from the 1930s or the 1940s, was ready to be challenged. First, however, the middle-aged Swiss blacksmith had one great climb still to do, for his angels had earlier told him to look around the Valley and he would see three superior climbs: Half Dome, the Arrow, and the north face of Sentinel. He had done two; now his eyes turned upward again.

Sentinel Rock, lying directly across from Camp 4, towers exactly 3,000 feet above the Valley floor. The extremely flat, slightly tapered north face

Sentinel Rock. The north face lies in partial shadow; the west face lies to the right, smooth and sunlit. (Photo: Steve Roper)

is distinguished by hundreds of flakes, cracks, and small, but long, ceilings. J. Smeaton Chase described the wall perfectly in 1911: "The Sentinel... is perhaps the least variable in expression of all the notable cliffs of the valley, standing resolutely muffled until the sun begins to sink to its eclipse behind the high promontory of El Capitan. Then his face glitters with fine Plutonian lines, hard and grim as steel on iron." The main wall itself, 1,100 feet high on its left side and 1,600 feet on its right side, is extremely steep and nearly devoid of big ledges. On the far right side of the wall lie its most prominent features: the Flying Buttress and, rising above it, the Great Chimney. The buttress, named (not well) by some aficionado of Gothic architecture, extends about halfway up the wall; its top forms the biggest ledges of the entire north face. The Great Chimney doesn't actually meet the top of the buttress, but instead begins 150 feet up and to the left; the blankish section in between is known as the Headwall.

Sentinel was not a totally unknown entity. The climbers of the 1930s and 1940s had climbed relatively few routes, and relatively easy ones, but the RCS members had a laudable trait: they loved to explore. Their mountaineering heritage was powerful indeed. Back in the thirties, Dave Brower, Morgan Harris, and others had hiked to the base of El Capitan, looked closely at the great face of Half Dome, investigated the Arrow from above and below, and actually thought about climbing Sentinel's great face. In 1936 Harris, Bill Horsfall, and Olive Dyer climbed the lower part of the face, an exposed series of ramps that led to Tree Ledge, a sandy slope just below the lower right side of the Flying Buttress. The wall soared above; here, obviously, was where the real difficulties of the north wall began.

After World War II, climbers became bolder. On the technical side, they used the new nylon ropes, and their hardware was better and more varied. Also, a new mood prevailed, a psychological frame of mind that said "go for it." The north face of Sentinel was obviously the next "great problem" after the Arrow Chimney since no one was seriously considering huge walls such as El Capitan at this time. Robin Hansen, Fritz Lippmann, and Jack Arnold made the first attempt on the wall in about 1948—they got 100 feet up. Jim Wilson and Phil Bettler, both grad students in physics at UC Berkeley and newcomers to Yosemite, were next; in the fall of 1948 they got a pitch higher.

Wilson and Bettler returned a year later with two of the strongest climbers of the day, Allen Steck and Bill Long, along with supplies for several days. At the end of their first day the quartet endured a miserable bivouac at the base of the Wilson Overhang, a dreadful-looking flared chimney about 400 feet up. A tilting chockstone at the base of the chimney served as a decent spot for one man to curl up on; but every time he moved, so would the chockstone, and this grating noise would wake up the others, perched in various niches. Bettler, however, had quaffed one of Wilson's backache pills and snored the night through.

Long and Wilson took turns nailing up the awkward chimney in the morning, but so slowly was the team moving that it soon became obvious that they wouldn't make the top. Although the four men had climbed only 450 feet of the 1,600-foot wall, they had, ironically, surmounted the major difficulties of the Flying Buttress. When Long and Bettler came back in May 1950, they found that thirty feet above the old high point the difficulties eased; by midafternoon on their second day they became the first to stand atop the buttress. Above reared the Headwall, a steep, crackless section. They retreated.

Allen Steck had watched this attempt with great interest—and was not unhappy with the outcome. "I lay awake many a night in Berkeley," he later wrote, "wondering what this north wall was like above the buttress; it was almost an obsession with me." Steck was no stranger to difficult climbing. He had begun his career, as so many youths did back in those days, in the High Sierra, hiking along trails and scrambling up rocky peaks. Then came a stint in the navy, where he bobbed around the South Pacific

Allen Steck rappelling by the Dülfer method, Yosemite Valley, 1953 (Photo: Allen Steck Collection)

on a destroyer escort during the waning months of the war. Discharged, he attended UC Berkeley, served as a ranger for the summer of 1948 in the Valley, and then spent the next summer bicycling through the Alps, climbing everything in sight. He became the first American ever to climb one of the fabled "Six Great North Faces" of the Alps when he did, with Karl Lugmayer, the face of the Cima Grande, in the Dolomites.

Steck's American record was not quite as bright. By the end of 1949 he had done many of the standard Valley climbs and established a new route on the Higher Spire. That was about it. But 1950 was to be his year: by May, following the first ascent of dramatic Castle Rock Spire in Sequoia National Park, the twenty-four-year-old Steck knew his time had come. Climbing mostly with his Berkeley friends, however, was not the way to success. Climbers such as Wilson and Bettler, lively people and excellent mountain companions, were not in the same league as Steck on a big wall: his season in the Alps had given him an enormous advantage.

Friendships are important, though, so Steck teamed up with Wilson to try Sentinel in June. They were in great shape, having worked out in the Berkeley hills as "charter members of the recently established 'Berkeley Tension Climbers' Running Club.'" The pair prepared for an all-out attempt but retreated almost immediately when a falling rock severed one of their ropes. (On October 23, 1949, a massive rockfall originating from a point just above and to the right of the Flying Buttress had smashed onto the third pitch of the route, and shards of whitened granite lay on every ledge, poised to fall.)

Where was John Salathé at this time? Though he had scouted Sentinel's north wall in 1948, with Nelson, he apparently displayed no further interest, regardless of what the angels had instructed him. Perhaps they nudged him in late June 1950, for when Steck asked him to go onto the wall, he instantly agreed. Though Steck had never climbed with Salathé except at the local Berkeley rocks, he had great respect for his abilities; the Arrow Chimney climb was legendary already. Most of the other members of the RCS had headed up into the High Sierra for the Fourth of July weekend, and Steck was getting antsy. Someone would soon make the climb: why not him?

Steck and Salathé drove up to the Valley in the blacksmith's old Model-T Ford on Thursday, June 29, roped up on Friday morning, and reached the top of the Flying Buttress late on Saturday. Ahead lay new ground: the Headwall. Salathé labored for more than ten hours on this pitch, placing six bolts and many marginal pitons. Finally, the two men were able to work across a slab and enter the Great Chimney, the gateway to the summit. This sinister slot, however, was repulsively flared in its lower part and claustrophobic in its upper part. It wasn't going to be easy.

Meanwhile, the pair had to deal with an even more malevolent enemy: the heat. The Valley later became famous among climbers for its sweltering summers, but by 1950 no one had yet commented on this phenomenon. On a one-day climb, hot weather was rarely a problem; one suffered temporarily and then returned to Camp 4 for a beer. On a multiday climb, however, heat could be enervating, as the Sentinel climb proved definitively. Since one could never carry enough water to replenish the outpouring of sweat, fatigue and cramps resulted. One quart per day per man had been considered adequate up to this point, and, on cooler days and shorter climbs, this proved adequate. Yet the temperature reached 105 degrees in the Valley that holiday weekend, and by day three the pair was not far beyond the halfway point.

The wall became a furnace, and since the customary afternoon breezes of the Valley never arrived, it became a windless furnace. As if this wasn't bad enough, Steck had to watch vacationers frolicking in the Merced River, 2,500 feet below. "If only those swimmers would stop splashing!" he later wrote. The fifty-one-year-old Salathé was stoical, but Steck knew he suffered also. "Standing there in slings, with his hammer poised over the star drill, John would turn his head and say, 'Al, if I only could have just a little orange juice!'"

The two climbers rationed their water carefully, but this meant that food was unpalatable; Steck estimated that, "as a liberal guess," they each ate but a half-pound of food on the entire climb. Although Salathé had carried along a two-gallon tin of dates, his favorite food, he jettisoned this, half full, into the bottom of the Great Chimney, where for decades subsequent parties could see the container rusting away inside the dark labyrinth.

On Monday morning, the start of their fourth day, Steck discovered that the lower flared chimney could be bypassed by tunneling into the interior of Sentinel and wriggling upward for 100 feet, a dark and lonely struggle indeed. (Few have ever gone this way; the outer chimney, though scary and exposed, seems preferable to caving.) Salathé took the lead on the next pitch, and he also chose a line few have ever repeated. A perfect back-and-foot chimney led upward from a fine chockstone ledge. Then, ten feet higher, it stopped. Above, the chimney narrowed abruptly at a ceiling. A hole, about as dark as a house chimney and nearly as tight, shot upward out of sight. Salathé, an aid specialist, naturally wanted nothing to do with this horror, later known as the Narrows, so he worked his way sideways to look at the Valley side of the back-and-foot slot. Chimneys, after all, always have outer edges—and these edges were but ten feet distant. The chimney widened immediately, however, and Salathé began pounding pitons up under the ceiling and standing in slings. An impressed Steck watched the action from his chockstone: "Using pitons upon which only he would ever rely (the double variety—back to back!), hanging almost horizontal, he was barely able to reach around to the outside of the chimney. The piton crack that he found made the lead. The Narrows were behind us!"

And the major difficulties were behind them, too, for steep sections alternated with easy chimney climbing and big ledges. Now only the heat could defeat them. At one point Steck spotted "a little bead of water" oozing out of a mossy crack. "It was barely enough to moisten my lips and wet my mouth," he wrote, "yet it was a wonderful sensation." Closer to the top, both climbers' mouths were so dry that they could barely speak. Steck tried not to watch as Salathé, at dawn on their fifth day, put his set of false teeth into a Sierra Club cup and used the last of his water to moisten them enough to insert. This was also the bivouac when an exhausted Steck was not especially pleased to hear Salathé say, "Allen, you should do the Arrow Chimney; now dot's a *real* climb!" By noon on July 4 they reached the top and staggered down the easy descent gully toward a stream below. Steck threw himself, fully clothed, into a shallow pool.

"The reason, the incentive, the motive for all this?" Steck asked in "Ordeal by Piton," his fine article about the climb in the *Sierra Club Bulletin.* "It is an intangible, provocative concept that I shall leave to the reader to explain." Steck was neither the first nor the last climber to avoid trying to illuminate the rationale for the peculiar sport of rock climbing. Steck's article, excellent though it was, contained one phrase he now wishes he'd never written: "... the second ascent should do better, if there should ever be one." Ironically, he himself was to repeat the route four more times during the next forty-four years.

The north face of Sentinel was Salathé's last big climb; in 1953 he temporarily crossed the border between eccentricity and insanity, and once again his life changed with drastic swiftness. One evening he showed up at Dick Leonard's house in Berkeley with a bag of prunes. "My wife has poisoned these with cobra venom," he exclaimed. "She is trying to kill me! I'll get her first!" A psychiatrist friend of the Leonards who lived a few doors away was quickly summoned, and he said forcefully, after Salathé had departed, "That man is dangerous—he should be locked up." The Leonards called Salathé's wife, Ida, and warned her. She stayed with neighbors that night.

Soon thereafter, Salathé abandoned his family and returned to Europe, living for some years in southern Switzerland in a one-room stone hut perched high above Lago Maggiore. He fell in with a newly formed religious sect called the Spiritual Lodge Zurich, and he devoted the rest of his long life to following the teachings of this group, a "Christian" one that believed in multiple incarnations.

In August 1958 Salathé ascended the Matterhorn, his last big outdoor adventure; back in Zermatt he gave all his equipment to the YMCA students he had climbed it with. By 1961 he was living in Zug, just south of Zurich, presumably to be closer to his sect's headquarters. He returned to the United States around 1963 and for the next twenty years wandered alone throughout the mountains and deserts of California, car-camping whenever and wherever the mood struck him. By this time he was remarkably self-sufficient. A tiny pension (about four hundred dollars a year in 1974) from the Swiss government enabled him to buy gas and staples, but much of his food came from the land. He became expert at discovering edible grasses and herbs; mixed with barley, rice, or pinto beans, and seasoned with parsley and garlic, these wild greens formed the main part of his diet.

Old friends such as Allen Steck, John Thune, Ax Nelson, and Raffi Bedayan would occasionally see the old Swiss, and I myself was lucky enough to meet him three times. His German accent, strong but charming, was barely understandable, though I soon figured out the theme of his meanderings. Although he mostly wanted to talk about his angel contacts, Medium Beatrice (the guiding spirit of his sect), or the evils of Catholicism, I sometimes managed to get him to talk about the old days. He utterly refused to believe that Sentinel had been climbed in three hours, smiling and saying, "Oh, now that the bolts are in, maybe three days."

Salathé, a simple, unpretentious man, lived in complete harmony with nature for many years. But in 1983 his vagabonding period ended, and he spent the last decade of his life in various rest homes in Southern California, dying on August 31, 1992.

Yosemite's climbing history is interesting in that entire generations of climbers seem to fade away at once. World War II, of course, was a natural break, and none of the prewar climbers did much at all after the conflict. Similarly, the immediate postwar generation disappeared around 1951: people such as Arnold, Hansen, Lippmann, Nelson, and Salathé never again did major rock climbs. The chief reason was that most of these men had started families and careers, which have always been incompatible with the time and commitment necessary to climb the bigger routes. Though they didn't stop climbing entirely, they tended to go into the mountains with their children or climb an old classic once a year. The same kind of mass exodus would take place several times in future years, most dramatically at the end of the Golden Age, around 1970.

The next Valley generation following Salathé's was made up largely of UC Berkeley science students and RCS people. The most active of these climbers were Bill Dunmire, Dick Houston, Dick Irvin, Bill Long, Dick Long, Will Siri, Allen Steck, Bob Swift, Willi Unsoeld, and Jim Wilson. Simultaneously, climbers from the Stanford Alpine Club (the SAC, which was founded in 1946 by Al Baxter, Fritz Lippmann, and Larry Taylor) became active, and though people such as Nick Clinch, John Harlin, Dave Harrah, Sherman Lehman, Jon Lindbergh (son of the aviator), John Mowat, David Sowles, and Jack Weicker rarely did first ascents, they visited the Valley several times each year, doing mostly the standard routes. Clinch later described the climbers of the period as mostly "introverted intellectuals.... The only approbation you got was from fellow climbers; the rest of the world thought you were nuts. And there was not a lot of natural athletic ability."

Clinch also recalls two events that radically increased his popularity: "I got a car and I got on the SAC qualified leader list." The latter meant that Yosemite rangers wouldn't question him or his party as to competence, as they did for those not "qualified." A qualified leader had carte blanche to sign out for any climb in the Valley. (Around 1948 the rangers had instituted a mandatory sign-out system for safety reasons; this lasted until about 1965, as I recall.)

Even with "qualified" leaders leading neophytes up the cliffs, climbing failures among Valley cragsmen had always been as much a part of the game as successes, dating back to the thirties. Almost everyone had stories to tell of epic retreats and embarrassments. Most such tales involved simply getting off route and coming down, or having to bivouac because of slowness. One story that entered into legend during this period concerned John Salathé, who once rappelled, at night, lost, down the Washington Column following some failed attempt on a route. Coming to the end of his rope while dangling in space below an overhang, he had to cut off pieces of his rappel rope and fashion prusik slings to get back up, a lengthy process. Salathé's partner, Phil Bettler, was quite deaf; the noncommunication between the two men was hilarious—in retrospect.

Nick Clinch has described one subtle aspect of retreating: "Nothing illustrated the basic irrationality of climbers better than the code that said you didn't leave good equipment behind. Rappel points were set up with the very pitons and sling rope that you considered too cheap and unsafe for climbing. To use expensive equipment for this was deemed an ostentatious display of wealth, a cowardly act, or inexcusably bad planning."

Most of the UC Berkeley and Stanford students quit climbing, or radically slowed down, soon after they graduated. Allen Steck, the undisputed leader of his generation, was soon to follow this pattern and settle down with a job, a wife, and kids. Yet for a few years—1950 to 1953—he stood out among his comrades, both as a rock specialist and a mountain man. For instance, seventeen days after he staggered into the pool below Sentinel, he stood atop British Columbia's Mount Waddington, having made the fourth ascent via a difficult new route.

Not a particularly brilliant climber back in the 1950s, Steck's forte was his willpower: he simply wouldn't turn back. It wasn't that he was foolhardy, pushing on no matter what. He simply had a marvelous ability to remain calm and say to himself, "Well, I'll just go up a little farther and see what lies ahead." Naturally, if one does this long enough, the result is success.

Steck's biggest Valley first ascent turned out to be Sentinel, a climb then and now judged to be equal to the Lost Arrow Chimney (Salathé himself—the only person to get up both routes until 1955—couldn't decide which was the more difficult.) But Steck had a few good climbs left in him, though he had groused to Salathé near the top of Sentinel that his next route was going to be a tourist stroll in a wheelchair. In March 1952, while in graduate school at UC Berkeley, he took a break from his studies in medieval German and established a strenuous aid route to the El Cap Tree, an eighty-foot pine growing in an alcove 400 feet up the southeast face of the monolith. Climbers had long noticed the tree, the only major one growing on the huge wall, and in the mid-1930s Bestor Robinson conceived of a plan to overcome the huge initial overhang: if a long pole could be lashed firmly to some lower pitons, one should be able to climb the pole itself and bypass much of the overhang. Dave Brower wrote about the abandonment of this plan: "Contemplation of the leverage which would be exerted on those pitons by such a pole served to dissuade more than a theoretical approach."

Park naturalists, eager to see if the El Cap Tree was a ponderosa or the similar Jeffrey, made an attempt around 1950, but quit after placing some aid pitons and a few bolts. Steck, Will Siri, Bill Dunmire, and Bob Swift spent two days on the climb, placing more bolts and pitons and then traversing across ledges that led up and over to the pine—a ponderosa. Steck looked up at the ceilings and sheer granite above the tree, commenting in his note about the climb: "The leads above the tree look interesting. A real opportunity for future rock engineers!" Twenty-six years were to pass before anyone attacked this upper wall.

Next for Steck came the first ascent of the beautiful Yosemite Point Buttress, the sweeping curve of granite leading to the rim just east of the Lost Arrow. Steck and Swift reached the prominent, high ledge called the Pedestal on their first attempt, in March 1952, turning back a mere ten feet above this because water was coursing down the steep and slippery face. An attempt two months later—this one by Steck, Bill Long and his brother, Dick Long, and Oscar Cook—ended only 100 feet higher, where an intimidating wall stopped them cold.

Steck, ever the tiger, convinced Swift to return to YPB (as the climb quickly became known) a few weeks later, and this time, even with a light rain falling, they soon sat on top, "our thoughts peacefully following the wisps of fog as they drifted through the trees." The climb, hardly in the same league as the Arrow Chimney or Sentinel, nevertheless marked the beginning of a trend, for buttresses such as YPB rose all over the Valley.

And, sure enough, Steck's roving eye soon turned to one of these, a beautiful black-and-gold buttress on the far eastern edge of El Capitan. The face of this great monolith, soon to be the most famous cliff in America, was so enormous and steep that no one seriously thought of possible routes. Yet the east buttress—not really part of the main El Cap face—brimmed with cracks and chimneys on its lower, distinct section. Higher, the buttress blended smoothly into the face, but here also the rock looked broken

Allen Steck on an attempt on the El Cap East Buttress, 1952; Middle Cathedral Rock looms in the background (Photo: Allen Steck Collection)

and probably climbable. In late October 1952 Steck teamed up with his old buddies, Dunmire and the two Long brothers. All went well until the third pitch, when Dunmire took off up an aid crack, belayed by Steck. About twenty-five feet up a piton pulled and Dunmire fell. To everyone's horror, the lower pitons popped, one by one: it was Yosemite's first "zipper" fall. The lowest pin held, however, and this saved Dunmire's life, for he had fallen upside down, stopping just before striking a blocky ledge. Covered with blood and unconscious—he had glanced off the rock on his way down—he came to minutes later, spouting, as he told me many years later, "gibberish about getting on with the climb and chiding my pals for standing around." He soon descended with the help of his friends and spent the night in the Valley hospital, suffering only from a bad concussion. When I asked if the accident had slowed him down, he replied with vigor, "You bet!

52

A typical Sierra Club group in 1955. Hervey Voge stands at right; Ed Roper, the author's father, kneels (Photo: Steve Roper Collection)

I never again climbed with abandon or total self-confidence, although I tried many times."

Understandably, Dunmire wanted no further part of the El Cap east buttress, so the next spring Steck went back with three friends, all named William: Long, Siri, and Unsoeld. Bivouacking twice on the route, and using lots of aid—but no bolts—the quartet had an uneventful climb, reaching the top on June 1, 1953. When they returned to the Valley, they heard the news that Everest had at last been climbed.

Steck's Valley heyday was over with this route, and the three Williams never again made Valley first ascents. All four men, however, hardly gave up climbing; they, along with Lippmann, Dunmire, Houston, and others, journeyed to the Himalaya the next year, making the first-ever attempt on Makalu, the fifth-highest mountain in the world. Willi Unsoeld further distinguished himself with a new route on Everest in 1963.

Dunmire's accident was an anomaly; because the Sierra Club RCS emphasized safety, the accident record in the Valley during the previous two decades had been exemplary: Dunmire's mishap was only the second serious one recorded. (The first had taken place in 1947, when SAC co-founder Al Baxter fell sixty feet on the Higher Spire, shattering both ankles.) Nick Clinch recently told me about an endless nighttime meeting in 1955 in San Francisco, where Sierra Club officials, worried about a few minor accidents, including Dunmire's, had gathered the leading lights of the day to discuss the problem. The climbers claimed the sport was intrinsically dangerous; the Club's spokesmen worried about the Club's image. An impatient John Salathé kept muttering in his thick accent, "Vy can't ve chust climb!" Bob Swift finally announced at midnight, "It's time we stopped this nonsense and all went home."

It is tempting to give names to generations, or eras, and Yosemite's early climbing history lends itself well to this kind of facile pigeonholing. The Leonard-Brower Era. The Salathé Era. The Steck Era. These labels almost perfectly sum up the 1930s, the postwar 1940s, and the early 1950s. But the labeling becomes complex from this point onward, for, with more climbers coming to the Valley, no one person or Sierra Club group dominated. The early and mid-1950s, for instance, saw the arrival of three "big names," and this period could be called, if the name were not so awkward, the Robbins-Harding-Powell Era. This era also forever marks the end of Northern California's domination of Valley climbing, for all three men were from elsewhere.

Royal Robbins is one of the true stars of the Valley; for twenty years he led the way toward an adventurous style of climbing. Coming from an unsettled home, as did many climbers in the years to come, Robbins was somewhat rebellious as a boy, given to stealing hubcaps and such. The Boy Scouts, founded as an outlet for youthful energies, proved to be significant in his life, and by 1949 Robbins was regularly going off with his troop into the rugged mountains of Southern California. This first look at the great outdoors changed his life. By 1951, at age sixteen, he had quit high school to be closer to the mountains. Working at ski areas and skiing as much as he could, he made enough money to climb often at Tahquitz Rock, that soaring hunk of white granite near Mount San Jacinto, east of Los Angeles. There he met Chuck Wilts, of Lost Arrow Chimney fame, who, realizing the talent of young Robbins, offered advice and friendship. Robbins stunned the Tahquitz climbing community one day in 1952 when he led a famous aid climb, the Open Book, without resorting to direct aid.

This was the hardest free climb yet done in the United States.

Not only a brilliant climber, Robbins also thought intelligently about the sport. While still in his teens he realized that the rating system then in use was obsolete. In 1937 Sierra Club climbers had more or less taken up the European rating system, developed in the 1920s by German climber Willo Welzenbach. All roped rock climbs were divided into but three classes: 4, 5, and 6. (Classes 1 through 3 represented trail walking through scrambling.) Class 4 meant easy climbing where pitons were unnecessary; Class 6 meant pitons were used for direct aid. Therefore, Class 5 represented *all* piton-protected climbing—called free climbing—and this was an enormously varied category by the early 1950s. Easy free climbs shared the same Class 5 rating as climbs such as the Open Book.

Obviously, a brand-new Tahquitz rating system was needed. Robbins and climbing partner Don Wilson decided to separate Class 5 into ten

Royal Robbins gives advice from a Camp 4 boulder, 1967. (Photo: Steve Roper)

subdivisions, 0 through 9. A rating of 5.0 would represent very easy piton-protected climbing; 5.5 would be at midrange; and 5.9 was reserved for the hardest of them all, the Open Book. Aid climbs were similarly rated, from 6.0 upward to 6.9; the higher the number, the harder the pin placement. This "decimal system" soon spread throughout California and the rest of the country, reaching the Valley around 1956. Much later it came to be known as the YDS—the Yosemite Decimal System.

Robbins quickly made his mark in the Valley; around 1952 he got off route on the first hard pitch of the Higher Spire; the resulting Robbins Variation was later rated a strenuous and scary 5.9. Then, with incredible hubris, he and two Southern Californian climbers, Don Wilson and Jerry Gallwas, made the second ascent of the Steck-Salathé route on the north face of Sentinel in 1953. Wilson, an arrogant young man, had collared Steck in Camp 4 one weekend, demanding to know details of the climb. Steck replied vaguely, never dreaming that an unknown climber, a mere kid, would have a chance on such a route. The trio nevertheless went up and did the climb in tennis shoes in just two days! In the Great Chimney, the team pioneered two new pitches, staying on the outside of the lower chimney and worming up through the Narrows on the upper section, the claustrophobic tunnel Salathé had avoided in 1950. In 1956 (not 1954, as has often been written) Robbins and the talented Southern California climber Mike Sherrick made the third ascent in a day and a half; Robbins thus became the first Valley climber ever to repeat a multiday route.

By the time I met Robbins, in 1959, he was held in awe throughout California's climbing community. An aloof-looking chap, Robbins had perfect bearing and a measured speech pattern—and these characteristics set him apart from the Berkeley crowd, who lounged around the local rocks or in Camp 4, laughing outlandishly, gesturing, shouting, drinking, farting.

Warren Harding was the second climber of this period who became a legend. Unlike most Valley climbers, who had started scrambling up rocks as teenagers, Harding came to climbing late. He had grown up in Depression Era California, not too far from Yosemite, but fishing and hiking were his only interests. "I couldn't catch a ball or any of that stuff," he once told a reporter; "I could only do what required brute stupidity." When World War II began, Harding failed his physical because of a heart murmur and became a civilian aircraft mechanic. During the late 1940s he got a job with the California Department of Highways as a surveyor, a position he was to keep, with a few breaks, for decades. After a fellow worker took Harding climbing in 1952, the sport pulled him in. "It was the first thing I was ever good at," he said. One of his first climbs was the Grand Teton, where he was a member of a guided party—and the weakest member of this group, an irony considering his later reputation as a person with incredible endurance. Harding's first new route came in late June 1953, when he and John Ohrenschall climbed the west face of Sugarloaf Rock, near Lake Tahoe.

Harding did his first Valley route later in 1953, and within two seasons he was established as one of the Valley's leading climbers. His first major new route in Yosemite was an interesting one indeed, the north buttress of huge and neglected Middle Cathedral Rock, the monolith directly across the Valley from El Capitan. An eighteen-year-old Bay Area climber named Frank Tarver had tried this buttress twice in 1953, taking leader falls on both attempts. Undaunted, he drove up to Camp 4 one morning in late May 1954, having been advised to look up a good new climber, Warren Harding. He saw a slight, dark-haired fellow weaving out of camp, obviously hung over. "Hi," said Tarver, "are you Warren Harding? I'm Frank Tarver. Let's go climbing." Incredibly, that same afternoon the pair set out for the north buttress. Reaching the base, they looked up to see, a few hundred feet above them, two other men, Craig Holden and John Whitmer, both from San Jose. "There was some sort of lapse of logic," Tarver later told me, "but it seemed like a good idea to go up and join them." They caught up with the surprised pair several pitches later, and together the foursome spent three thirsty days making the 2,000-foot climb. Though the difficulty was not particularly great, the routefinding proved complex—and the climb went on and on and on: it was the longest Valley climb yet done.

In mid-July 1954 Harding made the second ascent of the Lost Arrow Chimney, with Tarver and Bob Swift, in a fine four-day effort. Harding didn't lead many of the aid pitches but performed extremely well in the narrow chimneys that made up half the route. "I was amazed on the Safety Valve Pitch," Tarver told me. "Warren never even saw the mashed bolts that Salathé and Nelson had destroyed in order to save the hangers for higher up. He climbed right on by, totally unaware of them. There was never any doubt as to whether he'd get up a jamcrack or chimney." When the team reached the Arrow Notch late on the third day, there wasn't enough time to continue upward, so they sat and gazed down at the Valley, 2,500 feet below. "We...watched fascinated," Swift wrote later, "as bulldozers, steamrollers and graders pushed new routes through old meadows. The consensus of our combined engineering genius was that the only solution to the road problem lay in paving the entire Valley floor. White lines could then be painted wherever roads might be needed."

Harding was on a tear; on Labor Day weekend in 1954 he teamed up with Swift and Whitmer for a try on yet another beautiful and unclimbed feature of Middle Cathedral, the east buttress. Although only half as long as the north buttress, this route was more concentrated in its difficulties. The trio fought their way through an ant-infested tree a few hundred feet above the ground and then arrived at a totally blank wall about thirty-five feet high. Out came the bolt kit, but down went the sun. They bivouacked, resumed bolting at dawn, but then, several pitches higher, ran out of steam and rappelled to the ground.

Harding waited nine months before returning. Little competition existed in those early days, and he knew the route would be waiting. Swift and newcomer Jack Davis joined him on Memorial Day weekend, 1955, and they quickly climbed to their old high point. After a bivouac high on the route, the trio finished the climb, one that became extremely popular in the years to come. I was in the Valley that holiday weekend, on my first-ever RCS trip to the Valley, but was only vaguely aware of the successful Middle Cathedral climb. Had anyone told me then that four years later I would climb the route, I would have scoffed: such big cliffs looked utterly impossible to my youthful eyes.

When Mark Powell, the third influential Valley climber of the mid-1950s, was released from the air force in early 1954, he decided that rock climbing was what he wanted to do. He became an air-traffic controller in Fresno partly to be close to the mountains. At Easter he made his first trip to the Valley, a trip that should have squelched his newfound love: over-weight and puffing cigarettes furiously, he barely managed to make it to the top of the Lower Spire, hauled up by Jerry Gallwas. This incident humbled him so badly that he quickly shed forty pounds. By July 1955 he had become so adept that he led the pitch off the Pedestal, on YPB, without aid, an excellent 5.8 effort. Powell was a fleet climber also; he and his partner, Fresno climber George Sessions, raced up the route in a day, only the second time that exploit had been done.

Powell's first big new route was the east buttress of Lower Cathedral Rock, a steep and forbidding wall. This ascent, done in June 1956 with Gallwas and Don Wilson, was notable because it was done in one day, the first time a truly hard new Valley route was so accomplished. Whereas Salathé and Harding seemed to thrive on long climbs, with their consequent big loads and slothlike speed, this trio didn't especially relish the idea of bivouacs. Wilson, in a later note, explained his team's philosophy: "Preparation was complicated by the conflict between outfitting ourselves for a night on the rock with the result we would certainly experience one, or going very light, in the hope of going very fast, risking an uncomfortable night." The gamble paid off: after nearly fourteen hours of climbing, they reached the top just before sundown.

Like Robbins, Powell also thought the old Class 1–5 rating system was inadequate. By 1955 he had moved to Los Angeles and had become familiar with Tahquitz and the new decimal system. Later, he championed this system for use in the Valley, which gave it a huge boost, for by 1956 Powell was a true Valley star; when he had ideas, everyone listened. A tall, blond man with an angular face and sparkling, ultra-blue eyes, he radiated charisma and enthusiasm. Few could resist when he came looking for climbing partners.

Powell also came up with yet another way to rate climbs. He strongly disliked the fact that a one-pitch 5.8 route, for instance, was ranked identically with a ten-pitch 5.8 route. Thus was born, in the late 1950s, the Roman numeral grades. (Powell's earliest version of his system used Arabic numbers, with occasional plus signs, but "Grade"—as contrasted to "Class"—was the operative word.) Grade I indicated an extremely short route, one accomplished in a few hours. It could be an ultra-hard route, but it wouldn't take long. The next two levels, II and III, represented longer and more committing climbs; the latter would take most of a day. The Royal Arches climb was a perfect example of a Grade III. A serious one- or one-and-a-half-day route was called a Grade IV. Even more demanding climbs, such as Sentinel, became Grade V's. (We rarely used the word "grade." Most often, in speech, we simply used the number: "Sentinel's a five.") Routes could still be rated 5.8, but now the difference between a I, 5.8 and a IV, 5.8 was understood by all. It would be clear, for example, that on a Grade IV you'd better get a dawn start! By 1961 everyone was using Powell's system, one still in use today.

Powell proceeded to put up several more demanding routes in 1956, but perhaps the high point was his climb of the Arrowhead Arête, a steep, white rib located to the right of Yosemite Point Buttress. He did this intimidating route in October with Bill Feuerer, an air force enlisted man stationed near the Central Valley town of Merced. Feuerer's relative slowness and clumsiness earned him the nickname "Dolt"—a name he relished, even using it as a trademark for the high-quality equipment he later made.

The Arrowhead Arête climb infiltrated the subconscious of many Camp 4 climbers because of a note Powell wrote for the 1957 annual *Sierra Club Bulletin:* "It is high-angle face climbing on very small holds requiring great finger and toe strength with excellent body balance and faculties keenly tuned to withstanding exposure. To the advanced rock climber this would be a very difficult test; to the less competent, a nightmare. This is possibly the most continuous difficult fifth-class climbing in this country."

———————————————————————— ■ ————————————————————————

It was Robbins, not Harding or Powell, who garnered the biggest prize of the mid-1950s: the five-day first ascent of the great northwest face of Half Dome, the first Grade VI climb ever done in the United States. Two thousand feet high and averaging eighty-five degrees, the wall was the definition of intimidating. The "frightful amputation"—as J. Smeaton Chase described the wall in 1911—of the world-famous dome didn't attract climbers until 1954. In that year Dick Long, Jim Wilson, and George Mandatory made a courageous but pitiful effort, turning back after only 175 feet. To them, however, goes the credit for discovering the start of the route, the junction of the huge face with a slightly more broken area near its left side. In 1955 a much stronger team arrived: Robbins, Harding, Gallwas, and Don Wilson. During a three-day outing this team moved like sloths, reaching only the one-quarter level, far below what appeared to be the major difficulties. Oddly, the climbing was not hard on this lower section—it was ordinary Yosemite climbing. Why, then, did some of the finest climbers in the land take so long to get nowhere? Anyone who has stood at the base of the great face of Half Dome knows the answer: the view upward is overpowering. It doesn't seem possible that humans can climb such an enormous cliff with normal techniques. The foursome moved slowly because they simply didn't want to move quickly. Although both Harding and Robbins wanted to continue, the others were less eager, and the team retreated, intending to return soon. Yet no one was to lay hands on the cliff for two more years.

Robbins and Gallwas didn't forget about the wall; in fact, they dreamed about it and laid plans for an all-out attempt in 1957. Since they knew sophisticated equipment would be necessary, Gallwas made some tough chrome-molybdenum horizontal pitons, the first hand-forged ones made since Salathé's. Wide cracks could be seen from the ground, so Gallwas also fashioned the biggest angle pitons ever made—steel monsters up to two and a half inches wide. Heavy these were, but they were to come in handy. Also to be carried were the new "knife-blade" pitons designed a few years earlier by Chuck Wilts. These postage-stamp-sized blades of steel could be pounded into ultra-thin cracks, ones that before this had to be ignored.

On June 24, Robbins, Gallwas, and Mike Sherrick started up the wall, carrying supplies for five days. Thanks to their knowledge of the route, the trio reached the previous high point late on their first day—no fooling around on *this* attempt. By early afternoon of day two the threesome came to a blank wall, a section that from the ground had seemed like the crux of the route. Up and to the right lay a giant chimney system, obviously climbable. But how to get there? Robbins led a difficult nailing pitch to a tiny belay ledge; then he and Gallwas began placing bolts across the blank wall. Late in the afternoon Robbins placed a few more pitons above the seven-bolt ladder and paused. Above rose an utterly blank wall. Dozens of bolts would have to be placed. Then he spotted, far down and to the right, a narrow ledge that shot across toward the chimneys. This was the key to what was immediately named the Robbins Traverse.

Sherrick lowered Robbins fifty feet from the highest piton, and the swinging began. Back and forth Robbins ran across the horribly exposed wall, only on his fourth swing managing to grab some holds over by the ledge. Yosemite's wildest pendulum traverse had been completed. Happy to have this feature behind them, the trio rappelled to a ledge and bivouacked a second time.

For three more days the team worked up the wall, encountering sections that would fascinate and intimidate future teams. The Undercling, for instance, was a block that jutted out alarmingly from a chimney;

Opposite: *The sheer 2,000-foot northwest face of Half Dome; the 1957 route lies more or less directly under the summit. (Photo: Steve Roper)*

Robbins, the acknowledged leader on the hard climbing, "walked" out this block, with his feet on the main wall and his hands grasping the underside of the block. Higher was what became known as Psych Flake, a forty-foot-high shard of granite the men had to chimney behind. Although this pitch was easy, stones rattled in the black depths of the slot, indicating that the flake was slightly loose (and fragile it was, parting company with the cliff during the winter of 1966–67). On day four, with Robbins feeling somewhat enervated, Gallwas did most of the leading up the Zig-Zag Pitches, three ropelengths of highly strenuous aid climbing. These led to an absolutely flat—but disturbingly narrow—ledge that shot across to the left, just below a dead-vertical blank section. By squiggling along this ledge for about fifty feet, the trio was able to bypass the blank part. The Thank God Ledge is now one of the most famous pitches in Yosemite.

Easier climbing the next day led to the top. At sundown on June 28, 1957, their fifth day, the tired and thirsty climbers pulled over the edge and stood on the broad summit of the dome. On hand to greet them was Warren Harding, who had hiked up the trail. Harding, along with Powell and Dolt, had planned to try the route soon, but they had arrived in the Valley too late: the others were already partway up the wall. Harding, however, harbored no resentment—at least no visible resentment. "Inside, the ambitious dreamer in me was troubled," he later admitted.

Mike Sherrick, describing the climb, wrote that the trio had returned home "fortunate to avoid publicity about an accomplishment which would only have been made into a sensation." Ironically, the *Sierra Club Bulletin* in which these words appeared was dated November 1958. In that same month, massive publicity, generated in large part by climbers themselves, erupted over the first ascent of the Nose of El Capitan—the project to which Warren Harding turned a few days after the Half Dome climb.

CHAPTER 3

Inside a Cut Diamond: 1957–1958

To apply human standards of measurement to this monarch of mountains is sacrilege. To attempt by mere words and figures to convey some idea of its stupendous massiveness, its nobly-defiant impressive individuality, is rankest folly.

—Herbert Earl Wilson, writing about El Capitan, 1926

As Denali, Mount Rainier, and the Grand Canyon dominate and define their respective national parks, so does El Capitan loom, tower, and rule over the entrance to Yosemite Valley. You can pick any synonym for "dominate" and it will still work. Overshadow. Domineer. Intimidate. Overwhelm. Not enough such words exist in our language to properly describe the effect this cliff exerts on climbers and tourists alike.

Long ago I heard a ringing phrase: El Cap was the "largest exposed granite cliff on earth." But this claim must have been put forth by a Yosemite public-relations person ignorant of the 5,000-foot-high walls lining the Great Gorge of Alaska's Ruth Glacier or of the Trango Towers, those monstrous peaks overlooking the Baltoro Glacier.

No, El Cap is simply a large cliff, a large and hauntingly beautiful cliff. It's hard to grasp the scale: one soldier who entered the Valley in 1851 thought that El Capitan was about 400 feet high, missing its true height by a factor of seven. Although it is indeed high, what distinguishes it most is its unrelenting steepness and its color. The 3,000-foot wall is composed for the most part of remarkably clean tan-and-white granite: the cliff face looks scrubbed, as if cleansed daily by the gods. From the ground one sees no vegetation or lichen or shattered rock. Only one significant tree, an eighty-foot ponderosa pine, grows on the cliff—and you'll look for fifteen minutes before spotting it. The overall sheerness—on certain facets the wall is close to ninety degrees—is astonishing. Virtually no visible ledges mar the monolith. A quick and easy description, then: El Cap is the world's cleanest steep granite monolith.

Climbers universally called it El Cap back in the times we're now speaking of, the late 1950s; "The Captain" later became popular, and this literal translation of the Spanish is wonderfully appropriate. The original Indian name, To-tó-kon-oo-lah, was never used by whites. In March 1851, pointing to a supposed likeness of a human on the cliff's face, Chief Tenaya of the Yosemite tribe told his army captors that To-tó-kon-oo-lah meant "Rock Chief." A translator, who happened to be a Spanish speaker, shortened this name to El Capitán. The officers, instantly understanding the word, readily took it up, minus the accent mark. The name soon took hold, though for a time both Crane Mountain and Giant's Tower were alternates.

Yet another version of the naming of El Cap exists, and climbers may prefer this one. To-tó-kon-oo-lah, according to the early Yosemite writer Galen Clark, is actually the Indian name for an inchworm. This heroic worm crawled upward to rescue two youths stuck high above. How then did we get "El Capitan" from this native legend? Don't ask; just think about the possibility that the first named Yosemite climber was a worm and also a rescuer.

Aside from this lone invertebrate, I think it's safe to say that no being before 1950 entertained even a moment's thought about climbing El Cap. It simply sat there, a definition of the impossible. Climbers weren't afraid of it, for they couldn't imagine themselves up there. No one brooded over possible routes or stared longingly at the monolith, for no possible routes existed. El Cap, distant as the moon, endured outside the climbing sphere, simply a famous tourist attraction. The world's largest clean and exposed granite cliff.

Warren Harding's name will forever be associated with El Capitan, for he climbed it first and thus, automatically, became a legendary figure. Thirty-three years old in 1957, Harding had been climbing only five years. A tenacious and visionary man, he had been an iconoclast from the beginning. While the two boldest climbers of the mid-1950s, Mark Powell and Wally Reed, pushed free-climbing standards with almost every climb, Harding often thought in grandiose "engineering" terms. While Powell and Reed climbed as fast as demons, Harding was content to spend days on the cliffs. While Powell and Reed climbed only with skilled companions, Harding grabbed anyone who knew how to belay—and some who didn't. These traits became far more pronounced in later years, but even in the mid-fifties, when I first met Harding, he was known to be "distinctive."

My father, a chemist, worked at Shell Development and had long listened to the wild climbing tales related by his boss, Hervey Voge, of Lunch Ledge fame. In 1954 Voge introduced both of us to the local Berkeley rocks, and this is how, a few years later, I came to be perched atop Pinnacle Rock at a Sierra Club gathering, watching a flashy Jaguar roar up and park in the nearby street. "It's Warren Harding," someone whispered. Out stepped a handsome, devilish fellow with a young woman draped on his arm. Short and classically wiry, he strolled over to our group, a furtive gleam in his eye. At this time Harding was locally famous for his feats in Yosemite two years earlier, notably the second ascent of the notorious Lost Arrow Chimney. So I stared closely, trying to measure the man. I thought I would see him swarm up our practice routes, but instead he sat down and began drinking jug wine and telling stories. A sociable chap, I thought, but why doesn't he climb? Though he wore army fatigue pants, like most of us, he had dyed his black. Looking at his black flashing eyes, his wild black hair, his jet-black pants, his sultry moll by his side, his wine, and his lack of interest in what anyone was climbing, I couldn't believe my eyes. I was fascinated, mainly because the other climbers I knew were spectacled scientists, staid folk who would never have dreamed of wheeling up to a rock with a sports car and a jug and a flashy dame.

That night, as was the custom following an afternoon of climbing, we gathered at someone's house for a spaghetti feed. I watched the gallon jug

Warren Harding, about 1969 (Photo: Glen Denny)

of Mountain Red disappear and Harding get looser and looser. Overflowing with stories, he was the center of attention. Intrigued, I was still miffed that he hadn't climbed on our tiny crag, for at the time I had seen few expert climbers at work.

In the next few years I found out much more about the fellow's personal life, as well as some details of his climbing career. The Jaguar, painted purple at the request of a woman Harding was romancing ("Miss Puerto Rico, 1935," Harding told me recently), figured in several stories. Pulled over by a highway patrolman once for passing a Cadillac at better than 100 miles an hour, Harding haughtily informed the cop, "I hope you don't think I was racing him; I could have gone much faster." This story was told to me by John Shonle, a grad student at Berkeley who lived with a group of six climber-skiers at a huge, two-story house they had named Toad Hall. This was a place Harding frequently visited on his trips down to the Bay Area from Sacramento, where he lived at the time. Shonle also craved the fast lane, and one time he and Harding took part in an official sports-car race. The Jag overheated, however, and Harding dropped out, never to return to the circuit. "I had the feeling," Shonle told me later, "that Warren simply couldn't cope with organized racing." Harding, always marching to a different tune, later told an interviewer that he and his buddies loved "to go screaming around, wearing out tires, going to wineries in the Napa Valley. Drinking was very much part of the thing."

Climbing, being less organized than racing, appealed far more to a person who "had an outrageous approach to all of life," to use Shonle's words. Although Harding had made several significant climbs in 1954, he became a household name because of El Cap. Harding of El Cap, as in Lawrence of Arabia. Was he a visionary far ahead of his time? I think a fair answer is that Harding was indeed a visionary—but one only a little ahead of his time. It's highly unlikely that El Cap would have remained unclimbed for long.

The 1957 first ascent of the northwest face of Half Dome proved that a huge, steep, and treeless wall could be climbed. Harding, greeting Robbins, Gallwas, and Wilson on top, was outwardly congratulatory, but his brain was churning. Upon his return to the Valley floor, Harding drove to the base of El Cap and stared upward. He had instantly thought of the monolith for his next climb, for it was now obviously Yosemite's "last great problem." But where on the 320-odd acres of mostly blank, vertical granite was a potential route? Discovering a possible route on most cliffs is not as easy as one might think. Certain features jump out at the knowledgeable viewer, but the trick lies in connecting them. El Cap, like most of Yosemite's big walls, had a myriad of cracks shooting skyward for hundreds of feet. These random features were obviously climbable, though some were wider than one might like. Yet all were annoyingly scattered across the great wall; none went straight from bottom to top.

Lying on their backs in the hot meadowlands beside the Merced River, Harding, Mark Powell, and Bill "Dolt" Feuerer spent a full day in late June 1957 scanning the wall with binoculars. Wayne Merry, a crew-cut seasonal ranger that summer, dropped by at one point and argued for the middle left side of the great southern escarpment, the route later to be known as the Salathé Wall. But the others had their eyes fixed on a more direct route.

El Cap has two major faces, the southwest and the southeast. These convenient directional terms are somewhat misleading, for the two faces intersect not at defined right angles, as their names imply, but more at an ill-defined sixty degrees. To an observer standing on the road directly below, this angle is vague, for both faces blend into each other. Only from the side can one fully appreciate the dividing line, a beautiful prow soaring upward, steepening always, for nearly 3,000 feet. Concentrating their attention on this sometimes subtle prow, or buttress, or nose, the trio spied ledges, crack systems, and broken areas that undoubtedly had never been studied before. If this potpourri of rock features could be connected, then the upper half of the wall could be reached—and it looked much more straightforward, if repulsively vertical.

The route they picked out, soon to become a world-famous one (but not called the Nose for several more years), was devious and inobvious on its lower 2,000 feet. If the individual sections hardly looked splendid from below, the sweeping curves of the lower face and the grand, endless dihedrals of the upper 1,000 feet made up for this. In short, the location was a stunning one. "I'd say we chose the Nose as much for its aesthetic appeal as for its practical features," Harding wrote later.

Harding and his friends did a good job that day. They envisioned the wild pendulums that would have to be made to connect crack systems on the lower half. They spotted the six ledges that would become Camps I to VI. Harding made only one small error: he thought that the formidable ceiling he later called the Roof Pitch (and later yet to be known as the Great Roof) could be bypassed by cracks to its right. These turned out to be water streaks, however, and the roof had to be attacked directly. By the end of the day Harding and his buddies realized that the Nose could be done. It would take time, and it would take an unprecedented number of bolts. But it was not impossible.

A week went by as Harding assembled equipment and laid plans. Surprisingly, the easiest part was finding companions for the rash venture. Powell and Dolt had been skeptical at first, even though both had previously eyed the face. Yet both men felt strong and confident, and Harding's grit and enthusiasm were even then known. The trio knew immediately that making the climb in one push would be impossible, absurd, unthinkable. This was not to be a several-day jaunt. Harding's longest climb was four days, and the others' even shorter. The longest anyone had ever spent

The great sweep of the Nose of El Capitan. The Salathé Wall is to the left; part of the shadowed North America Wall is visible. (Photo: Glen Denny)

on an American rock wall, without support, was five days—the Steck-Salathé route on Sentinel. Water and supplies for much longer than that simply couldn't be carried.

And thus siege climbing on American rock was born. As Harding has pointed out repeatedly, the climb required a new philosophy: an expedition mentality. If one were to climb short sections at a time and then rappel to earth, leaving ropes in place, then supplies could be transported ever upward. Well-stocked camps could be established on the bigger ledges, and the fixed ropes—and more and more supplies—could slowly be pushed higher and higher. This technique had worked in the Himalaya. Would it work on the Nose? The climbers themselves would have to act as Sherpas, but since there were no real weather problems, little hurry, and an extraordinarily easy retreat (a few hours' worth of rappels, a ten-minute walk, and a ten-minute drive would take you from halfway up the face to Yosemite Lodge's bar), this would hardly be an insurmountable problem.

On July 4, 1957, the trio started up the wall. Their first goal was Sickle Ledge, a comfortable, curving platform some 550 feet above the base. Not surprisingly, the route began immediately with direct aid. Though the wall here was not particularly steep—perhaps seventy degrees—it was smooth and basically holdless. A fairly good crack system shot upward, and belay ledges appeared when needed. Not too bad, the climbers thought, but as they neared their goal the cracks petered out, and two pendulum traverses, the first of many to come, were needed to reach Sickle.

Three days were spent on these initial pitches, with the men alternating leads and then rappelling their fixed ropes each night to the comfort of the Valley floor. On the fourth day, as on a Himalayan expedition, the team moved up into Camp I. Sickle, soon covered with ropes, water bottles, clothing, and food, became home for the next four nights.

The wall steepened appreciably above Sickle Ledge, and the next section of the route was characterized by disconnected cracks and horrific exposure. Wild pendulums led across sheer walls to sling belays. Wide cracks shot upward and then ended. Dolt, an engineer interested in equipment, had manufactured some heavy, wide-angle channel pitons—up to two inches wide—and these came in handy in many places, for the climbing was getting serious. On four separate occasions the leader fell after pitons had popped out; Harding sported a badly rope-burned hand and several bruised ribs from one of these tumbles.

On day seven the team encountered the feature that came to be known as the Stoveleg Crack, a 300-foot series of two-to-three-inch-wide slits on the eighty-degree wall. Fortunately, Harding had spotted this landmark from the ground and had brought along several specialty pitons, ones acquired in a strange way. During the fall of 1956, Frank Tarver, the youth who had climbed with Harding in 1954, decided to search a local dump for old angle-iron stock from which to fashion wide-angle pitons. Working his way through a labyrinth of old bedsprings and rusting appliances, Tarver spied four enameled stovelegs, separated from an old-fashioned stove. Buying these for a song, he and a friend smashed one end of each U-shaped leg and brazed the flattened section. Next, they drilled a hole through the steel and attached a ring. Voilà! A sizable angle piton was born, one much larger than the ones Gallwas would later make for Half Dome, or that Dolt would make for the Nose. Nine inches long, and wide enough to fit cracks between two and three inches, the device weighed fifteen ounces. Naturally, the metallurgical qualities of this gadget were suspect, but it would obviously work—and that was what mattered.

In the spring of 1957, Tarver, heading for Alaska and knowing that Harding had big plans for the upcoming season, gave his friend the four stoveleg pitons, and these devices quickly entered into legend. Many years later, as Tarver told me about the origins of the pitons, he added, "You know, it's ironic that of all the climbing equipment I fabricated over the years, the piece that gained notoriety is the one I never used myself or considered very noteworthy at the time."

But the monster pitons allowed Harding to nail his way up much of the 300-foot section. Since the pitons were few and the cracks uniform, he had to leapfrog the devices upward, a frightening situation. One can imagine Harding, seventy feet above his belayer, standing in slings on this absurd piece of a Hotpoint stove, looking down at several more of the devices pecked into the crack directly underneath. Below the bottom one he'd see the rope billowing out free of the wall in the wind, for he'd had to remove many of the lower pitons, stovelegs and others, to use them again higher up.

Time for a safety bolt, even if placed next to a perfect crack. The danger was simply getting too great. Back in these Dark Ages climbers mostly used bolts that were three-eighths of an inch in diameter, and drilling each gigantic hole by hand proved to be a time-consuming and strenuous process. Nevertheless, Harding was not frugal: he and his mates fixed 125 bolts into the cliff during the ensuing months. Safety took precedence over risk.

The stoveleg pitons became battered and twisted, even losing their enamel after a few days of this maltreatment, so the trio returned to earth on July 11, having fixed their ropes to 1,050 feet, a ropelength short of Dolt Tower, the prominent ledge named for Feuerer and destined to become Camp II. Harding, Powell, and Dolt had climbed for a total of seven days, managing an average of 150 feet a day. Though this seems slow, we again must remember the state of the equipment in those days. And the laborious drilling. And the hauling of supplies. The fear factor also contributed to the lack of progress, for belay spots were wisely made bombproof, with two bolts and several pitons used as backups. This conservative technique was used especially at the sites of sling belays (or hanging belays), places where not a trace of a ledge existed.

A nonclimbing problem arose immediately upon the trio's return. As Harding later put it, "it seemed that our climbing presented quite a spectacle and had attracted a crowd of tourists, which created a traffic jam at the road-junction near the base." The authorities were not happy, and, after a conference with the chief ranger, Harding's group agreed to postpone their climb until after the Labor Day weekend, in those days the traditional end of the tourist season.

But it was actually Thanksgiving before Harding got back onto the Nose. One of the reasons for the delay was a sad one: Mark Powell had badly injured his left ankle on September 20. He had taken a young woman climbing on Arrowhead Spire, an easy climb near Yosemite Point Buttress. Moving fast—and thinking more about a prospective liaison than the climb—he carelessly popped off the rock, falling some thirty feet onto a ledge. Since the woman was a beginner, she couldn't get down on her own and go for help. Because of a wind, their shouts drifted every which way but down. At dusk someone finally heard the screams, and rescuers arrived in the middle of the night. By that time Powell's wound, a compound dislocation of the ankle, had been grinding into dirt and granite for nearly twelve hours. I once tactlessly asked him if this thrashing had anything to do with carnal activity. "How I wish," he said with a big grin.

A full day passed before doctors examined Powell, and the delay proved catastrophic, for infection already ruled the wound. He spent weeks in a county hospital ward, his stinking purple limb awaiting the surgeon's saw. This was avoided, but he would limp for the rest of his life.

With Powell out of the El Cap picture, Harding cast about for partners. He sent Royal Robbins a card: "Why don't you join us?" Robbins declined, later telling an interviewer that he didn't wish to join Harding "because it was his scene, and because I didn't want to do it that way [with fixed ropes], even though I didn't think it could be done any other way."

Harding then asked Wally Reed, a modest and talented climber who worked at Yosemite Lodge when he wasn't going to college; he agreed. Allen Steck heard the siren call of Harding, and he, too, came to the Valley. He now remembers the event as a strange interlude in his climbing life. With two babies in his household, and with job responsibilities in Berkeley, the veteran of Sentinel hadn't climbed in several years. Now he was asked to go up onto the most fearsome wall in Yosemite. "Harding said not to worry," Steck later told me. "He'd do all the leading; he just needed a belayer. I thought it might be fun. It wasn't."

Thus two newcomers joined Harding and Dolt for the next phase. One high point of this four-day jaunt was a turkey dinner, prepared by Harding's mother and hauled by the foursome up to Sickle Ledge. An inordinate amount of time was taken up with hauling supplies, a laborious process in

The pendulum into Stoveleg Crack, Nose of El Capitan (Photo: Glen Denny)

those days before mechanical ascenders. Prusiking on less-than-vertical walls, one's knuckles constantly scraped against the rock; and on diagonal fixed ropes, common on the lower part of the route, strange forces and torques came into play, making the effort especially awkward and strenuous. Not fun at all, especially with a forty-pound haul bag attached to the waist.

Although the climbing ropes were nylon, of course, the fixed ropes were manila, a far cheaper material. The manila ropes left in place had swayed in the breeze for several months by this time, and Reed learned firsthand of what long-term abrasion can do to a rope. He had just begun prusiking up a section of rope when suddenly he plummeted back onto a ledge: the rope had broken. Luckily the ledge was a fair-sized one and he didn't roll off. "Henceforth," Harding wrote later, "all fixed ropes would be nylon—and expense be damned!"

It took a day and a half just to reach the previous high point, and Harding managed only sixty feet of new ground late on day two. That night marked the first sling bivouac in Yosemite climbing; the foursome simply held their positions and stood in their slings or slumped against crude fanny belts. Twelve hours of darkness; a night to remember.

Steck had a horrible time. The exposure appalled him, and he felt worthless. In the middle of the night came a grating sound followed by curses. Harding, some fifteen feet above Steck, had chosen to bivouac with his weight mainly on a gigantic T-bar "piton" fashioned from construction stock. Harding had used an oversized hammer to implant this monster into the wide crack, but the three-inch-wide device, weighing some two pounds, had shifted radically. Although the men laughed it off, one can imagine the quality of the rest of the night's sleep.

The next day began poorly for Steck, who was peed upon by Harding. How does one relieve oneself on a big wall? It comes down to this: gravity rules. But as the sun crept across the beautiful white wall, illuminating each and every crystal, the incident was quickly forgotten.

Harding nailed ninety feet to the top of Dolt Tower, a classic bivouac spot, flat and spacious. Just as he began clambering onto this ledge, a near-tragedy occurred. Stepping out of his aid slings to make the transition to easy free climbing, he grabbed a huge boulder, one presumably well lodged in a wide crack. It wasn't. As it started to roll outward, Harding fell back onto his last piton and prayed. The boulder stayed put, and a breathless Harding soon found a way around it. He quickly placed a bolt and then spent ten minutes lashing the boulder to it.

The four men, extremely happy to be on a level surface after some thirty straight hours standing in slings, settled in for a far more comfortable night. On the next day, their fourth, after a little upward exploration, it was time to head back to the city. For Steck, this retreat came none too soon; he had never felt truly comfortable. Still, it was a great thrill to rappel 1,200 feet to the ground in a matter of hours, not worrying about anchors or having to retrieve ropes. Some of the diagonal rappels, however, were frightening, as were some of the hanging rappel transfers. And the manila ropes hardly inspired confidence.

Winter arrived. The manila ropes continued to sway and fray, so in March 1958 a wary Harding, with Dolt, replaced the lines with seven-sixteenths-inch nylon, a necessary measure if they were to persuade anyone else to accompany them. Powell, meanwhile, was eager to join the action. His ankle still festered, but he figured that since aid climbing dominated, he might as well be standing in slings as standing around watching. So in mid-April the threesome headed up the wall once again, this time equipped with the "Dolt Cart," a lightweight, two-wheeled device built by Feuerer. This contraption soon had to be abandoned, for, as Harding wrote later, "it required four people and thousands of feet of rope to run the thing!" The team was discovering one of the sobering realities of siege climbing: since most of the effort is expended in supplying the upper camps, little time is left for exploring new territory. This particular weekend excursion was a fine example—they had climbed only sixty feet of virgin rock.

About this time I went up to the Valley with a small Sierra Club group. We were vaguely aware of the El Cap activity, so after our Saturday climb several of us hiked to the base of the wall, a ten-minute jaunt, and stared at the single fixed rope vanishing upward into the shimmering whiteness. I snapped a photo of this odd sight, as strange to me as an alien spaceship.

When I recently saw this slide again, for the first time in decades, its banality amused me. A rope fixed onto the flanks of El Cap? I saw so many in the next few years that the image of the thread snaking up the wall seems almost natural, part of the cliff itself. Yet, obviously, I had been transfixed by the sight in April 1958: the first siege rope ever set up in Yosemite.

We sat quietly for half an hour, walking over and touching the rope on occasion and even giving it a tug. The wall was overpowering when seen up close, and we thought the project insane. Naturally, to disguise our emotions, we spewed forth glib comments. Harding was a dreamer who'd never finish the project. Harding was stalled. Nine months so far? This wasn't a climb, it was an engineering feat. A circus. We "experts" gathered at the base of the great cliff, fresh that very day from the 200th-odd ascent of the trade route on the Lower Brother, knew in our hearts that we were witnessing the doomed, grandiose scheme of a madman. These were our public comments. Privately, I think that all of us would have shed a finger or two to have had the vision and courage of the renegade Harding. I felt this way, yet I had no intimation whatsoever that a year later I myself would be playing Sherpa up fixed ropes on yet another Harding route.

In May the team made better progress, this time up more amenable rock. El Cap Tower, a fabulous ledge at the 1,400-foot level, became Camp III and was stocked with hundreds of pounds of water and gear. Texas Flake, the perfectly named shard of rock just above, went quickly, for behind it lay an easy, hidden chimney, one of the easiest sections of the entire route. Above this was flawless rock, and the team had to spend a day establishing a diagonal ladder of bolts. This took them to one of the classic pitches of the climb, Boot Flake, another perfectly named slab of rock. Harding nailed his way up the right edge of this fifty-foot-high feature, quite aware that the crack tended to be an expanding one. He led the pitch slowly and carefully, placing no bolts for protection. A long fall, in which the wide pitons would zipper out, was an ever-present possibility, and this lead established Harding forever as a masterful and bold aid specialist.

By May 25, the end of this particular effort, the fixed ropes extended midway up the cliff to the bolts atop Boot. The rangers once again became upset with the team's progress, for the solstice beckoned and tourists flocked, and, for the second time, they implemented the summertime ban. Harding's team, demoralized by both the enforced delays and the lack of progress while on the cliff, began to unravel. Dolt, according to Harding, "began making ominous biblical quotations: 'Those who live by the sword,' and so on." He dropped out, and Powell's chutzpah began to evaporate with the reality of his slow-to-heal injury.

One might imagine that by this time Harding would have been desolate and desperate, with his ropes, reputation, and energy on the line, wondering what to do next. He couldn't quit. He couldn't go up on the Nose alone. What to do? Incredibly, he laid siege to yet *another* wall.

The east face of the Washington Column is no El Cap. Located at the opposite end of the Valley, the 1,100-foot cliff, ignored by climbers and tourists alike, is just one of many supersteep cliffs in the Valley. Harding, and Harding alone, had already picked out a route up the often-overhanging wall. A crack system shot up and right all the way to the top, with only a few breaks. The cracks were wide; overhangs loomed; and, like El Cap, few ledges marred the verticality.

In June 1958 Harding convinced two friends from Fresno, Rich Calderwood and George Whitmore, to give the wall a try. Calderwood was a relative beginner; Whitmore was a practiced mountaineer; neither had ever dreamed of being on such an intimidating wall. Armed with a thousand feet of rope and a hundred pitons, they reached a four-foot-wide platform known as Overnight Ledge in two days. The last 150 feet up to this ledge proved spectacular, for the route lay up a crack in the back of a classic open book. Since this crack was an inch-and-a-half wide for much of its length, Harding had to nest one-inch angles together and also use some of the wide-angle pitons made by Dolt. Calderwood, following Tarver's example, had manufactured three new stoveleg pitons: now there were seven, and they were used constantly in the wide cracks.

Overnight Ledge, the only decent one on the first 1,000 feet of the 1,100-foot route, was about 500 feet above the talus, and it became a staging area for the efforts that followed. Later, Calderwood and Harding pushed the route a few hundred feet higher, to the base of a fearful-looking overhanging squeeze chimney later to become notorious as the Harding Slot. They turned back here, leaving ropes dangling some 700 feet to the ground. The summer soon ended and El Cap beckoned. The Column would have to wait.

Harding now had equipment plastered over two major walls. When the time came to go back up on the Nose, in the fall of 1958, all seven stoveleg pitons hung from a sling at the Column's high point. Harding and Calderwood prusiked up the ropes to retrieve these, and other equipment, but to their great surprise the stovelegs had vanished! Down they went to search the talus below. After two hours of methodical exploration, they were just about to give up; then they spotted the pitons, nearly hidden in a hole. The frayed and broken sling told the story: rodents had chewed the sling in half. (It's hard to believe that small creatures, most often mice, spend their entire lifespan living *inside* Yosemite's big walls.)

Given all this siege-climbing activity, one might wonder if any of these climbers had jobs. Yes. Harding worked for California's Department of Highways as a surveyor; Whitmore was a pharmacist, Calderwood a student. Although all three could get time off when necessary, most of their climbing was accomplished on weekends. This in large part accounts for the slothlike progress on the Column. A weekend might be "wasted" hauling supplies to a high ledge. Drills might break or dull high on the route, forcing an early retreat. Weather could be a problem: either a storm or a heat wave. Partners might not show up. Girlfriends pleaded for lowland activities.

■

On the Saturday after Labor Day weekend in 1958 a huge effort began to finish the Nose Route. Powell showed up, as did Wally Reed and Calderwood. Two newcomers to the expedition were Wayne Merry, the summer ranger who was now a student at San Jose State College, and John Whitmer, the San Jose climber who four years earlier had accompanied Harding on the north buttress of Middle Cathedral Rock (Whitmer should not be confused with George Whitmore, who had earlier joined the Washington Column team). Harding was desperate to finish. "I continued," he wrote later, "with whatever 'qualified' climbers I could 'con' into this rather unpromising venture."

Nine days passed, days of repetition and boredom punctuated with moments of terror. Haul, haul, haul. Drill, drill, drill. Thunderstorms lashed the team for two days as they cowered in their crude plastic shelters. When it wasn't storming, the heat was stifling. The biggest thrill of this particular effort was the spectacular pendulum off Boot Flake. The top of this feature, an airy but table-flat ledge about fifteen inches wide, was an ideal belay spot. From the ground, a year earlier, Harding had realized that something radical would have to be done here, namely some sort of traverse to the left. Thus was born the King Swing.

"I was damned intimidated by the exposure up there," Merry told me later. "It was just a clear shot to the ground—absolutely dead vertical." Harding once again took charge and a strange lead it was, since it lost about fifty feet of hard-earned elevation. Merry lowered Harding this distance until his feet were about level with the bottom of Boot. Then he began sprinting back and forth across the wall in great arcs, trying to reach something, anything, out to the left, around a subtle corner. Time after time he did the pendulum, sometimes asking for a few more feet of rope to be let out. Finally, on about the fifth try, he jammed his fingers into a short crack and managed to lodge a quick piton.

Then he looked upward. The crack ended in a few feet! Now what? Off to the left was a broken area, but twenty feet of utterly blank wall lay in between. Another pendulum was called for, so Harding yelled for more slack. The two climbers couldn't see each other by this time, and even the shouts were ambiguous. Merry related the gist of the ensuing "conversation" many years later.

"What's going on?" Merry yelled.

"Lower me some more," Harding screamed. "Slower, goddamn it!"

"I can't hear you!"

"Slower, you idiot! Stop there!"

One of the loneliest and most dependent feelings in climbing is to be doing a wild and exposed pendulum out of sight of your belayer—and this was perhaps the wildest pendulum traverse ever done. Twenty feet below the piton, and now about seventy feet below the top of Boot, Harding began swinging once again. Since the next goal, shattered flakes and ledges, was visible and secure, this second swing was easier than the first and Harding soon finished it, climbed up a ways, and set up a belay station.

Though the key to the upper wall had been found, the problems were hardly over. Following a pendulum is as lonely and scary as leading it, and the procedure is far more difficult in terms of rope management, especially when you are trying to establish fixed lines. Hours passed before Merry arrived, and one can appreciate that the pair checked knots and procedures dozens of times. The belay station soon sprouted ropes and bolts. A day was spent connecting this airy spot with El Cap Tower, and the fixed ropes soon stretched diagonally across the sickeningly steep wall near Texas Flake.

Even with all this furious activity, the high point was pushed only a few hundred feet higher, to just beyond Camp IV, a series of barely adequate ledges at the 1,750-foot mark. Above loomed the Great Roof, the most prominent feature of the Nose. This obstacle would have to wait. Down the six men went. This was to be the last trip for Reed, Whitmer, and Powell, whose ankle still bothered him.

Two more attempts in October proved equally fruitless, at least as far as gaining new ground. As before, much of the time was spent rerouting ropes, cringing from storms, and stocking the upper camps. The park rangers were once again getting antsy, not because of the traffic jams this time, but simply because of the interminable delays. Harding was given a deadline: finish by Thanksgiving. "I have never understood how this was to be enforced," he later wrote.

On Saturday, November 1, Harding, Calderwood, Merry, and George Whitmore (joining the climb for the first time) began what was to be the final push. That day they reached Camp IV after dark, following a 1,900-foot prusik. With perfect weather and unlimited supplies, there could be no excuses this time. The team had but 1,100 feet to go and they could string their umbilical cord clear to the top. Harding and Merry would be in the lead at all times, pushing the route. Calderwood and Whitmore would be granite Sherpas, hauling loads up the ropes day after day.

"The following seven days," Harding wrote, "blurred into a monotonous grind—if living and working 2,500 feet above the ground on a vertical granite face can be considered monotonous!" One of the highlights of the first week proved to be the worrisome Great Roof. This monster ceiling, easily visible from afar, looked awesome, but a perfect crack leading up to it, and then horizontally under it, allowed Harding to make short work of the obstacle. With its subtle curves and dramatic planes, the roof proved to be the single most aesthetic section of the whole route.

On the Great Roof Pitch, Nose of El Capitan (Photo: Glen Denny Collection)

The team reached Camp V, a spacious ledge a few pitches higher, on November 4. A pitch higher lay a small but comfortable niche, named by Harding the Glowering Spot. As Merry came up to this shallow hole, he saw Harding crouched in the niche, a sullen look on his hairy, dirt-streaked face. He had just broken his hammer and was in a foul mood. "Harding," Wayne Merry wrote me recently, "named the Glowering Spot the minute he got there, because it suited his eldritch humor." Others might have named the nice little ledge Sunrise Niche, or Thank God Hole, or Crystal Ledge—but not the inventive and imaginative Harding.

Camp VI, a fine triangular platform at 2,400 feet, saw its first humans a few days later; Whitmore and Harding celebrated by sharing a tenth of port, which they had treated as gently as a baby during the long hauling sessions.

The upper third of the Nose is one of the most soul-satisfying places in Yosemite. Planes of marble-smooth granite shoot upward toward infinity. The various dihedral walls, dead vertical at this stage, converge in broad, angular facets, and climbing through this magical place is like living inside a cut diamond.

For hundreds of feet at a time Harding never had to think twice about what to do. The routine was so simple: stand in the top loop of the aid slings, gaze for five seconds at the size of the crack three feet above, remove a one-inch angle from the hardware rack, smash the pin hard with fifteen or twenty blows, hammer-test it with a cursory downward "whop," clip a carabiner into it, and then move an aid sling upward. This sequence was repeated scores of times in these upper dihedrals.

The first week of November passed rapidly. Why, with all the easy nailing, did this section take so long? Several explanations come to mind. The wall was frightfully intimidating, and this led to overdriven pitons that then had to be painstakingly hammered out. The cracks were often packed full of dirt and grass, and this caused delays. The days were short, the mornings cold. Each day's prusik up to the high point, sometimes 300 feet above, seemed to take forever. Rope management was a nightmare, with all the various ropes and anchors. Sling belays took a long time to set up, and belay transfers took half an hour to effect. The leader, either Harding or Merry, placed bolts routinely every once and a while for safety reasons, even next to perfect cracks. The belay anchors usually consisted of two large bolts, each of which took at least forty-five minutes to place. Drills dulled, and leaders cursed. With these myriad problems, it was no wonder that the team averaged only 100 feet per day.

Adding to the snail's pace was a shortage of equipment, especially bolts and drills. Calderwood rappelled all the way to the ground one day, called the Ski Hut in Berkeley, received a special-delivery package the following day, and prusiked back up the next day with his valuables. Such effort, however, was wearing the twenty-one-year-old Calderwood down. On Saturday, the eighth, he fled down the ropes to the ground, later telling a reporter, "The pressure just got too heavy." What he didn't mention was that he had been casually moving around on the relatively spacious Camp VI without being tied in to the rock. In a moment of inattention he had almost pitched off the ledge. He immediately jumped onto the rappel ropes and started down. According to Wayne Merry, "He told us later that partway down he found himself sobbing uncontrollably, for no reason he could fathom, maybe other than missing work, missing classes, and missing his pregnant wife." Calderwood thus became the first person to be humiliated by the overpowering wall, but he was hardly the last: within a decade dozens of brave and not-so-brave climbers had turned tail. Much later, Calderwood told me that it wasn't the exposure that had bothered him; it was the idea of playing around endlessly on a cliff while he should have been studying and working. "My work ethic," he told me wistfully, "got to me. My powers of concentration were just not assembled in the right place."

So now there were three. George Whitmore, a calm and shy loner, was content to haul loads, and Harding and Merry didn't see him for days on end as he worked and slept lower on the route. He spent one long and dark night alone in a wild rain- and windstorm on Dolt Tower, calling it one of his most miserable nights ever in the mountains.

Wayne Merry, a competent and steady climber, was by now a conservation/education major at San Jose State College. Neglecting his studies (he barely passed physics that semester), he had opted to join the team, knowing that Harding was in need of reinforcements. Though relatively inexperienced, he nevertheless had, like Harding, a calm mind and an extremely pleasant personality. Merry was to lead his fair share on the upper section.

It is impossible to see the rim of El Cap from high on the route, since the sheer walls block out the upward view. Still, Harding and Merry knew they were getting close. On Monday, November 10, a storm moved in and pounded the duo with sleet and snow; no progress whatever was made. On Tuesday they set off at dawn from Camp VI with high hopes, though with only two bolts left. By late afternoon Harding and Merry stood on a tiny ledge only 120 feet below the top, encouraged by shouts from above—friends had hiked up the monolith's back side to greet them.

What followed during the next fourteen hours is now legendary: the most famous single episode in Yosemite's illustrious climbing history. Whitmore caught up to Harding and Merry at six o'clock with a fresh supply of bolts, and at dusk Harding set off with his headlamp. The frightfully exposed wall above overhung in tiers. A crack led upward for a short distance, but it ended in a blank wall—one that extended up and out of sight toward the still-undefined rim. In a short while Harding was hammering away on his drill, an act that he was to repeat twenty-seven times that night. The Iron Man placed many of the bolts hurriedly; only one out of three was inserted all the way in. This saved precious time and was not as dangerous as it sounds, though later parties were somewhat unnerved by the protruding bolts. (All the bolts were replaced some thirty-three years later, and one of the originals, carefully hoarded by the replacer, fetched eight hundred dollars at a recent auction.)

Merry told me about this memorable night: "I remember being absolutely miserable, standing on that little ledge. But seeing that Warren was dangling under an overhang all night, I couldn't bitch. I kept falling asleep standing up, and shivering, and starting to fall over until the anchor caught me. George spent the night impaled on a sharp point, so I guess I was the most comfortable. I remember hearing the sound of the wind and that little tink-tink-tink up above, and seeing that little black spider hanging under the overhang up there in the glow of his headlamp."

All through the frigid night Harding worked, and shortly after first light he wriggled his way out of his slings and crawled onto the gentle summit slabs. It was six o'clock on November 12, 1958. Dozens of people sprawled over the sloping summit cap: friends, hangers-on, reporters, and Harding's girlfriend of the year, Ellen Searby. "I was pent up," Harding confided to a newsman later that day. "I sure grabbed that girl of mine."

Yosemite rock climbing would never be the same. First, an "impossible" wall had been vanquished, and climbers immediately saw the consequences: huge, unclimbed "impossible" walls lay in every direction—

and climbers had now demonstrated that they could spend twelve days living on a vertiginous wall. Also, the enormous publicity given to Harding's climb meant that the general public learned about a crazy new sport for the first time. It would be fatuous to claim that the El Cap epic led to a stampede of new climbers, but within a few years Camp 4 swelled with would-be climbers eager to make their mark—and eager to tell the nonclimbing world about their accomplishments. It would be equally fatuous to claim that we who frequented the cliffs before the El Cap adventure scoffed at commercialism. Or that we didn't succumb later. Or that everything would have been just dandy if Harding had never climbed El Cap. In reality, the event was just another step in the evolution of rock climbing. The sport can't stay the same for long—and thus it changes. Whether a change is "good" or "bad" is often impossible to say, especially at first. Still, favorable publicity (and maybe even unfavorable publicity) always increases a sport's participants, and this in turn leads to crowding, resentment, a longing for the "good old days"—and almost always a surge in the quality of the sport.

War-sized headlines blazed across the San Francisco afternoon papers of November 12. "Yosemite Climbers Make It" roared the *News*. "El Capitan Conquered" blared the *Call Bulletin*. Huge photos showed Harding pulling over the rim, looking remarkably like a street bum. Generally accurate articles spilled over into the papers' interiors, with numerous sidebar stories attached.

An editorial in the *News* lauded the climbers and their ideals, also adding a plea for global peace: "If [mankind] doesn't kill himself first—on a mountain or with a bomb—he just may learn how to inhabit the earth as God planned."

The *Oregon Journal* echoed this sentiment: "If these three have done nothing else, they have proved that men of our day possess stamina, courage and determination equal to those of any age." But the editorial writer issued a warning: "It is to be hoped that their feat will not inspire the uninitiated to like endeavor."

The publicity, though startling because of its volume, was not really surprising. In July of 1957, after the initial attempt, several small Central Valley papers had covered the story. In September of the successful year, during the nine-day attempt, an account with photos by Wally Reed had appeared in the *Oakland Tribune,* the first Yosemite climbing story since the Higher Spire climb of 1934 to attain front-page coverage in a metropolitan newspaper.

During the final November effort, the Nose story was mentioned on eight separate days in the *San Francisco Chronicle*. Was Harding a publicity hound who instigated this flood of news accounts? Not directly, perhaps, but it was understood that his girlfriend, or another companion, would track the progress on the cliffs and phone details to the newsman.

Climbing publicity is not intrinsically sinister. Yet for those who regarded climbing as a type of "pure" sport, as many of us in those halcyon days were wont to do, publicity was something to be shunned. Outsiders couldn't possibly understand our motives, so you climbed for yourself. You dealt with the cliff alone—and for your style and actions you answered only to yourself. You wanted peer recognition, of course, but you *never* went outside the immediate group for acceptance. Harding, who obviously felt differently, later came to call us "Valley Christians" for our high-minded beliefs regarding publicity and other matters.

Harding had few compunctions about publicity and was on the phone soon after his return to the Valley floor. *Life* magazine paid the group several thousand dollars for photographs, but the election of John XXIII as pope two weeks earlier knocked the climbing story out of the way, and the pictures were never used. (The money, however, enabled Merry to get married, an idea that had come upon him one shivering night at Camp IV. "Well, why *not* marry Cindy?" Harding had asked.) Merry and Harding collaborated on a story for *Argosy,* a men's magazine, and this was published the following April.

The National Park Service's director, Conrad Wirth, told newsmen that his agency wanted to "cut out the stunt and daring trick climbing that people go into hoping to be able to commercialize on what they accomplish." Perhaps because this attitude was shared by most rockclimbers, the climbing press remained relatively silent. The *Sierra Club Bulletin,* long noted as *the* repository of California climbing events, never mentioned the first ascent of the Nose. Neither did *Summit,* at the time the only American monthly devoted exclusively to hiking and climbing. The only contemporary account ever published (in the climbing press) of the world's most difficult rock climb appeared in the *American Alpine Journal* of 1959. Harding's understated four-page article, simply titled "El Capitan," attracted little attention; the journal, basically an Eastern-oriented publication, had a highly limited circulation. Still, Harding's piece garnered the distinction of being the first modern-day Yosemite article to be featured in this respected national journal. Soon dozens would follow.

CHAPTER 4

Weekenders No More: 1957–1959

[Outsiders] seem to picture Yosemite climbers as walking up to the base of a 2,000-foot buttress (which undoubtedly overhangs somewhat) and pounding up a lone direct-aid crack which extends upward for as far as the eye can see and farther!... What these critics fail to realize is that some of the finest 4th and 5th class climbing to be found anywhere makes up the major portion of the buttress climbs.

—George Sessions, 1958

Not all attention, of course, was focused on El Capitan in 1957 and 1958; most climbers regarded the ongoing Nose saga as a side show and went about their business as usual. But a subtle change was taking place during these two years. Until this period, climbers had occupied Camp 4 only on weekends. People went elsewhere for their climbing vacations: the Tetons, Canada, the Northwest. Rock climbing was still generally thought of as simply a facet of mountaineering; you trained in the Valley on spring weekends and then migrated to the mountains in the summer. Exceptions existed, naturally, but rarely had climbers *lived* in the Valley.

Mark Powell, however, had saved some money and, for a few months in 1957, lived in Camp 4 full time, the first climber to become a Yosemite resident rather than a visitor. Powell was at loose ends that year, unmarried and restless. He knew that a person who didn't mind a little hardship had no need of a full-time job. Life was cheap in the Valley: one didn't pay camp fees, didn't need any shelter besides a flimsy tent, and didn't even think of suits and ties. One had no real need for a car, or insurance policies, or haircuts. If one cooked in camp, in lieu of grabbing a burger at nearby Yosemite Lodge, a dollar a day would suffice. Those who worked in the winter and saved even a few hundred dollars might have six months a year in which to play around. The best incentive for a long-term visit,

Mark Powell, 1965 (Photo: Glen Denny)

sensed early by Powell, was that by climbing four or five times a week one could get into magnificent shape, something that weekenders couldn't. In retrospect it's easy to see how the standards began to shoot upward with the arrival of resident climbers.

Powell whirled up the cliffs like a dervish in 1957, almost as if he knew this would be his last productive summer. On July 18, a week after he, Harding, and Dolt had retreated from their first attempt on El Cap, he and Wally Reed put up a new route on Pulpit Rock. While the Improbable Traverse route proved insignificant in the overall picture, it certainly showed the direction in which Yosemite climbing was going. For seventeen years people had been nailing their way up the two normal routes. Powell searched the pinnacle carefully, selected a likely free line, and boldly went up on it—and made it. Not content to follow in others' footsteps, he experimented with the unknown, pushed his limits, and often went out on the proverbial limb. The best climbers were to emulate this attitude during the remarkable decade to come.

Two days after Pulpit, Powell and Reed chose a far more harrowing wall, the northeast face of Middle Cathedral Rock. Harding, as recounted, had garnered the two buttresses on either side of this broad face several years earlier. Powell wanted the wall itself, for beautiful it was, covered

Joe Fitschen, 1965 (Photo: Glen Denny)

with hundreds of tiny ledges and flakes visible only in the oblique light of sundown. He knew a route could be worked out, and two days later he and Reed had it, a climb Powell called "comparable with Sentinel Rock's North Face."

Powell and Reed behaved like kids in a candy store. Next came the first ascent of Lower Watkins Pinnacle, an oft-tried spire. Reed must have been busy a week later, for Powell teamed up with Dolt to capture the north buttress of Lower Cathedral Rock, a steep, scary, and dirty route with little to commend it. Still, the 1,000-foot climb required two days and some horrendous aid climbing—and some easy aid climbing. Powell, masterful at pitoncraft, must have levitated up one pitch, described later by Dolt: "An excellent crack enabled Mark to overcome a 70-foot slightly overhanging wall in the corner in 15 minutes."

Two weeks later Reed was again ready for action, and he and Powell climbed a route that later became a true classic: the south face of North Dome. The thrilling, continuous liebacks at the top of this hard-to-reach climb remain in the memories of all who have been there.

Five days later came Powell's climb of Bridalveil East, a steep wall just left of the most ethereal of Yosemite's many waterfalls. Powell grabbed Harding for this one, and they used only four direct-aid pitons in the 600 feet of sheer, water-polished rock. Once again Powell demonstrated a mastery of free climbing. He later wrote a sentence about this climb that to me symbolized the daring direction Valley climbing was taking: "Higher, the necessity of clinging with both hands caused a 70-foot overhanging face to a gnarled tree to be led bereft of pitons."

Labor Day weekend of 1957 proved to be a three-ring circus. Royal Robbins and Joe Fitschen made the fourth ascent of the Lost Arrow Chimney in two days of climbing. Fitschen, Robbins's main climbing partner in the late 1950s, was a twenty-year-old, blue-eyed college student from the Los Angeles area. A slight fellow (as were most of the climbers of this era), he moved up the rock with a quiet fluidity, never grunting or groaning, and always in control—the very definition of an intellectual climber. Most of his climbing had been accomplished at Tahquitz Rock, where he and Robbins had done some amazing routes together. Fitschen had been scheduled to go on the first ascent of the northwest face of Half Dome in June, but at the last minute he couldn't get free from work; Mike Sherrick went in his place.

Knowing the army would soon call upon them, both Robbins and Fitschen wanted one last big climb. With the pair's experience and drive, it was no surprise that they roared up the Arrow Chimney so fast on this holiday weekend, even though Robbins later wrote that he was "almost dizzy with fear contemplating that horrendous gash topped by the unreal pinnacle...." The first four ascents had taken, respectively, five, four, three, and two days. Robbins wryly noted that this tradition of subtracting a day from each party's time "puts rather a strain on the next party." Ironically, six months after these words appeared, the route was indeed done without a bivouac.

Powell and Reed put up a new route on the East Arrowhead Buttress at the same time, but the biggest gem of the holiday weekend was Monday's climb of the Worst Error. The name Harding once again surfaces—in a new context. Harding the Crack Climber is not as well known as Harding the Iron Man. This is fair, since his crack-climbing career was short compared to his big-wall career. Harding always insisted that 5.8 was his maximum, and this was often true. He tended to pound in aid pitons whenever an open face above looked difficult, yet cracks and chimneys proved a different matter; he was superb in these, as he proved in the Labor Day episode at Elephant Rock. This formation, overlooking the Merced River outside the confines of the Valley itself, was an unknown quantity to climbers. From the highway Harding had spotted a gigantic slab, some 500 feet high, plastered like a monster finger against the main rock. Since such exfoliation slabs always have cracks separating them from the mother cliff, Harding and Wayne Merry went to investigate.

The third pitch of the Worst Error, as Harding later named it, turned out to be a twenty-inch-wide slot that soared upward without a break for 115 feet. No protection whatsoever was possible, and Merry led this section, telling me years later, "I was feeling far too claustrophobic to worry about falling." Not particularly difficult for a chimney expert, it is a highly scary pitch to this day. (In 1961 I led this chimney in a state of metabolic uproar. At the base of the pitch I smoked several cigarettes—the first and last ones of my life. This was to calm me. Then I spooned half a jar of honey. This was to ensure superhuman strength. Mort Hempel, my partner, watched this silly ritual with mouth agape and eyes exploding with fear.)

But this sinister slot was a minor obstacle compared to what lay above. Harding disappeared around a corner, and soon Merry realized the rope was no longer moving with authority. Up, down, up, down. Six-inch movements. "I figured I was going to hold a fall, for sure," Merry said later. "I must have checked my anchors a dozen times." Then he heard hammering. And more hammering. Harding, at the base of a horrifying bottomless slot, was trying to nail a short section. Finally he placed a bolt, stood on it, thrust his bantam body into the slit above, and wormed his way up to the top. Though several aid points were needed, this was indeed a sterling effort, demonstrating that Harding was certainly among the first courageous crack specialists. He called the upper pitch "the most difficult stretch I had ever led."

Just weeks after this flurry of activity, Mark Powell's career basically ended with his Arrowhead Spire fall. During an incandescent fifteen months he had established fifteen new routes, including four classics: the northeast face of Middle Cathedral, the Arrowhead Arête, the south face of North Dome, and the east side of Bridalveil Fall. On the latter three climbs he used a total of only eight aid pitons, an outstanding accomplishment. Powell's commendable Valley career included twenty-one first ascents and two first free ascents. He still put up first ascents as late as 1966, but the earlier period was his particular Golden Age.

Obviously, not all Valley climbing of this time involved serious adventures. Rockclimbers had always enjoyed themselves on the smaller cliffs, taking friends up easy routes, or simply taking a "rest day" by doing a standard route in the afternoon. Occasionally a noteworthy or frivolous event took place, one that climbers spoke of for months. The most-talked-about incident of 1957 concerned some well-known (or soon to be well-known) climbers. ABC's "Wide World of Sports" wanted a brief but live Yosemite climbing segment in late March for a "Spring Comes to America" program. They contacted the Sierra Club, who in turn called upon Bob Swift. Hearing that free ropes would be his payment for merely climbing for a few hours, he drove swiftly, as it were, to the Valley and was informed by the ABC director that since he had arrived first he would be the climbing leader. Others had also heard the news. John Harlin raced up from Stanford; he was judged by the film crew (as remembered by Swift) as "not as good as the leader but still competent." Jules Eichorn, of Higher

Spire fame, showed up next: he was "a new man and clumsy looking." He was informed he'd literally be the fall guy, since a staged fall was part of the scenario. A shy, long-faced Frenchman who happened to be in the Valley (giving lectures around America, including one in Berkeley the previous night, which I had attended) watched the whole scene, but Gaston Rébuffat, the most well-known climber in the world, was not asked to join the team. The film crew chose a clifflet near Lower Yosemite Fall, and, after many rehearsals, Eichorn duly popped off. The American public, those few who saw the pointless escapade, once again believed climbing to be a crazy pastime.

With this business over—and no free ropes forthcoming—Swift, Harlin, and Eichorn traipsed over to the Washington Column to show Rébuffat, on his first and only trip to the Valley, what the great granite walls were all about. "Harlin and Gaston were on the lead rope going up to Lunch Ledge," Swift told me recently, "and Gaston seemed to be enjoying himself. Still, I was amused to see that when he came to a tree that John had wormed his way through, for purposes of protection, Gaston would simply untie the rope, climb around the offending branches, then tie on to the rope once again."

With Powell out of the picture, with Robbins and Fitschen incarcerated in the army, and with Harding and his compatriots thinking mostly about El Cap, 1958 was a slow year. No major first ascents were completed, except, of course, the El Cap extravaganza described earlier. Nevertheless, it was hardly a dull year. Occasional out-of-state visitors arrived, and some new faces appeared, ones that would be around for a decade.

Most out-of-staters still shunned the Valley. Easterners had barely heard of the place, and the mountaineers of the Pacific Northwest had mountains and cliffs aplenty within a day's drive. Rockclimbers didn't travel much in the days before interstate highways, but a more insidious reason for the lack of visitors to Yosemite was the general misconception about Valley climbing and traditions. For example, Harvey T. Carter, an eccentric Colorado climber, had visited the Valley in the spring of 1957, full of hubris. He alienated Valley climbers immediately when he left a slip of paper in a summit register (on the Lower Spire, as I recall) reading: "Removed the register for further study." It never reappeared and is perhaps still being analyzed in Colorado. A few days later, Carter managed to work his way up only a few pitches of Steck's route on El Cap's East Buttress before turning tail and fleeing home, much to the amusement of the locals. Apparently he had expected the route to be festooned with fixed pitons, for he wrote to *Summit* with an odd complaint: "I was rather shocked by the apparent lack of climbing and developed routes in [Yosemite]." Sensing his tenuous position, he then proceeded to put his foot firmly in his mouth: "Although I teach a modern advanced standard of climbing I do not care to engage in controversy with people who have no knowledge of the methods which constitute advanced technical climbing."

Outsiders would soon flow into the Valley, but not quite yet. California-based climbers had a few more years of picking the Valley's plums by themselves, and 1958 saw the arrival of one of these climbers, a man who became one of the finest rockclimbers of midcentury, the prototype of the Camp 4 resident "bum," and a master of first ascents, scoring a grand total of forty-eight during his career. Chuck Pratt, nineteen, struggled with physics at UC Berkeley. He didn't really like the discipline, but, since he was barely aware of this, he would stick with college for a few years longer. Meanwhile, he would climb during weekends and summers.

Pratt happened upon climbing in the traditional manner. As a kid in Salt Lake City he devoured mountaineering books in a local library and then experimented with clothesline and lag screws on local rocks. Then his parents made a serendipitous decision: they moved to the San Francisco Bay Area. While in high school in Oakland, circa 1956, Pratt met a self-effacing fellow named Charlie Raymond, who also had illusions and delusions concerning mountain climbing. They scrambled around local cliffs. They enrolled at UC Berkeley together, and there, in the dank basement of Eshleman Hall, the headquarters of the UC Hiking Club, they met others with similar tastes.

Trips to the Valley followed. Pratt's study of arcane theories involving

Camp 4 on a quiet spring weekday (Photo: Glen Denny)

motion and gravity suffered, at perhaps a great loss to physics, for he showed promise. He early sensed a trap, however: excelling at physics might lead eventually to a full-time job, a full-time commitment, and a certain loss of freedom. Pratt, a true romantic, had seen his parents strive for the American dream; he saw their limited success, their nominal happiness, their incomplete existence. Slowly, he began to question the concepts of money, children, and mortgage payments. He was hardly alone in these sentiments, for the Eisenhower years had lulled so many Americans into complacency and visions of material richness that a backlash was inevitable.

While Pratt awaited an epiphany, he climbed. He instantly displayed his talents with an early free ascent of Phantom Pinnacle, a difficult crack climb near the Cathedral Spires. Then, on July 15, 1958, he made his initial first ascent, number one of forty-eight. Though the new route on the northeast face of the Lower Spire hardly shook up the climbing community, I well remember it, for it was also *my* initial first ascent in Yosemite.

I had encountered Pratt several times at the local Berkeley rocks during the previous winter, and we had agreed to head for the Valley after the school year ended, the school year in my case being high school. By early July several of us from Berkeley had migrated to Camp 4. Though we were fairly good climbers, especially Pratt, the big cliffs intimidated us and we stuck mostly to the old standards.

Naturally, we met other climbers. Wally Reed, for instance, was working at Yosemite Lodge during the summer of 1958, and we youths were flattered when a person who had actually climbed on El Cap spoke with us and even climbed with us. Appreciating the Yosemite backcountry as much as he did the great Valley walls, Reed was one of the first to see the possibilities of climbing in Tuolumne Meadows. On July 18 he and Pratt made an attempt on the north face of Fairview Dome, Tuolumne's biggest cliff. They failed but returned in August to finish this elegant climb.

Other members of the UC Hiking Club visited the Valley, some staying for weeks. Krehe Ritter, a math grad student and a French-horn player, was my main climbing partner. (We had driven to the Valley many times in the spring on his underpowered and overloaded Lambretta motorscooter, a ride that took about seven hours, though it seemed twice as long.) In July we struggled up the old classics with trepidation and joy.

It was Pratt, however, climbing brilliantly that summer, who shone like a star, and we stood in awe of his abilities. Quiet, short, barrel-chested, he was the most natural climber any of us had ever seen. We would watch him slither up a jamcrack with seemingly no expenditure of energy. We relaxed while belaying and told ourselves that the route didn't look bad. Then our turn came. I remember once striding confidently up to a crack he had led, sticking my hands into it, lifting a foot—and stalling out. I tried another combination. Faced another direction. "Pratt," I screamed, "you bastard. Which way did you face?"

"I faced left, but I'm sure it goes both ways," Pratt yelled diplomatically.

"Shit! Big help! Does it get easier above that bulge?"

"Not really."

"Okay, here I go. Keep the rope real tight!"

My frustration grew; I wanted to cry, or scream, or simply be lowered to the ground and curl up into a fetal ball. I managed at last to thrash up the crack, but barely. My hands, bloody and cramping, dangled uselessly as I reached Pratt, who graciously allowed that it had been hard for him, too.

With this crack genius's arrival, the evolution of Valley climbing reached another turning point. First it had been the prominent pinnacles that climbers sought. Then walls with trees and ledges. Then bigger walls with prominent crack systems. Then lesser spires and lesser walls. But 1958 marks the emergence of short, hidden crack climbs, often on minor exfoliation slabs, and often outside the confines of the Valley itself.

In September, Pratt found and climbed two such routes, the Cookie and the Cleft, across from Elephant Rock. These short crack routes led nowhere and had no real summits. You simply grunted up a crack to a ledge, then rappelled. Difficulty for its own sake. I well remember regarding these climbs as "practice" routes, utterly failing to see them as an emerging trend. Pratt and a new cadre of crack climbers established dozens upon dozens of such routes during the next ten years, and this activity led directly to an increase in free-climbing standards. Although the top of the rating scale had stayed for years at 5.9—partly because of the reluctance to move up to the mathematically absurd 5.10—this formerly rare level was becoming absolutely routine for people such as Pratt and Reed.

The success of the El Capitan climb was uppermost in our minds during the early months of 1959: the big walls suddenly had become possible. By this time I was suffering through my freshman year at Oregon State College, but friends sent me the many Nose clippings topped with banner headlines. Letters flashed back and forth between Corvallis and Berkeley—and, of course, between other places and people—outlining plans for the next season. Highly excited about our climbing future, partly because of our minor successes the previous year but also because of the El Cap climb, we teemed with ideas and plans.

By April I found I couldn't take the triple pressures of calculus, a girlfriend in faraway Berkeley, and the siren call of the Valley. I walked away from my dorm one morning with a bulging suitcase and stuck out my thumb, destination south. In my hysteria (and poverty) I had decided to become a temporary migrant farm worker, so I ended up a few days later in a Sacramento skid-row hotel near the employment office. A fire erupted that night, April 7, in a nearby flophouse, and I stood shivering in the street as the coroner's wagon hauled away a charred body. A racist ghoul next to me panted, "I hear it was just a nigger." At that moment I decided to forego the orchards and head on toward more pleasant surroundings.

I ended up in Yosemite Valley three days later, lonely and wondering about my future. Luckily it was a Friday night, and within hours Ritter and Pratt arrived on the Lambretta for their normal weekend outing. We had a splendid reunion, but Saturday and Sunday passed too quickly, and soon I was alone again. I, it turned out, was the sole dropout that spring.

I wrote my father on Monday, April 13: "I am the only occupant of Camp 4. I slept until 11 A.M. this morning. I think I'll hike up El Cap tomorrow." Three days later I wrote: "Not much to do up here alone. Yesterday I hiked up to the base of the El Cap Tree looking for dropped hardware—I found none. I might be home next Monday."

Life in the Valley without climbing companions was grim. I was eighteen, self-centered, and insensitive to nature. I soon retreated to the city, reconciled my nonacademic lifestyle with my skeptical but supportive parents, argued about this new lifestyle with my skeptical and soon-to-be-gone girlfriend, endured odd jobs, went to the Valley on weekends, borrowed money, and prayed for summer. I was at loose ends, but when I thought of my narrow escapes from the dreaded calculus and the hot, hot almond orchards, I figured I was better off mowing lawns in the Bay Area.

There had always been a hierarchy of climbers, and the spring and early summer of 1959 showed this to good effect. As in the old days, Sierra Club groups from the Bay Area arrived on weekends, as did UC Berkeley and Stanford students. Such people, for whom climbing was pure recreation, tended to do the classics, as I had been content to do the previous summer. Traffic increased on such routes as the southwest arête of the Lower Brother, the Washington Column, both Cathedral Spires, the Royal Arches, and the Overhang Bypass route on Lower Cathedral Rock. These were—and are—all excellent climbs, but they were not especially severe. Still, many weekenders aspired only to this level. By this time I was a Qualified Leader in the Sierra Club's Rock Climbing Section, an honor grudgingly bestowed on me by the section's elders, who not so secretly felt that I was a little immature to be taking beginners up multipitch climbs. (And they were right; I tremble now to think of my nonchalance.) On a typical spring weekend in 1959, I would take three or four Sierra Clubbers up the Royal Arches on Saturday and the Church Tower or Pulpit Rock on Sunday. This was all great fun, and I also got into shape.

At the next level above the regular weekenders, most of whom preferred to be guided (though it was never called this explicitly), were the competent climbers who sought the more difficult traditional climbs, such as the Lost Arrow Spire and Yosemite Point Buttress. These climbers occasionally put up new routes, though often not in the best of styles. One example of this was the 1959 climb of Ahwahnee Buttress, a nebulous feature rising to the rim above the Ahwahnee Hotel. A group of Fresno climbers had spent many days over several months on this route, fixing ropes and moving slowly. In May they finally finished it off. George Sessions, one of the team members, wrote up the climb, ending with this sentence: "It is difficult to conceive of an ascent of the buttress being completed in less than two days of sustained climbing." This was seen as a challenge by better climbers, and not too long afterward the second-ascent party roared up the climb in eight hours. Sessions and his crew were excellent fellows and safe climbers, but Sessions's partners moved like slugs—and this was one of the main differences between this middle-level group and the next one up the line.

The newer crop of climbers were not only good technicians, but highly motivated. People such as Pratt, Raymond, Ritter, John Fiske, Herb Swedlund, and I lived in the Valley, climbed almost every day, practiced aid climbing on the boulders of the campground, and within a few weeks were in superb condition. Those who get into decent physical shape tend to have sharp mental attitudes. Though we still feared the big walls, the lesser ones became our playground. We climbed fast and efficiently compared to our predecessors; sometimes we managed *both* of the Cathedral Spires in a day and had enough energy to do the lowly Church Tower on the way back down the hill. I don't wish to imply that we were supermen that summer, or that the weekenders were beneath contempt. Simply put, we were cocky and fit, two attributes not shared by most of the more conservative weekenders.

A price had to be paid for such hubris, I suppose, and the first to fall was Don Goodrich, a UC Berkeley grad student who had done several innovative first ascents on the Glacier Point Apron in previous years. On June 12, 1959, he and Ritter and two others attempted the southwest face of Mount Conness, a shimmering white wall in Yosemite's backcountry. They had barely begun when Goodrich, in the lead, pulled up onto a large block. It rolled outward. This was long before anyone wore a helmet, and the rock crushed his skull.

Greatly sobered by this tragedy, the first such of our young lives, we left the Valley and spent a few quiet days in Berkeley. At "Ritter's Pad," a cottage where climbers hung out and where Goodrich had lived, we divided his gear among us. My long-suffering mother, who admired Goodrich because he had been a stabilizing influence on her wayward son, thought this calamity would signal the end of her offspring's crazy climbing career. I, the crass idiot, instead showed off my new gear to her.

Young people are resilient, and soon we all were back in the Valley once again, this time for a month-long stay. Ritter, trying to forget the bloody nightmare, bravely pretended he still loved climbing. He, Pratt, and I were the only climbers in Camp 4 for a short while; then we got word that Southern Californians were about to invade "our" domain. Oddly, the two groups had never really gotten together in the Valley; Robbins and his cohorts had done their great Valley routes, then vanished, a year or so before we Bay Area climbers had arrived. We Northerners were excited, for naturally we'd heard rumors of young Southern upstarts who swarmed up horrible routes on Tahquitz Rock, that fine dome of granite east of Los Angeles.

Around June 20 a few Southerners arrived, and we gathered in the boulders to introduce ourselves. TM Herbert caught our eye first. His first name was simply TM, something we found difficult to believe. What's your *real* name?" we insisted. "Come on, you can tell us." "Tough mother," he replied. Within days Herbert became known as the resident wit of Camp 4, performing at a frenetic level, making outlandish faces and gestures as he talked about his previous sufferings on the crags. His antic demonstrations on how he planned to handle the notorious smooth Valley cracks had us rolling on the ground. "Those cracks won't stand a chance," he cried. "I'll pull 'em apart; I'll smash 'em; I'll make 'em scream with pain." Gawking at his rippling torso and biceps, we had no doubt he would tame the slippery devils.

Herbert's near-manic behavior and plastic face contrasted dramatically with that of movie-star handsome Dave Rearick and wiry, crag-faced

TM Herbert, about 1967 (Photo: Steve Roper)

Bob Kamps. Both men were known to be superb free climbers, and both were quiet and shy. We had already heard of this pair, for they had made the fifth ascent of Sentinel's north face the previous year—and in so doing had inadvertently entered into legend. Knowing little of the route, and knowing no one to ask for information, the pair had begun climbing some 800 feet below the traditional rope-up spot, Tree Ledge. The lower part of the north face, dirty and featureless but quite steep, had never been climbed. Rearick and Kamps had thus really made a first ascent, one unlikely to be repeated. Realizing their mistake only at the end of a long day, the pair retreated. Shortly thereafter, they approached correctly via Tree Ledge and completed the Steck-Salathé route in admirable style.

Having told us this story, Rearick mentioned that someone named Yvon Chouinard would be showing up in a few days, hot for the Arrow Chimney. Not knowing this name, and hearing it as "Yvonne," I perked up and asked brightly, "Where is she now?"

Chouinard showed up, and though he was not of the female persuasion, I forgave him the moment he opened his car's trunk and showed us the gems therein, almost as precious as the delights a putative Yvonne would have offered. During the previous winter he had hand-forged several dozen beautifully crafted pitons, modeled after the tough ones Salathé had fashioned a decade earlier. We caressed these objects, made of chromemolybdenum steel alloy, over and over, looking at them from every angle. Claiming they would stand up to repeated use, Chouinard demonstrated his wares on the Camp 4 boulders and then let us have our whacks. "Smash it as hard as you want," he begged us, seeing that we were hammering one specimen gingerly. We all took turns bashing the hell out of this pin, pounding it in and out of crooked, incipient cracks. Chouinard was right: it was the crack that was destroyed, not the piton. Our soft, bendable European pitons became obsolete that very day. Trouble was, our new friend had none of these fabulous toys for sale.

During the next week we Northerners got to know Chouinard quite well. Born near Lewiston, Maine, in late 1938, he had moved to the Los Angeles area with his French-Canadian family right after World War II. As a teenager he scrambled all over the local cliffs, seeking falcons. This inevitably led to climbing, and he next gravitated toward the most famous mountaineering spot of the mid-1950s, the Tetons, where he did many of the classic routes. He hadn't done much in Yosemite, though at age twenty he was easily the most accomplished mountaineer among us. Short, friendly, inquisitive, and talented, Chouinard became an instant friend to us all.

Within days we all were climbing together and climbing hard. It was a classic example of the theory that the whole is greater than the sum of its parts. The exchange of ideas, the talk of equipment, the differing skills— all these led to a new psychological frame of mind. The Valley suddenly didn't seem quite so big.

In late June, Chouinard and Herbert climbed the Lost Arrow Chim-

Yvon Chouinard, about 1968 (Photo: Glen Denny)

ney, a place where his pitons worked like magic in the bottomed, decomposed cracks. More important to me, however, was the fact that the two men had bivouacked at the base to get an early start. They had left their sleeping gear there, some 1,200 feet above the Valley floor, and upon their return they were in no mood to recover the cache. Chouinard hired me to retrieve their belongings, and I treasured my reward: three hand-forged pitons that all summer long I regarded as talismans.

New equipment, new partners, new freedoms. The stage was set for the burgeoning of the Golden Age of Valley climbing.

━━━━━━━━━━━━━━━━━━━━━ ■ ━━━━━━━━━━━━━━━━━━━━━

A graph that plotted the frequency of ascents in Yosemite Valley would show a marked increase in 1959, for this was the year climbing took off. The Lost Arrow Chimney, for example, had been repeated but three times in the dozen years following the Salathé-Nelson first ascent. But in 1959 alone four parties managed this strenuous and unpleasant route. The north face of Sentinel had a similar record: by 1959 only four ascents had been logged since the first—and 1959 saw four more. Other climbs of the early fifties, such as the El Cap Tree and Yosemite Point Buttress, received heavier traffic also.

Perhaps the older classics beckoned because we all were a little unsure of ourselves. As it turned out, 1959 was not an especially good year for first ascents—only three major ones would be done. It seemed we needed further honing, and our plans were laid accordingly. Chouinard and Herbert had an agenda, for instance. So did Pratt and Raymond. Both teams quickly did the Arrow Chimney and Sentinel, routes they had dreamed about for two years. Others, including myself, had lesser goals, routes such as the Arrowhead Arête and Bridalveil East, two of Powell's classics. These routes, shunned by most weekenders, were occasionally climbed by us, with trepidation. The aura surrounding some routes was so powerful that months and even years would go by without an ascent.

The Arrowhead Arête, for instance, had, by the summer of 1959, seen only two further ascents since 1956; perhaps we all still remembered Powell's words from his *Sierra Club Bulletin* account. A nightmare for the less competent? Great finger and toe strength? These were heady words indeed, and I for one dreaded the moment someone would suggest doing the climb. Who was I to attempt such a route? But when Pratt casually said, on July 16, "Let's go do it," pointing up at the sweeping white profile visible from Camp 4, I agreed instantly. Hours later, deep inside the West Arrowhead Chimney, the rope-up spot, I looked up at the now-grotesque swoop and its blankness and its mystery—and I rebelled. "We'll die!" I screamed. "Why are we here?" My words echoed off the walls of the claustrophobic chimney while Pratt sat quietly, sorting gear and staring out at the Valley far below. Finally, in a tight voice, he yelled, "Goddamn it, are you finished?"

We did the route and did it well. My elemental terror vanished once I set hand to rock, to be replaced by a potent sensation of wariness—a strong-enough emotion in itself, but controllable. The lessons of this day I should have learned at once, but I never did. Until the end of my Yosemite career, I lost sleep and trembled before every hard climb. I thought I was alone in this regard, but, talking with other climbers over the years, I discovered I wasn't—not by any means.

Of the three major first ascents done in 1959, the first of the year was done by an "outside" team. Although weekenders rarely did the big climbs by the late fifties, and almost never the big *new* climbs, an exception occurred in early June. Most of us were absent on the weekend when Dick Long, Terry Tarver (brother of Frank, who had fashioned the stoveleg pitons), and Ray D'Arcy climbed the forbidding northeast buttress of Higher Cathedral Rock. This 1,000-foot-high prow of granite, burnished golden by iron oxide, turned out to be one of Yosemite's classic climbs. Long, who had eyed this wall for years from one of his favorite haunts, the Higher Spire, had picked out an obvious if sheer route up crack systems that shot upward to join a huge, flared open book. The team took two full days for their ascent, using only a little direct aid in the flared section. Because the trio were weekenders, word of this gem spread so slowly that years passed before the quality of the route was recognized.

Dick Long, a high-school teacher in 1959 (but soon to begin medical school), was a fabulous mountaineer and free climber, but because he rarely visited the Valley, this fact was hardly known outside a select group. He was also an on-and-off piton manufacturer, turning out decent horizontals and large angles. In fact, on the Higher Cathedral Rock ascent he brought along some prototype angles that were three inches wide, the largest ever made. Climbers on the Higher Spire who had heard these pitons being driven into the rock told Camp 4 climbers about the "bonging" sound emanating from the cliff, and the name "bong-bong" (quickly shortened in informal usage to "bong") soon became the name for any piton wider than two inches. To make these steel monstrosities lighter, Long had drilled holes all over them, another first. Chouinard, seeing these angles after the climb, was mightily impressed: his widest angle measured only an inch and a half.

The three Cathedral Rocks are hardly as imposing as Half Dome and El Capitan, but they are huge and dominant in their own right. Each has "schizophrenic" qualities. Some of the best rock in the Valley is found on each—and some of the worst. Some of the most beautiful colors in the Valley exist on each—and some of the drabbest. Each has ugly and fearsome routes—and each has beautiful routes. Each has a sheer wall facing more or less north—and each has a walk-off route on the south. At certain times each captures the light so perfectly that one wishes to run up to the wall and start climbing immediately. At other times one wants only to flee the somber cliffs, tilted and faded like old tombstones in a midnight graveyard.

The second major first ascent of the year also lay on the Cathedral Rocks. Pratt and I had been idly considering the huge north face of Middle Cathedral, and apparently so had Bob Kamps. Bill Dunmire had been the first to think of climbing this dark wall; in 1952 he had written that it was "a cliff which no reasonable climber will attempt unless prepared to spend several days (and nights) on the wall."

One warm evening in late June, Kamps suggested we go down and look it over. "It'll go, no problem," said Bob. So the three of us piled into his car after a hurried dinner and drove down the Valley. The setting sun bathed the face in oblique golden light, warm and friendly. How pleasant it was to sit in the meadow at dusk and plot a route! How easy it was to find bivouac ledges, crack systems, even belay spots.

"Shit, we'll run up that part."

"Hey, look at the ledge to the right of that big bush! That could sleep ten!"

"Two days, what do you think? But maybe take stuff for three?"

What we didn't realize was that north faces rarely got sun. Lack of sunlight, we were soon to find out, meant decomposed rock, damp cracks full of grime, and tottering flakes hanging like guillotines over chimneys. The route we accomplished was the least pleasant big one I've ever done. The rock was loose, the pitches unaesthetic, the dirt eye-filling, the mood somber. No whoops of joy ever echoed across the concave cliff. Serious business, this climb, and I felt a little out of my league. We bivouacked the first night on a short, eighteen-inch-wide ledge, simply sitting there like three morons on a park bench. Our asses ached and froze. Below lay 800 feet of ghastly exposure. Above rose a series of sickening slits, steep and rotten. I've had better nights.

In the cold gray dawn, Kamps led the most nerve-wracking direct-aid pitch I'd yet seen. Pratt and I could sense the difficulty with our eyes closed: the pitons rarely rang with authority as they were driven. Instead, they thudded and scraped and thunked. Down constantly came the sound of Kamps testing pitons: tap-tap-thunk-tap. As grit fell upon us like rain, so, too, came gentle curses and reminders to be alert: "Watch me, man! This pin is shifting!"

"I got ya, dad!"

An hour or two went by. Then: "Whose idea was this, anyway? Kamps, you bastard, hurry up. We're freezing!"

"Hey, don't worry, the sun will be on us in about ten hours."

Above this desperate aid pitch, Pratt led a horrifying slot with scant protection: 5.9 and ultra-dangerous, we all agreed. Kamps and I didn't dare utter a word during this hour-long struggle, not wishing to interrupt Pratt's concentration. (Robbins, who along with Joe Fitschen made the second ascent a few months later, was duly impressed; in October he wrote that Pratt's pitch was "certainly one of the most remarkable leads in the history of American mountain climbing.")

Luckily, the angle eased off above this and the rock's quality improved somewhat. After another bivouac, this one on spacious but equally frigid ledges, we topped out at noon of our third day. The first of the great Cathedral north faces had fallen.

The third—and last—major first ascent of 1959 was not long in coming. Fixed ropes had swung in the breeze for a year on the Washington Column's east face, the route Harding and his cohorts had begun the previous summer during the ranger-enforced ban on climbing El Cap. In the spring of 1959 Harding and a Stanford grad student named Gerry Czamanske had prusiked back to the high point, intending to push the route to completion. Nearing the entrance to the grossly overhanging slot that now bears his name, Harding began placing nested angle pitons, a technique, possibly first developed by Salathé, wherein one stacks or nests pitons together to accommodate a wider crack. About fifteen feet above Czamanske, Harding stood up on one such fabricated contraption. It promptly popped and Harding fell twenty feet. Czamanske remembers the scene vividly: "He came rattling right down on top of me, brushing my body. If that huge rack of hardware had been on his other side, I would have taken it right in my face." Somewhere on the way down, Harding's left hand became entwined in a loop of the rope. Blood oozed from the wound, a fairly minor one, and Harding said at once, "Seeing blood makes me uneasy." The pair immediately retreated.

Soon it was July and Harding was getting desperate. How long was *this* route going to take? Luckily, the obscure cliff wasn't subject to the summertime ban; only El Cap merited this restriction. Searching through Camp 4 for gullible climbers, Harding's piercing black eyes settled upon Pratt and me, fresh from our victory over the evil north face of Middle Cathedral. At this moment Pratt and I were just about the only resident climbers left; a virulent heat wave suffocated the Valley and the smart ones had left. We two had no money to head elsewhere. Weighed down by lassitude and baked by the heat, we simply waited for something to happen. Maybe we'd win a Bingo game over at the lodge.

Harding, always an entertaining and persuasive talker, just happened to have a jug or two of wine in his car. In the relative cool of evening he talked up the greatness of his plan. "There are plenty of cracks—and perfect ones too," he announced. "I haven't seen a speck of dirt, and Overnight Ledge is super; plenty of room for three." Then, playing his trump card, he purred, "It's in the shade after two o'clock and really nice and cool up there!"

The next day I looked at the cliff carefully for the first time. "Holy shit, Harding!" I exclaimed. "The whole thing overhangs. In two directions yet!" Indeed, the wall leaned beyond the vertical. In addition, the upper half of the route diagonaled to the right, which would make for strenuous leading, following, and prusiking. The greatness of the plan suddenly didn't seem so compelling. I also remembered some of Harding's stories from the previous night, especially the one about the frayed fixed ropes, chewed by voracious rats supposedly the size of marmots. This story was not nearly so amusing in the light of day. Subdued, I drove to the grocery store with Harding. "I'm not sure about this, man. Looks way too damned big to me."

"Hey," Harding said suddenly, "let me buy you a beer and a dead chicken." Minutes later, as I attacked an entire barbecued fowl, life once again appeared tolerable. When someone is particularly nice to you, I have since learned, be on guard.

Harding issued our marching orders on July 21 and we fell into step. First we all would transport big loads of water and gear up to Overnight Ledge, 500 feet above the talus. Then Pratt and Harding would try to overcome the narrow chimney just above the high point—the Harding Slot—and probe the untouched rock above. I, chief Sherpa, would keep the two climbers supplied.

Campfire smoke hung motionless in the meadows as we toiled up the half-hour approach that morning. No birds sang, and the pines creaked and cracked from the dryness. The temperature stood in the high nineties by the time we arrived at Overnight Ledge, around noon. Water was obviously going to be a major problem—we sucked at our canteens constantly—so down I rappelled and trundled back to Camp 4, covered with sweat and dirt. I managed to borrow a few water bottles, but I knew we needed more. My eyes lit on an empty gallon wine jug, likely one of Harding's. Feeling like an utter ass, I filled the jug at a faucet, hoping no climber was watching. A heavy glass container on a climb?

Somehow I horsed the thing, unbroken, along with an additional ten quarts, up to the ledge by late afternoon. Harding's claim about the shade proved true: the air was still stifling, but the radiating glare had vanished. I was happy again. Far above, I could see my two friends swaying in their aid slings, fighting slanting overhangs and wide cracks. At dusk, with the Harding Slot behind them, they retreated down their fixed ropes to join me at Overnight Ledge.

"So, how was the slot?" I asked. "It looked absolutely horrible from down here."

"It looks absolutely horrible from up there, too," said Pratt. "Warren did a great job. He just wriggled up that thing like a snake."

We settled in for the evening on two-tiered Overnight Ledge, watching darkness invade the Valley. Hundreds of tiny fires slowly emerged through the haze, and we could almost smell the steaks sizzling on the campfires. Promptly at nine o'clock, as usual, came that most famous of manmade Valley spectacles: the Firefall. Following a teasing ritual of long-distance questions, answers, and pauses between the rim and the Valley floor, a functionary of the Curry Company, the park concessionaire, slowly pushed a hundred pounds of glowing embers over the lip of Glacier Point, 3,200 feet above the Valley floor. For 890 feet (a distance measured with string in 1949 by rangers who had nothing better to do) the red-hot coals cascaded down splendidly before settling onto a wide ledge. Although wildly inappropriate for the natural setting, it still presented an unforgettable sight. It also caused confusion. I once heard a tourist ask a ranger, "Sir, can you tell me which waterfall the Firefall comes over?"

We had the best seats in the Valley for the show. Then it was time for "bed." Bivouacking in a T-shirt was pleasant, and it would have been a perfect night, except for two things. Fearless mice the size of mice, not marmot-sized rats, scurried about constantly, eager to sample our sweaty ropes and clothing. Then, all night long, came the sound of gurgling and sucking, as if aliens were stealing our precious bodily fluids. Canteens tipped into mouths frequently and surreptitiously; our water supply fell alarmingly.

At dawn Pratt and Harding sullenly went up to work on the route, but the heat intensified and they soon gave up and rappelled to Overnight Ledge. We all fled back to dusty Camp 4.

A week passed and the temperatures retreated to merely scorching.

Warren Harding prusiking to Overnight Ledge, east face of the Washington Column, 1959 (Photo: Steve Roper)

Early on Monday, July 27, Pratt and Harding ascended the ropes once again. By this time it had become obvious that I was to be a Valley-to-ledge Sherpa, not a ledge-to-high-point Sherpa. The two climbers would come down each night to comfortable Overnight Ledge to sleep, and they wanted it to be fully stocked with water and food.

"You'll need some help," Harding told me. "I know a couple of guys at the lodge who know how to prusik. Get 'em if you can. Maybe they'll have a day off." This is how I came to meet Glen Denny, the articulate six-foot-three-inch redhead who figured prominently in the Valley's history in the years to follow. Denny, a twenty-year-old busboy at Yosemite Lodge, didn't have a full day off, but he and another employee named Rob McKnight volunteered to go up onto the Column *before* their lunch shift. If this seems a casual way to treat a big Yosemite cliff, well, it was. The pair claimed to know how to prusik and rappel with efficiency, and this was enough for me. I shudder now to think of what could have happened, but in those days we regarded our immortality as a given and thought rappelling great fun, not dangerous at all.

So at dawn on Tuesday, Denny and McKnight prusiked up the 500 near-vertical feet to Overnight Ledge, carrying many gallons of precious water. Thinking himself extremely clever, Denny had filled a three-gallon milk can, borrowed from the lodge's cafeteria. Partway up, the lid of this unwieldy canister worked loose and water went coursing down the granite. Only two quarts remained by the time he righted his load. Denny told me this story back on the Valley floor, a sheepish expression on his face. "I'd go back up, but I gotta work now."

After the sun went behind the cliff and the heat slackened, I quickly ascended the ropes with ten quarts of water and fruit juice. Harding and Pratt had come down after a long day's work; they had made moderate progress that day up constantly overhanging rock and were only about 250 feet from the rim. I wanted to stay, but Harding ordered me down, this time not for more water. "Take these to the post office first thing in the morning," he said, handing me several rolls of exposed film. "Mail them special delivery to the *Oakland Tribune*. Then call them and report our progress."

Earlier, I had taken numerous photos of the climbing team with Harding's camera, thinking these would be good to have for our personal collections. To our surprise, Pratt and I discovered that Harding had already informed the media about our attempt. When I joked that I had taken most of the shots, Harding said, "Well, I guess you could use the money if we sell 'em."

Down the ropes I went once again, carrying the precious film and feeling like a courier on a special mission. When I got back to the lodge, I found a frenzied Denny hurling plates and glasses into his cart. "I just asked the boss for a few days off, and he said okay! I'm going up in a few hours, as soon as I finish these goddamn tables."

"Tonight? You crazy?"

"They need more water, and it looks like they'll get close to the top tomorrow. Maybe I can go with 'em."

Slightly miffed at this, since I was supposed to be the number-one Sherpa, I paused—but only momentarily. What with all the mindless and strenuous prusiking, the thrill was wearing off. I also had to fulfill my media obligations. I wished Denny luck.

At two in the morning of July 29, Harding and Pratt were woken out of a deep sleep by a huge apparition struggling over the lip of Overnight Ledge, dragging a monster pack full of water and goodies. Party time on the Column. The trio wolfed candy bars and fruit juice until dawn, sitting on the exposed ledge, watching the shooting stars.

Pratt and Harding started up the ropes early, feeling a little weary of the game themselves. Denny waited on Overnight Ledge to see what would happen higher. Though only 250 feet separated the highest rope from the top, great slanting dihedrals containing wide cracks prevented easy progress. Harding, the master bolter, placed fifteen in this horribly exposed and strenuous section. He had also fashioned some huge pitons out of an aluminum T-bar and placed them again and again. The by-now-famous stoveleg pitons were also used, for the final time: superwide angle pitons were soon to become commercially available. Near dark the two men reached a sloping ledge just below the top. Denny soon joined them via the fixed ropes, and the trio spent a wretched night, mitigated only by the fact that they were close to success.

A difficult aid pitch at dawn Thursday took the trio to the rounded, sandy rim, and an hour later, after plunging speedily down the easy descent route, they relaxed on the Valley floor, posing for the camera. Pratt's clothes were in tatters; Harding looked even more emaciated than usual, his dyed-black army fatigues dangerously close to slipping down his never-large hips. Head Sherpa Denny looked remarkably fresh, considering he had prusiked 2,000 feet in forty-eight hours, carrying huge loads.

The *Tribune* had received the special-delivery film and that afternoon splashed the entire front page of the second section with my photos. I soon received a check for thirty dollars, the first money I'd ever made climbing. Proud to have played a minor role in the climb, I submitted a short article to *Summit*, ending my account with the statement: "[It is] one of the greatest climbs in the world." A few months later, when I held the issue in my hands, I saw to my amusement that the editors, oblivious to the renaissance in Yosemite climbing, had deleted the last three words.

CHAPTER 5

Nirvana:
1960–1961

Our ascent, of course, does not end the possibilities for new accomplishments on El Capitan. The day will probably come when this climb will be done in five days, perhaps less; and a younger generation will make a new route on the west face.

—Royal Robbins, after the second ascent of the Nose, 1960

On January 27, 1960, a letter postmarked Los Angeles arrived at my house with no return address and no signature. "As of December 1959," the letter began, "a new climbing club was formed called the Yosemite Climbing Club. This letter is an invitation to you to become a member. The club will be kept small by having extremely high standards. Seventeen persons because of their outstanding climbing ability and devotedness to climbing have been invited to join.... Until the club's first meeting in Yosemite Valley sometime this spring, the club will operate as follows: no officers, no constitution, or by-laws, and no dues."

The sixteen names listed (someone couldn't count) represented the elite of California climbers at the end of the 1950s: Yvon Chouinard, Harry Daley, Bill Feuerer, Joe Fitschen, Tom Frost, Warren Harding, TM Herbert, Bob Kamps, Mark Powell, Chuck Pratt, Charles Raymond, Dave Rearick, Royal Robbins, Steve Roper, Herb Swedlund, and Charles Wilts.

The hand of Yvon Chouinard was visible, though not literally, for the calligraphy was not his wretched scrawl. (The actual manifesto had been penned by Feuerer, I later found out.) But Chouinard had earlier talked about such a club. Flattered by the invitation and amused by the anarchic tone, I was still somewhat resistant to the idea. Most of us had learned to climb with organizations such as the Sierra Club and/or various university clubs. We appreciated those groups, for they had taught us well and even managed to instill safe climbing practices into our rebellious brains. Yet we had also come to realize that the club members tended to socialize more than climb. Rather than seek new adventures, they generally preferred the status quo. We young lads wanted to attack new walls like commandos, not follow the tried-and-true rules of drill sergeants.

The idea of joining a new club was the last thing on my mind. Nevertheless, I wrote Yvon and agreed to join, for his goals seemed admirable: "Assemble together devoted climbers interested in raising the standards" and "Work on a guidebook to Yosemite Valley." As for the former goal, who could possibly argue against it? And how intoxicating to be thought a "devoted" climber! As for a new guidebook, this need was quickly becoming obvious: all we had at the time was a thirty-five-page chapter in the Sierra Club's 1954 High Sierra guidebook. Only seventy-five roped climbs were described—and the same number of new climbs had been accomplished in the six years since the book's publication. Chouinard knew that a new guidebook, if done right, would be a huge job, one probably best done in a communal effort.

The YCC died in infancy; more properly, it was stillborn. Chouinard's next letter, less than a month later, bore his own handwriting and conveyed less enthusiasm. The letter opened: "I guess it's up to me to get things rolling on the YCC.... Pratt, Royal, and Fitschen have not bothered to answer." And it closed: "I know this letter sounds like an autocratic type deal but somebody has to start things going."

"Next thing you know, he'll want some dues," I complained to Chuck Pratt one spring day at a local Berkeley rock.

"Then he'll call the meeting on a perfect climbing day," complained Pratt. "We'll sit around arguing and raising our hands."

"And you'll be elected secretary and get to take minutes. Shit! And I'll be put onto a committee!"

Rebels don't like authority, or committees, or rules. I had hoped to *escape* this sort of thing. While I more or less had to follow certain rules set by my parents and teachers, I didn't have to do so with climbing. As I recall, the proposed meeting never took place, and the YCC was never again discussed after the spring of 1960. Chouinard briefly mentioned the club in the back-of-the-book notes in the 1960 and 1961 issues of the *American Alpine Journal,* but this was the only time the name ever appeared in print.

If the YCC was a momentary historical curiosity, the sentiment behind it proved visionary. Chouinard had reached out to the community beyond Southern California: five of the sixteen people lived in the north. From now on we would be California climbers, not regional rivals. He also showed prescience about the need for an up-to-date guidebook solely for the Valley. "We must have it next summer," he had urged in his second letter. This was not to be, but Chouinard's idea took hold, and Pratt and I soon began taking notes for an eventual guidebook.

If Chouinard faltered as an organizer in early 1960, he surely recovered his confidence a few months later when the denizens of Camp 4 began to rave about his inventiveness. We'd been impressed with his pitons the previous summer and now he had many for sale, at the outrageous price of $1.55. Most commercial pitons—made either in Europe or by small American manufacturers such as CCB, Gerry, Holubar, and Klockar—went for a dollar. In addition, Chouinard's new angle pitons, up to an inch and a half wide, looked professionally made and eminently useful. But these didn't surprise us, for we'd seen prototypes before.

What *did* surprise us was a new toy, one that changed Yosemite climbing almost immediately. Chouinard's "rurp" was obviously something special. An acronym for "realized ultimate reality piton," this ludicrously small fragment of heat-treated steel opened our eyes to untold possibilities. True, we all had used knife-blade pitons, invented by Chuck Wilts in 1953 and by 1959 available commercially. But this razor-thin device buckled into an accordion shape the moment the tip encountered a tight bend or a crystal. In a deep and clean sixteenth-inch-wide crack the tool worked perfectly, but such a crack usually had wider spots nearby where regular thin pitons could be smashed in. Wilts's pitons and their imitators, theoretically splendid, had not caused a revolution in aid climbing.

Chouinard's rurp did just that. He realized that Yosemite granite contained far too many "incipient" or "bottomed" cracks. The Cretaceous Period cooling of the granite batholith had not been performed with the best interests of Yosemite climbers in mind. Distinct cracks in granite, the ones visible from afar, most often form by exfoliation—the breaking apart of monolithic chunks of rock by repeated frost action. These cracks, often perfect, formed the more obvious routes. A different type of crack could be seen if you looked closely, however. These, the ones originally in the batholith as it first rose to the surface, tended to be seams or folds—far too trivial for ice to pry apart. Yet in a sense they *were* cracks: the seam was a weakness, a 70-million-year-old weakness, in the very structure of the granite.

Chouinard thought that a thin-bladed, slightly wedge-shaped device of superhard steel could be pounded far enough into such seams to serve as an aid piton, and so, in April 1960, he brought a few samples to the Valley for testing. He and Tom Frost, a young engineer from Southern California, had spotted a likely crack for their first experiment. Kat Pinnacle, several miles outside the Valley, was a soaring, square-sided pillar that had first been climbed in 1940. To Chouinard the unclimbed southwest side looked feasible—half of it, anyway. A fairly straightforward crack shot upward fifty feet on an overhanging face. At this point, as the angle eased back to the mere vertical, the good crack simply petered out. An incipient seam, a hairline crack, a shallow wrinkle—call it what you will—led up about thirty-five feet to a huge platform at the base of the summit block. Chouinard had tried the route once before and had been stymied by the ultra-thin crack. Now he was ready.

After nailing the strenuous but easy lower section, Chouinard pulled out his prototype rurps, fashioned from sections of brittle, industrial-size hacksaw blades. He smashed one into the crack and pondered his next move. The size of a large postage stamp, the piton jutted alarmingly from the crack, 90 percent of it still visible. The ground-down, tapered blade (where the hacksaw teeth had once threatened) had penetrated the crack about a quarter of an inch.

Chouinard clipped a carabiner into the rurp's tiny attached sling, connected an aid sling, and eased upward, sure the wafer would pop loose and strike him in the eyeball. It held. He placed another. Then, where the crack opened slightly, a knife-blade. All told he built a ladder of four rurps and four knife-blades; each one stuck out an appalling distance from the seam. A fall would have meant a zippering of every one of the thin pitons and a sixty-foot ride downward, but Chouinard knew the bombproof pitons at the lip below would hold—and the incredible steepness of Kat meant that he wouldn't hit anything. He finally moved off his last blade, made a few free moves, and mantled onto the big ledge.

Without Chouinard's rurps, no one could have done this climb without placing four bolts. For a few months Kat was the most difficult direct-aid route in the Valley, probably the world, and the rating was instantly controversial: 6.8 or 6.9? (The Yosemite Decimal System for aid climbs—a progression in difficulty from 6.0 to 6.9—was the current system in 1960, though within about a year it was abandoned in favor of the present A1 to A5 system.) Since Chouinard hadn't pulled any of the pins, the lower figure seemed appropriate; one wished to reserve the top of the line for a truly horrendous death climb. On the other hand, several 6.8 routes existed already, and Kat was surely a step upward in the evolution of difficulty. By the time the A1 to A5 rating of aid climbs took hold the next year, harder climbs than Kat were commonplace, and Kat became A4 in the next two guidebooks. Still, if plaques had a place in a natural setting, one could be installed at the base of this now-legendary climb: "Here, on April 2, 1960, superdifficult aid climbing was born."

Chouinard and Tom Frost—who would become the most respected equipment manufacturers of the 1960s—both had amazing creative streaks, though usually it was Chouinard, the artist, who came up with an idea and Frost, the engineer, who figured out how to design it. This combination of talents led immediately to innovative gear, and within five years every serious rockclimber on earth either used the Chouinard-Frost equipment, coveted it, or copied it.

A few other items appeared that spring. Chouinard's aluminum carabiners proved the least exciting to us, for we all owned similar ones by this time—Raffi Bedayn (he had changed the spelling of his last name by this time) had made superb aluminum carabiners for close to ten years. Yet Chouinard's were stronger, and one could open the gate while stand-

Tom Frost, 1964 (Photo: Glen Denny)

ing in slings from the carabiner, a subtle advantage for aid specialists. But basically, a carabiner was a carabiner.

Frost had, for his own use, fashioned some bigger angle pitons, up to about two and a half inches wide—the first quality ones ever made from aluminum. Soon the Chouinard-Frost team had them for sale. These bongs became instantly popular and allowed fearsome jamcracks to be protected. Each year during the early sixties bigger bongs were produced; they stopped at four inches eventually.

Nineteen-sixty was also the year when 120-foot ropes became antiquated. For reasons now unknown, this had been the standard-length rope for three decades. Without a murmur, we all instantly adopted 150-foot ropes, which this year were being touted by manufacturers. The shorter ropes were not mourned, for Yosemite pitches seemed always to be a little longer than 120 feet. Soon, of course, the pitches on the new climbs all seemed to be a little longer than 150 feet! Only two types of the longer ropes were available: the standard white nylon ropes, made especially for climbing by the Columbian Rope Company, and goldline, a stiff synthetic rope made by the Plymouth Cordage Company. Goldline soon faded from the scene, though it had its adherents.

———————————————————— ■ ————————————————————

If the spring of 1960 marked a huge equipment advance, it also became a milestone of another sort. No one had yet died actually climbing in Yosemite Valley. Hikers scrambling on cliffs where they had no business had been killed. A Stanford student named Anne Pottinger had died of exposure after a climb of the Higher Spire in 1955. As related, Don Goodrich had died climbing in the Yosemite highcountry. The Valley, however, had not yet claimed a person using ropes—a remarkable record, given twenty-seven years and thousands of climbs.

The death of Irving Smith, on March 19, began an unfortunate trend: he was the first of fifty-five rockclimbers to die in the Valley during the next thirty years (all but four of these occurred after 1970, the end of the Golden Age). Smith, a blond, crew-cut high-school junior from Fresno, had been climbing with enthusiasm for a year and wanted to be the youngest person to stand atop the Lost Arrow Spire. "How old were you when you did it?" he asked me one night in the coffee shop at Yosemite Lodge, two months before his death. After I replied "eighteen," he grinned shyly and confided that he would soon—at age seventeen—be attempting the spire with a group of Fresno climbers. I raved about the route and predicted he'd have no trouble whatsoever.

Ironically, he never even set foot on the actual spire: he was killed on the "approach." A pair of long and frightfully exposed rappels must be made to reach the airy notch separating the Arrow from the main cliff. Smith, first down the second rappel, never got to call "Off rappel!" No one saw what happened; a brief howl echoing from the depths marked his last moment. He may have rappelled off the end of the rope; perhaps the rope knocked a loose rock down onto him. More likely, however, is that he had reached the notch and was making the transition from rappel to the shattered granite gap when he lost his balance or grabbed a loose rock. He plunged into what I regard as one of the most sinister places in the Valley: the Arrow Chimney. This slot, prehistorically dark and damp, is a place to avoid. Certainly it is not a good place to die. Smith ricocheted down this dreadful crack for 500 feet, lifeless long before he smashed onto a chockstone ledge.

The body, first spotted by Smith's friend George Sessions a few hours later, was thought to lie in an "inaccessible" spot by the rangers; they and the lad's father opted to leave the corpse where it lay. To justify his position, the father told reporters the standard cliché: "This is the way Irving would have wanted it." What else could a grieving dad believe? Warren Harding, uneasy with the decision, immediately volunteered to rappel and recover the remains. The rangers declined his offer and placed the Arrow Chimney off limits to climbers for a year. Chouinard and I were first up the Arrow Chimney after the death, and I was in the lead when I came upon the desiccated remains. To break the tension, I yelled down to Chouinard, "Goddamn it! His parka doesn't fit me!" The body had quickly decomposed and within a few years would be washed down the chimney by winter storms.

We immortal ones shrugged off Smith's death. "The guy couldn't even rappel right, for God's sake," I remember saying glibly. We thought accidental death could be avoided by sound methods: if you checked knots, checked anchors, checked each other—then all would be well. Only incompetents died. It could never happen to us.

Thus, by May, Smith had been long forgotten by most of us. The excitement for the coming season was palpable. Pratt and I had quit college forever; Robbins and Fitschen had finished serving their country (the former as a clerk at Fort Bliss, Texas; the latter as a reveille bugler and band player at Fort Mason in San Francisco). Everyone was hot to climb, and most wanted to train at Tahquitz Rock in southern California. This immense dome of the purest granite had become famous over the previous few years. The Southerners, of course, climbed at the place often, and their stories of superlative routes had naturally influenced us. It seemed time to visit their area. Chouinard, who always encouraged us to visit Tahquitz, later wrote a sentence that was believed by outsiders years after climbing at the rock was no longer fashionable: "Every spring even the native climbers [of the Valley] spend a week at Tahquitz getting in shape...."

During the first week of May several caravans of Yosemite climbers headed south. Chouinard, Fitschen, Frost, Pratt, Robbins—they all took off. For some reason I didn't join this exodus, instead staying in the Valley and enjoying the finest month of climbing of my life, as close to Nirvana as I'll ever get. A fellow named Dick McCracken, a relatively unknown Berkeley climber of about twenty-five, showed up, and we vowed to climb every day. We almost did, making second ascents of significant routes and even making three minor first ascents. McCracken and I were perfectly matched: we climbed fast and capably, especially on aid pitches. We didn't push the free climbing too hard, but on 5.7 we sprang upward with dispatch.

We took delight in accomplishing some of the harder standard routes, whooping with satisfaction when we did well. If climbing on the bigger walls was sometimes fearful and a lot of work, then doing pleasant half-day routes within our capabilities easily made up for this suffering. Moving well over rock, feeling our muscles respond to the challenge, was one of the great pleasures of life. We basked on sunlit ledges, told jokes, and planned future climbs. That month we wondered if we could climb in that fashion forever.

Dick McCracken, 1965 (Photo: Glen Denny)

Silence reigned, and without our comrades no peer pressure interfered with our simple pleasures. Each morning we awoke to a bright new world and chatted excitedly about what climb to do. On weekdays we were the only climbers in Camp 4; we shared the place with perhaps five groups of tourists. On weekends the campground's population soared—to about ten climbers and twenty sets of tourists. Camp 4 was never full that month.

May 1960 was also a pivotal month for news. Caryl Chessman inhaled the peach-sweet fumes of potassium cyanide at San Quentin Prison, amid worldwide protest. I named a slab-pinnacle on Sentinel Rock for this criminal that very afternoon, but because it looked remarkably like a pawn, people later assumed I was a chess fanatic, not an opponent of the death penalty. The first public mention of the Pill caused much alarm—and gave many of us furtive hope for future and babyless pleasures. The House on Un-American Activities Committee, a congressional group that seemingly had never heard of the Constitution, met in San Francisco's City Hall to deride professors who had refused on principle to sign loyalty oaths. Police goons hosed down peaceful demonstrators on the marble steps of the building in the first such event of the sixties, the forerunner of dozens to come. I distinctly remember poring over all these headlines while sitting in the lodge's quiet lounge, a haven on weekday nights, one infinitely far removed from gas chambers and screaming crowds.

By early June the Tahquitz climbers returned and attacked the walls with alacrity. Their training had paid off: they were in magnificent shape, tired of short routes, and raring to go. High on the agenda of some of this group was the northwest face of Half Dome, not repeated since the first ascent three years earlier. Fitschen, Frost, and Pratt climbed the intimidating wall in mid-June, bivouacking but twice. Robbins congratulated his friends, but, as he later said with a smile, "I'd love to own Half Dome." With this proprietary interest in mind, two weeks later he and Dave Rearick made the third ascent—with only one bivouac.

Five major new routes were also established during this period, before the summer heat drove everyone out. Two of these routes, big walls though they were, hardly rocked the boat. The north face of Higher Cathedral Rock, a sheer 1,000-foot cliff, fell to Pratt, Chouinard, and Bob Kamps. Then Camp 4 Terror, the amorphous wall behind the campground, saw its first humans, Kamps and Rearick. (This pair soon left for Colorado, where, to the dismay of the locals, they made the first ascent of the Diamond, on Longs Peak, the most coveted route in the Rockies.)

Three long, serious routes, however, stood out. The north face of Lower Cathedral Rock, a huge and unpleasant-looking wall, beckoned. Out of the army the previous November, and having just a month earlier quit his job as a bank teller in Berkeley, Robbins began his meteoric rise to stardom with this climb, his first major new route since Half Dome. He, Pratt, and Fitschen spent two and a half days on the 1,200-foot wall, working out a circuitous and difficult line. The high point, if one can call it so, was a detached flake encountered on day two. This proved no ordinary obstacle, as its name, Gong Flake, testifies. Several hundred feet high, forty feet wide, and varying from three to ten feet in thickness, the gigantic flake seemed to vibrate when someone struck it with the heel of his hand. Yet the only route lay behind the flake, inside a claustrophobic chimney. Visions of roadkills flashed through the climbers' minds as they toiled up this slot; all three would be road pizza if the monster decided to choose June 3 to exfoliate. It didn't. Robbins wrote later that "the combination of poor piton cracks, rotten and very loose rock, dirty and messy gullies and cracks, and dangerous climbing problems, plus other disagreeable aspects, has prompted us to consider this the most unpleasant, yet one of the most challenging climbs we have ever done." Needless to say, the route never became a popular one.

A few weeks later Robbins and Fitschen did yet another horror climb, Arches Direct. The 1936 route called the Royal Arches was actually misnamed: the pioneer climbers, for good reason, had avoided the great arching swells, keeping far to their left. The two men knew that the lower part of the new route (immediately named Arches Direct, in keeping with the custom that the second route on a wall must be more direct) would be straightforward enough: simply follow the line of the innermost arch upward until it began to curve over toward the horizontal. But where and how to penetrate this arch and the remaining ones?

On June 24 the pair climbed 750 feet up dirty, wet, and difficult rock to investigate an apparent weakness breaking through the initial arch. A "slimy, grassy, and rotten overhang...then faced us," Robbins later wrote. Five hours passed as Robbins cleaned mud and grass from the decomposed cracks and placed knife-blades and other suspicious pitons. He finally got in a perfect piton and decided to free-climb up easier-looking rock. This particular technique, one that has always faced climbers—and always will—requires courage and confidence. Standing on a pin, one must step out of the security of the aid slings and move off into unknown territory, feeling naked and unsure where the next rest will be—or where the next protection might be. A nervous Robbins soon discovered he was essentially stuck twenty-five feet past his last piton. Standing on a tiny hold, he quickly placed a marginal knife-blade behind a flake. The flake, however, didn't appreciate this invasion and chose suicide in hopes of damaging its violator. The flake popped and down Robbins plunged through midair. Fifty feet he fell, the longest Valley drop yet. Such was the steepness of the wall, and so great was the friction through the many lower pitons, that Fitschen, far below, barely felt the jolt. Robbins, shaken but unscathed, marveled at the fact that he hadn't been hurt—as was usual in those days, he had but one turn of the rope around his waist.

This dreadful pitch, completed the next morning by Robbins, involved another five hours and two shorter falls. In all, the lead required twenty-eight pitons and ten hours, and the two climbers quickly realized they had completed Yosemite's hardest aid pitch. The remainder of the climb proved slightly easier, but the pair reached the rim, with "dirt-filled mouths and throats," only late on their third day. This route, too, sunk into obscurity ("Never again," said Coloradan Layton Kor after the second ascent five years later), and it was excluded from the guidebooks of the 1980s.

The third significant climb of 1960 proved to be quite an exception to the ugliness of the two previous climbs, and it soon became a prized route, one repeated fifteen times during the 1960s. From Camp 4 all of us had stared endlessly at the north face of Sentinel, especially at dusk, when the oblique light lit up thousands of tiny features, creating a lovely sight indeed. So entranced were we by the possibilities on this face that we ignored the right-hand profile: the west face. This narrow prow of white granite, some 1,600 feet high, is not particularly steep—perhaps only seventy degrees. Yet smoothness is the middle name of Sentinel's west face. Hardly a ledge mars the upward sweep; not a single tree or bush disturbs the integrity of the soaring cliff. Chouinard and his main partner that year, Tom Frost, thought the route could be done, though they worried about an obvious feature soon to be known—and feared—as the Dogleg

Crack, a narrow slit that bent ten degrees halfway up its 200-foot length. The route, which took two and a half days (the pair climbed the lower 800 feet of the face to Tree Ledge, something that was rarely, if ever, repeated), involved difficult aid climbing, ten sling belays, and wild free climbing. One highlight was an expanding flake low on the route. Pitons had to be placed straight up underneath it, and each pin tended to loosen the previous one. The trick was to be extremely gentle with the hammering. Higher, the first section of the Dogleg Crack brought raves from Chouinard: "Frost made the finest lead I have ever seen up an 80-foot long 8-inch wide jam crack with only a wooden block for protection." The climb marked the first major Yosemite success for Chouinard and Frost, and their names became forever intertwined, both because of the climbs they did together and their later ten-year partnership in the equipment business.

Tom Frost was the quietest and most modest person to inhabit Camp 4 during these early years. Only much later did I learn that he had been a champion sailboat racer in his early twenties. Bright and superclean both in looks and in language, he preferred to stay out of the limelight, rarely arguing, rarely writing about his exploits. Robbins later described Frost "as one of those spirits I cite to illustrate that the quality of people in climbing is one of the reasons I love the sport. Tom, besides being an outstanding climber, is a walking emanation of good will. He doesn't waste his time in negative talk...."

At least three superhard aid pitches existed by midsummer: Kat Pinnacle, the crux overhang on Arches Direct, and the expanding flake on the west face of Sentinel. Yet free climbing was coming into its own also. Nine first free ascents were made in 1960, a huge increase from previous years. We actively, for the first time, went up on the cliffs with the intention of freeing routes. Most often this meant simply eliminating a few aid pitons from a mostly free route. Previous climbers had started using aid at the 5.8 level, and since most of us were capable of doing 5.9 by 1960, some of these new free routes were minor in significance. One exception stood out, for it was the first 5.10 route ever done in the Valley—and one of the first in the country. The initial pitch of the east chimney of Rixon's Pinnacle, climbed originally with four or five aid pitons, was a slightly overhanging corner that had been burnished to a glasslike texture by eons of running water. Awkward enough to nail, the thirty-foot section looked intimidating to climb free, since few resting spots were available. Liebacking up this slippery open book, Robbins took a good fall at one point, lifting his belayer off the ground. He persevered, however, and made it on his next try; even today the pitch is rated 5.10.

———————————————— ■ ————————————————

Even though 1960 was distinguished by major equipment advances, sterling free-climbing progress, and several stupendous big-wall routes, the year's greatest adventure took place on a cliff known to all, climbers and public alike: El Capitan. No one had seriously considered repeating Harding's Nose route for nearly two years, but by September four men thought the time had come for the first continuous ascent—that is, from ground to rim without resorting to fixed ropes. The quartet—Fitschen, Frost, Pratt, and Robbins—were among the finest climbers in the land by this time. (Chouinard, Kamps, and Rearick qualified at this level also, but they had other things to do at this juncture, such as earning a living in the city, maintaining a family, or going to grad school.)

Robbins, the acknowledged leader, believed that fixed-rope climbing lacked adventure. Given enough time, any determined climber, however competent, could manage to commute up and down an umbilical cord that stretched from ground to high point. In short, Robbins believed in commitment. This attitude, as visionary as Harding's original El Cap plan of three years earlier, was to have far-reaching implications during the next few years, leading to stern words and actions among two camps: those who thought fixed ropes were fine, and those who thought them wholly unnecessary. For a few years this polarization caused friendships to suffer, certain climbers to retire in disgust, and countless discussions in Camp 4 and in various journals.

Robbins thought four people would be ideal for the job: two would climb on a given day, trailing a few ropes; the other pair would prusik these ropes with their huge loads. Then, the next day, the teams would trade off so that everyone shared in the leading. Robbins also thought ten days would be needed for the effort. Thus, as with the first ascent, logistics, rather than climbing difficulty, worried the four men. At a quart and a half of water per man per day—the bare minimum needed to survive for such a long time—this alone added up to 132 pounds. With food, extra ropes and equipment, and sleeping gear, the total baggage would be close to 200 pounds. Two men would have to horse a total of four duffel bags, starting at fifty pounds each, up several hundred feet per day, often spending twelve hours ensnared in aid slings while prusiking or waiting.

The team expected heat in mid-September and they got it: the sun beat down unmercifully on the glaring white granite. By the second day Robbins wondered if they could remain strong and confident under such punishment. But because they were climbing faster than expected, this meant they could drink more water each day—a marvelous incentive for going fast.

Clouds scudded across the sky the next day, and given this reprieve and the new ration of two quarts of water per man per day, Robbins knew they had it made. It even rained briefly on the afternoon of the fourth day, as they approached the Great Roof. The packs got lighter, wildflowers appeared in the cracks, and Scorpio appeared nightly, just above the south rim. For the first time laughter rang out across the wall. Frost, according to Robbins, "kept us nearly in tears with his straight-faced hilarities." The expedition was obviously going quite well. So competent and harmonious was the group that the ascent was routine, except for one close call when Pratt, wrongly thinking he was anchored, came close to pitching off a ledge to his death. By three in the afternoon on the seventh day, summit well-wishers were offering lukewarm champagne to their heroes.

It is difficult to imagine now what a psychological breakthrough this Nose climb was. Without fanfare, the best rockclimbers in the world had simply gone up and done the planet's toughest climb without using fixed ropes. In a single stroke this changed Valley climbing permanently: never again did top-level climbers string fixed ropes from ground to rim. This tactic would have been like using a horse-and-buggy in the thirties, or wearing a homburg in the sixties. Harding, always a renegade, continued fixing ropes for a while, but on his later climbs he, too, swore off siege climbing.

■

Even by late 1960 not many climbers from out of state had visited the Valley, and the ones who did tended to be mountaineers quickly discouraged by the slippery jamcracks and polished slabs. One such outsider was Mike Borghoff, once a juvenile delinquent and later a Purple Heart Korean War vet and a fine poet. Mike tried for years to get up the Yosemite

Mike Borghoff, 1965 (Photo: Glen Denny)

classics, most often failing. I first met him in 1958, halfway up the Lower Brother; he was trying to meld his big mountain boots onto smallish holds, a look of bewilderment on his face. In the fifties, in Washington and Colorado, Mike had been an accomplished rough-rock climber, priding himself on moving well over loose Class 4 rock without a rope. On smoother and more difficult rock, however, he floundered. He confided to me a few years later that he well knew his shortcomings: "I'm the eternally youthful half-ass who will always try, better with words than with hardware…. No confidence, no poise; no poise, you get nowhere." Fortunately, Mike had a few happy moments in the Valley over the years—and he genuinely loved the place.

Borghoff we tolerated, since he was trying to comprehend the Valley and its unique character. Many of us laughed at other outsiders, especially those who had an "attitude" problem. Some would arrive with grandiose plans—and announce these to anyone within earshot. More often than not, these fellows would literally sneak out of the Valley after a failure, not wishing to endure the smirking faces back in Camp 4. Cruel we were to some of these people, but when we heard that Layton Kor was soon to arrive, we knew he would be different.

Kor, a towering twenty-two-year-old bricklayer from Colorado, was already famous—even in California. That he was the finest climber ever to come out of the Rockies no one doubted for an instant. He had laid waste already to Eldorado Springs Canyon, that superb area near his home in Boulder, establishing dozens of daring routes. He had made the first ascent of the sheer wall called the Diagonal on Longs Peak, and surely would have made the first ascent of the fabled Diamond, on the same peak, if Kamps and Rearick hadn't done it first.

Kor arrived in late September 1960, only two weeks after the second ascent of the Nose, and immediately teamed up with Chouinard on the first ascent of the Valley's most breathtaking slab, the Glacier Point Apron. Serious free climbing on this 1,200-foot-high sprawl of featureless granite had begun only three weeks earlier, when Bill Amborn, Joe McKeown, and Rich Calderwood wound their way up 500 feet of ultra-smooth rock to a tiny protrusion they christened Coonyard Pinnacle. (This name resulted from one climber's distortion of Chouinard's name, correctly pronounced "Sheh-nard.") Amborn, the grandson of 1920s pioneer William Kat, came back a few days later with a hot seventeen-year-old Bay Area climber named Jeff Foott, and they continued up the blank slab, tilted at about fifty degrees, for an additional 600 feet, turning back finally just one pitch short of the Oasis, an all-year spring at the top of the Apron.

Chouinard and Kor's ascent all the way to the Oasis a few days later thus covered only one new pitch and can hardly be considered a significant first ascent. Still, any doubts about Kor's ability vanished instantly. At six-foot-four, the gangly kid, known for speed, not delicacy, might have been expected to have trouble with the most slippery piece of rock in

Yosemite. He didn't—and the Kor legend began immediately.

By early October most Camp 4 residents had departed, and I found myself in a situation faced by dozens of climbers in the years to come: the enthusiastic big man looming over me, insisting we go climb. Now! Anything! Pack up! Kor, cursed or blessed with an overabundance of energy, simply could not sit still. In all the years I knew him I never saw him read a book or newspaper, or look contemplative. He paced; he told filthy jokes with childlike glee; he chased women. He was successful chasing women. He ate with great zest, one time wolfing down a hamburger we had cruelly stuffed with a thin sheet of cardboard. He nudged people constantly. He talked and wrote in choppy sentences, flipping from subject to subject as his mind raced ahead of his mouth or pen. One letter I received from him shows this stream-of-consciousness style, here reproduced verbatim: "I will be leaving for Europe April first so wish me good luck on the walls, what do you have planned for next summer? suppose you will crash up the big mountains. What has been happening in the great white valley of yosemite. Any new routes? or great repeats? Suppose Royal is at Sugar Bowl...."

I loved Kor's natural and frantic behavior, and he and I hit it off on our first meeting. Hot to climb also, I instantly had the feeling that going along with Kor guaranteed safety: he seemed born to climb. I could go off with

Layton Kor, about 1965 (Photo: Glen Denny)

him anywhere and come back alive. We did a few big routes together that fall and promised each other to tear the Valley apart the following spring.

Kor never showed up in 1961; suffering from a serious lung fungus, he was "taking the cure" in a Texas clinic where a starvation diet would apparently effect a cure. We imagined that quacks ran such places, but by summertime Kor once again attacked his home cliffs with a vengeance. Whether it was the diet prescribed by the Texas doctors, or the thought of missing a summer of climbing that restored Kor, we shall never know.

I had saved about five hundred dollars by late 1960 and decided to spend most of 1961 in the Valley. I arrived on New Year's Day and was still there at the end of the year. I climbed about sixty routes that year, with long absences only in August (a trip to Wyoming) and November (odd jobs in Berkeley). Caught between going back to school, or getting a real job, or doing something constructive, I simply existed in a state of limbo, as if waiting for someone to drag me away from the great granite rut. No one did, so I lived climbing and thought climbing and dreamed climbing.

It was a great year, full of adventures of every kind. Right away came a controversy, one ongoing to this day. The key word was "bolt." When were bolts justified? In the old days the answer was simple: if you didn't have a piton that would fit a crack, you drilled a hole for a bolt. But now pitons came in all sizes, from rurps to bongs. Some of these new tools, however, took great skill to place—and this led to the central question: If less skilled climbers simply placed bolts whenever the going got tough, wouldn't this lead to an unsightly and unnecessary increase of bolts? Yet who should decide if bolts were needed?

Chouinard, the most thoughtful climber of the period, decided to vent his opinions on the subject, and in March 1961 he published an article in *Summit*. He immediately stated his thesis: "The problem is not one of individual taste, but rather one which must be determined by the entire climbing fraternity and adhered to by everyone who climbs." Bolts not only mar the beauty of the rock, he went on, but many climbers now feel "undressed" without their bolt kit handy. A less-than-expert leader is "never" an excuse for using bolts. Lack of equipment is "never" an excuse for placing bolts. An angry Chouinard raved on and on, not mincing words. He described the desecration of the Lost Arrow Spire, where climbers of the mid-1950s, not as capable as John Salathé, had placed nine additional bolts. Chouinard indirectly called for insurrection when he mentioned that Mark Powell had chopped all nine so that the climb would revert to its first-ascent level of difficulty.

Needless to say, letters to the editor poured in to *Summit*. Chuck Wilts, for instance, knew that the best climbers had sometimes made ascents that were unprotected and thus unsafe. "Should [such a] climb," Wilts asked, "be forever forbidden to sane climbers? Who is to be the judge?"

Washington climber Gene Prater claimed that arrogant experts can simply bypass "unnecessary" bolts, leaving them in place for the less competent. Robbins chimed in: "Generally speaking, bolting is not climbing; it is the elimination of climbing difficulties by the tedious hit-twist method." Knowing that the rigid "rules" set forth by Chouinard wouldn't work—since climbers despise rules—Robbins called for "a change in values," a phrase he used three times.

The subject came up many times around the Camp 4 tables that spring. I postulated that any strong-armed person could simply walk up to the base of El Cap and place a ladder of bolts clear to the top—the most spectacular and direct route in the world. Yes, this would take time, but think of the fame, I raved sarcastically. Think of the publicity! Money! What was to stop such an egotist?

Totally agreeing with Chouinard's point of view, and believing that actions would speak louder than words, I soon struck. In 1959 Herb Swedlund, the Valley's finest raconteur and usually a highly competent climber, had placed a ladder of seventeen bolts while establishing a new route alongside Lower Yosemite Fall. I watched him occasionally during the ten or so afternoons he worked on the route and noticed he always wore bright red or yellow shirts. He explained that the route, visible from the path below, attracted many gawkers, among them ravishing young women. Our handsome hero would place a few bolts on a given afternoon, then rappel swiftly on his fixed rope and dance down the talus toward his admirers.

"Ah, does this sort of thing work?" I asked hopefully.

"Ask a hundred," said Swedlund, smiling, "and you'll get one."

The bolt ladder, placed right next to a prominent crack system, was simply Swedlund's way of delaying the climb for as long as possible in order to further his sexual career. While this reason may have been unique, his overuse of bolts had bothered me in 1959—and still did two years later. In May I led the offending pitch in a few hours, placing decent pitons in disconnected, dirt-filled cracks and shunning the bolts as if they were radioactive. Joe Oliger, my partner, then spent two hours chopping all seventeen.

A few people applauded this decisive action; a few people thought I was an ass. Most wondered why I had bothered—and Swedlund never mentioned the incident. Bolt chopping became a popular pastime in the ensuing years, though bolt *placing* became equally popular. Two factions developed, and the matter was never really resolved.

■

Only one distinguished route was established in the spring of 1961: the near-vertical northwest face of the Higher Spire. Robbins and Fitschen had attempted the route the previous September, turning back after completing two-thirds of the 1,000-foot route. They had had no pitons that

would fit a long, wide crack, and, according to Robbins, "bolts were anathema." Shortly after this, Fitschen went off to Europe to become a bohemian and faded forever out of the Yosemite picture. Robbins grabbed Tom Frost the following May, and they nailed the wide crack using Frost's new bong-bongs. A short, blank wall then appeared and Frost reached for the bolt kit. He searched his pockets. "Royal," he yelled down. "I don't have the bolts. Tie 'em onto the haul line!"

"You must have them," Robbins yelled up. "Look again!"

They were not the first climbers to have forgotten vital gear—and they were assuredly not the last. Down they rappelled.

A few days later the pair went up and finished the route, bivouacking once and rappelling the standard 1934 route in the dark. Fixed ropes were not used, and bolts were used sparingly—six in all. The climb gained instant notoriety for one pitch, the Chimney of Horrors, a nightmare Robbins had first led on the 1960 attempt. Sixty feet high, narrow, overhanging, and flared, with nary a crack for protection, this slot absolutely deserved its name. Robbins described the sight as "psychologically devastating" in a *Summit* article. Nevertheless, he struggled upward, retreated slightly to place a protection bolt, and then continued, heart in mouth. "The consolation which climbers have in most tight chimneys," he wrote, "namely the possibility of jamming to a standstill if a slip occurs, was not present in this one.... Near the top I felt I was extending myself to the utmost and an eighty-foot fall was the alternative to adhering to the rock." At the top came that most unsettling of techniques: placing an aid pin far, far above the last protection and gingerly standing up on it. This lead set a standard for boldness, and from this day onward I was not alone in regarding Robbins as Yosemite's best climber.

Robbins's next big new route proved this beyond doubt, though he quickly gave equal credit to his companions, Pratt and Frost. Brilliant though these two were, Robbins once again was the driving force behind the ascent of the "world's finest rock climb."

Opposite: *Layton Kor leads the White Flake Pitch on the northwest face of the Higher Cathedral Spire, 1965. (Photo: Glen Denny)*

CHAPTER 6

To Siege or Not to Siege: 1961–1962

*It has become popular in other parts of North America, espe-
cially in the Northwest, to lay fixed ropes up a climb to avoid having to bivouac or take a chance with the weather. These ropes create
an umbilical cord from man to where he truly belongs and to where
he can quickly retreat if things get tough. This manifests American
love of security and shows that the climber should not be there in
the first place.*

—Yvon Chouinard, 1963

Years after his climb of the Nose, Warren Harding claimed in print that
Royal Robbins, Tom Frost, and Joe Fitschen—three of the four men
who made the second ascent—were "contemptuous" of the methods used
on his historic climb. Not only do the three climbers deny this allegation;
they claim great respect for Harding's achievement. At the time the Nose
was done, siege climbing was the only possibility, and everyone recognized
this. The probable truth: Harding's *later* fixed-rope climbs came in for heavy
and justified criticism, and this has undoubtedly clouded his memory.

In the early 1960s even Robbins was unsure about the role of fixed
ropes on routes as intimidating as El Cap. Far from deriding Harding,
Robbins in fact chose this tactic for the initial section of his first new El
Cap route, the Salathé Wall. Climbers had looked at the broad face left of
the Nose for years: Wayne Merry had seen crack systems as early as 1957;
Chuck Pratt had also spotted a potential route. Yvon Chouinard, constantly
prowling the Valley in search of routes, had gone so far as to name the
entire wall in honor of his hero, John Salathé. Robbins and Frost, looking
at the cliff early in September 1961, "came to the giddy conclusion that a
magnificent route lay there."

Days later, Robbins, Frost, and Pratt began climbing. Robbins realized that stretching fixed ropes from ground to top would mock the es-

sence of climbing: unknown adventure. Yet the wall was huge, perhaps too huge to do in one push. What to do? Perhaps if the trio fixed ropes over the 800-foot lower section—from the ground to the prominent ledge at the base of the huge, heart-shaped feature known as, yes, the Heart—then they could regroup on the ground and later take supplies to the high point, cast loose from their umbilical cord, and strike out for the rim. "Since we wished to avoid a siege-type ascent with fixed ropes from bottom to top," Robbins later wrote, "this plan...seemed the best compromise between what was possible and our desire to keep the enterprise as adventurous as we could. By adventurous I mean, essentially, uncertain."

This sentiment, hardly dreamed of yet by most other Valley climbers, seems to me now to exemplify a noble and calculated philosophy. Where Harding simply wanted to have "fun," endlessly prusiking ropes with food and wine, not caring whom he was with or how competent they were, Robbins saw that climbing big walls in good style could do wonders for the soul. Climbing, for him, tended to be a spiritual exercise: not man overcoming the rock with garrison tactics, but man striving and reaching for a deeper meaning. If you pushed into the unknown, then perhaps you'd discover something about yourself. Robbins may not have been consciously seeking such goals, yet he sensed that subduing a wall with siege tactics would be an exercise in self-deception, for, given enough time, *anyone* could siege a wall. He wrote that fixed ropes and overuse of bolts would guarantee "the certitude which tends to diminish our joy in climbing."

The first part of the route went as planned: after three and a half days the team reached Heart Ledge, tied six ropes together, and rappelled to the ground. Several blank sections 500 feet up had required a total of thirteen bolts.

Three days later, after resting and acquiring more equipment, the trio prusiked up their ropes to Heart Ledge. Then came the bravest act of all. Keeping just three ropes, the team hurled the others into the void. The umbilical cord had been severed.

Because the Salathé Wall route was done by the best climbers in the world, few stories have arisen concerning the first ascent. No stoveleg pitons. No ranger bans. No nighttime bolting marathons. No suspect climbers. No Dolt Carts. Three experts moved masterfully up vertical rock, sharing the leads and humping the loads ever upward. Each day brought difficult climbing, involving 5.9 and A4. A complex pitch would take perhaps five hours, but once it was done, it was done. Ever upward.

During the six days of the final push from Heart Ledge, September 18–23, the three men climbed the 2,000 remaining feet to the rim. Jamcracks, chimneys, pendulums, delicate nailing—you name it, they found it. One highlight was the long, exposed pendulum into the intimidating off-width crack leading to Hollow Flake Ledge. Robbins, by now a master of the pendulum, led this pitch, which proved to be the key to the

*Royal Robbins doing a pendulum above Lung Ledge, Salathé Wall
(Photo: Tom Frost)*

Looking up toward the Roof and the Headwall, high on the Salathé Wall (Photo: Tom Frost)

central part of the route. Another landmark was the Ear, halfway up the wall. This tremendously exposed bomb-bay slot, was later described by Robbins as a "frightening formation," one that made for an "anxiety-producing pitch." Shortly above this they reached the most aesthetic bivouac ledge any of them had yet seen: the twelve-by-twelve-foot, absolutely flat top of El Cap Spire, a pillar separated from the main cliff by a three-foot-wide gap.

Most impressive of all were two awesome, and connected, sections near the top: a tiered ceiling they simply called the Roof and the overhanging wall just above, dubbed the Headwall. These two sections didn't need complex names; they are classics of the genre. The ceiling jutted out perhaps twelve feet, yet the tiers contained hidden but near-perfect cracks, and Frost nailed this quickly. Above lay a 150-foot headwall, tilted five degrees beyond the vertical. Bottomed and flared cracks shot up this sober and grainy expanse, but pitons nevertheless stuck long enough for upward progress. The exposure defied description. An object let loose from here will spin free for about 400 feet before brushing the near-vertical cliff below. Seconds later it will kiss the wall two or three times before exploding into the forest, 2,000 feet below.

The last classic section was Pratt's pitch at the very top. Near the end of their final day, the last thing the trio wanted to see was an unprotectable jamcrack. But who better than Pratt, that master of crack climbing, to make short work of this? Robbins later described not the efforts of Pratt, but of his follower, Frost: "Tom…followed Chuck's lead and came up sweating, cursing, and praising Chuck's uncommon talents." Mild-mannered Frost cursing? This is surely an indication of the difficulty.

And so ended what Robbins was soon to call the "finest rock climb on earth." Nine and a half days; two pushes; less than two weeks elapsed. Fixed ropes had lain on the cliff for only three days, and the thirteen bolts placed low on the route became the total for the entire route. Could Harding have done this? Of course not. Would Valley climbing have suffered if Harding had spent a couple of years fixing the route and placing scores of bolts? Absolutely. The time was ripe for evolution. Harding pioneered the big-wall concept; Robbins refined it.

It would certainly make a good story to claim that Harding retaliated instantly with his ascent of the west face of the Leaning Tower, completed with siege tactics just three weeks after the Salathé Wall climb. But the ever-restless Harding had actually begun this wildly overhanging route, located on the south side of the Valley next to Bridalveil Fall, ten months earlier. The lower part of the Tower averages one hundred ten degrees; the upper section about ninety-five degrees. Without question, the Tower is America's most overhanging wall. And the wall is as blank as it is steep; hardly a single crack mars the lower part. Why did Harding choose this feature, one that would require so much bolting? "It was a face I'd long wanted to do," he wrote later. This simple and honest appraisal typified Harding's approach to climbing: find a nice wall, grab some novices, and carry lots of rope and bolts.

On the last day of 1960, Al Macdonald and Les Wilson, two young climbers from Berkeley, accompanied Harding on the first attempt; they intended to spend three days on the wall. Harding, the Pied Piper of Yosemite, had lured these two relative beginners onto this 800-foot monster on the strength of his name. What apprentice could resist? The first effort, however, ended quickly. While Harding was bolting and nailing away on the first pitch, he loosened a flake that broke off and smashed against his head. "My neck. I think it's broken," Harding moaned.

"Can you move your head at all?" Macdonald yelled up.

"Yeah. All the way around. I can see pretty good too—two of everything."

Harding managed to get down under his own power and the team gave up, leaving a rope dangling from the high point, some seventy feet up.

Nearly six months passed before Harding and Macdonald returned. With the aid of Glen Denny, who had learned a lot since his Sherpa efforts on the Washington Column, and George Whitmore, the quiet porter of the Nose, Harding, who was to lead 80 percent of the route, spent a week bolting and pitoning.

The June temperatures soared. Days passed in a blur. Television crews arrived; an epic was in the making. Macdonald spent one of his days off in the parking lot of Bridalveil Fall, listening to tourists explaining to one another exactly what was happening on the cliff above. "Some," he wrote later, "actually believed that we stood on the ledge and threw the rope up the cliff, and that after the rope mystically attached itself to the rock, we pulled ourselves up hand over hand."

Each night the team would retreat from the climb either to the Valley floor or to a bivouac spot in the nearby forest. Progress was slow for a good reason: the wall was mostly devoid of cracks. Bolt after bolt was placed, and occasionally Harding ordered his partners to remove bolts and their hangers. Purportedly to save the hangers for later, this was simply an act of impertinence. Robbins placed bolts for future climbers; Harding sometimes placed them for a one-time use, a pattern to become clear in his future ascents. Fried by the 105-degree heat, the team temporarily called it quits on day seven, having reached comfortable Ahwahnee Ledge, some 450 feet up. Many bolts had been placed; many difficult piton placements had been made also. Harding, as usual, had done some superb nailing.

By the time the team—now composed of Harding, Denny, and Macdonald—returned to the Tower in October to finish the route, the Salathé Wall had just been completed. The threesome admired this climb, knowing they weren't in the same league as Robbins and his group. Harding was as quick to praise the skills of others as he was at claiming himself just a plodding incompetent.

The trio spent an entire week on the wall, bivouacking on Ahwahnee Ledge each night but the last one, spent just below the summit. Finally, on October 13, the three men pulled over the top: the route had taken eighteen days in all. One hundred eleven bolts had been placed; fixed ropes stretched over the entire route.

Many of us watching this spectacle unfold from the ground didn't like what was going on. The Salathé Wall climb had shown us what was possible; the Tower route already seemed an old-fashioned approach. Find a blank wall and spend a year bolting up it: was this the future? We were harsh on Harding, the prime exponent of this style. Yet, in retrospect, it's hard to imagine the Tower being done, in 1961, without sieging. Bolting took lots of time, and the wall was so severely overhanging that rappelling was impossible: one had to prusik *downward* as well as upward. It would have been ludicrous to try to retrieve all the ropes each time the team retreated from working on the route high above. And, what with all the bolting, they simply couldn't have done the route in one continuous push. Should the climb have been done at all, considering it was half bolted? Maybe not, but it was.

Because of its striking appearance, the climb became extremely popular in the mid-sixties—once the missing bolts and hangers were replaced by Robbins on the second ascent. A consensus about the Tower later emerged: if Harding wanted to go to all that trouble to establish a route, let him. All the better for us lazy ones to enjoy a beautiful location without doing too much work!

On the same day Harding's group topped out on the Leaning Tower, a historic event was unfolding on Elephant Rock, downstream from the main Valley. Chuck Pratt, the crack specialist, outdid himself on this Friday the thirteenth. To the right of the already-climbed Worst Error, a pair of dramatic-looking cracks shot up a sheer wall. Pratt had spotted these months earlier, and he and Mort Hempel, a superb climber from Berkeley, had hiked up the talus to investigate. The left-hand crack seemed more alluring than the right-hand one, so up they went. The first pitch, led by Hempel, overhung slightly and involved a 5.9 lieback; the next pitch, a terrifying slot, overhanging and flared, went to the master crack man and was 5.8, though no protection was possible. The hour was late, so the pair retreated with promises to return soon.

On October 13 they returned. Above the former high point, another long and difficult chimney pitch took the duo to a final problem, a short but awesome jamcrack just below the top. Even Pratt had trouble here: the shallow, flared crack overhung gently and was slightly grainy. He squirmed up this obstacle an inch or two at a time, locking his arms where possible while positioning his feet just so on the periphery of the crack. Both strength and finesse are required for off-width cracks, the kind where no appendage seems to fit well. Pratt, as strong as Hercules, also had the grace of Achilles. Sometimes a foot bridged tenuously across the crack's outer lip; sometimes he had to stack both feet in clever combinations for them to stick long enough to scrunch his body an inch higher. "Pratt never said anything on other leads," Hempel recalled recently. "But this was different—he said 'Watch me!' a number of times. When I took out the protection, it was barely in place, and the crack just stopped at the top and I had to maneuver over a tiny overhang. I just climbed the rope. I knew I couldn't climb the crack. Pretty exciting."

Known as the Crack of Doom, this climb stood for several years as Yosemite's hardest crack climb. Though I later wrongly called the route the first 5.10 ever done in the Valley—Robbins's free lead of the east chimney of Rixon's Pinnacle was actually the first—it can be argued that Pratt's on-sight lead of a route never before done was the better achievement. Elimination of a few aid pitons from an established route such as Rixon's is surely difficult, but Pratt's bold lead into unknown territory stands in a class by itself.

Many styles of climbing existed during 1961, as can be seen from the three routes described above. Feeling left out by autumn, I decided to assert myself by doing something grand. So I chose two neglected areas: solo climbing and ice climbing. A voracious reader, I had been heavily influenced by the heroic Alpine exploits of Hermann Buhl, Gaston Rébuffat, and others. Rock climbing was fine, but, by God, we had to branch out and become alpinists! This, in essence, meant moving fast and unroped up difficult rock and difficult ice. The books I had devoured extolled the beauties of such efficiency, but they were short on practical details— such as *how* to solo aid climbs, or *how* to climb thin ice. Although I was determined to learn these modes of climbing, my new career lasted only sixty days.

I ran up the Royal Arches alone in less than an hour, mostly unroped, an event that led to instant hubris. Make way for me, Gaston! So I next turned to the Lost Arrow Spire, knowing nothing about how to solo an aid route. Having done the climb five times already, I was hardly worried about the difficult piton placements, but at the base of the wildly exposed first pitch, subdued and shaky, I tried to recall if I had ever read about solo aid techniques. Paralyzed by the knowledge that I knew absolutely nothing, I considered retreat—but I could already hear the hoots of laughter that would greet me back in Camp 4. Furthermore, I sensed that Janie Dean, the lodge's coffee-shop manager and my girlfriend-of-the-moment (and one of the few women to have climbed the Arrow), might refuse to mate that night with a known coward. No, I would go on; I *had* to go on. I could probably learn as I went. Perched in my slings near the top, several hours later, I suddenly realized my methods were unsound: I had invented a clever but flawed system. Had a piton popped I would have slid downward for half a rope length, not to my death, but to the bottom of the loop of rope that formed my makeshift belay. No piton popped, however.

But success breeds even more hubris, and a short time later, after a series of December storms, I looked up to see the immense but disconnected slabs beneath the face of Half Dome covered with a skinny layer of snow and ice. I immediately cornered a new friend, a physics major I had met at the Berkeley rocks the previous winter. Frank Sacherer was a superb rockclimber already, but a virgin on ice. Knowing that he had also devoured Buhl and Rébuffat, I raved, "It'll be perfect cramponing up there, man. Great practice for the Alps." Sacherer hesitated.

"I'll go first, show you how it's done," I said, having strapped on crampons about six times in my life—but six times more than Sacherer.

"Well...okay," he said, frowning. "But we're taking a rope, aren't we? It looks slippery up there."

"A rope!" I screamed. "Jesus, on that little slope? You think Buhl would want a rope? No rope! Besides, if you fall off, you'll drag me down with you!"

Irony. About 2,000 feet up, near the top of a flawlessly smooth and treeless 600-foot slab, my crampons skittered off glare ice that barely kissed the granite, and, with sparks flying from my ice axe's futile self-arrest on the granite underneath, I shot down the fifty-degree slope like a rocketship, achieving Mach 1 as I sailed over a cliff 500 feet below. Sacherer, sure I was a goner, didn't even bother to shout down. Relieved he hadn't insisted on being joined by a rope, he morosely began inching upward toward the safety of nearby trees and ramps.

I awoke to find myself splayed out crucifixionlike on a snow-covered ledge, 600 feet below Sacherer. Struggling to comprehend my injuries, I soon gave up and began howling for my out-of-sight friend. Once he heard my pitiful shrieks, Sacherer began tiptoeing courageously down the now-fearful slope. Later, displaying a strange mixture of anger, competence, and diffidence, he ushered me down treacherous slabs to safety, 1,500 feet below. The idea of a ranger rescue never once entered our heads: we both knew that Buhl would have simply started down without a complaint.

I spent thirteen days in the tiny Valley hospital, pissing what seemed to be pure blood for the first ten days due to a brief courtship between a broken rib and a kidney. Harding, in to visit once, grew ashen observing my output. "Roper," he exclaimed, "you're pissing your life away!" My father felt the same, but figuratively, not literally: "Your poor judgment," he wrote me three days after the accident, "has caused a great halt in my personal Xmas affairs; there are going to be a considerable number who receive Xmas cards late on account of you." Two days later his mother died. It was quite a Christmas.

Following these brief forays into Buhl territory, I quit both solo climbing and ice climbing and lived happily, on and off, in Yosemite for the next decade, climbing only with companions and only on warm rock.

Nineteen sixty-one saw yet another controversial style of climbing emerge, one that I had more success with: speed climbing. This activity, while hardly new, was refined this year and caused a few problems. As Chouinard put it a few years later, "Climbers climb not just to see how fast and efficiently they can do it, but far worse, to see how much faster and more efficient they are than a party which did the same climb a few days before. The climb becomes secondary, no more important than a racetrack." As a naturally fleet climber, I often chose companions with the same trait. We sometimes would pick a climb that hadn't yet been done in a day and race up it without bivouac gear, feeling smug afterward. One-upmanship figured in some of this action, to be sure. On the other hand, we were thrilled to move efficiently. A question asked more and more this year was: "How long did you take?" I was guilty of this, trying hard to make my mark doing what I was good at.

The finest example of speed climbing competition in this period—the one Chouinard obliquely refers to above—concerns the north face of Sentinel, that long and strenuous route pioneered by Steck and Salathé in 1950. The wall had been done fourteen times by September 1961, but without a bivouac only once—a ten-hour 1960 ascent by Robbins and Fitschen. Excellent though this deed was, it had been Robbins's fourth time up the wall and Fitschen's second; they knew the route by heart. By this time the route was all free except for a short aid section on the Headwall; with lots of strenuous jamcracks and chimneys, it was a Valley test piece for crack specialists.

Sacherer and I climbed efficiently together, forming a no-nonsense team. Not often did we relax on ledges, dangling our feet into space and discussing the meaning of life. Instead, we prided ourselves on moving quickly up steep rock, hammering pitons with blows worthy of Thor himself and setting up belays within a minute or two. When I suggested in early September 1961 that we try the Steck-Salathé route, a climb neither of us had done, Sacherer didn't even bother to ask me about bivouac gear. In fact, he was more of a fanatic than I, insisting we take only one rope and only two quarts of water. I balked. "What happens if we have to retreat?" I asked plaintively.

"We won't. We don't." Sacherer, a college junior majoring in physics at the University of San Francisco, tended toward arrogance. He believed in the power of the mind to overcome all obstacles and utterly disdained frailty. Once, as he was making some 5.7 moves fifty feet above a worried partner, without a single piton between them, the partner yelled up, "Frank, for God's sake, get a pin in!" Sacherer slowly turned downward, stared at his quivering friend for a full five seconds, and then snarled, "Shut up, you chickenshit."

We did Sentinel in eight and a half hours, strolling into Camp 4 well before dark, disguising our tiredness with a jaunty swagger. Robbins strode over to our table with a bottle of champagne in his hand. "That was well done, you guys! I watched you all day. Congratulations! Drink up!" We found this act commendable indeed. Sacherer, an unsophisticated lad, took his first-ever sip of bubbly, scrunched up his face, and said, "It tastes like Coke."

Robbins had been generous, but he was not about to allow two twenty-year-old punks to retain a Sentinel speed record. He politely waited a full day before swinging into action. Then it was our turn to watch through binoculars as he and Tom Frost raced up the wall, often climbing simultaneously, the first time this tactic had ever been done on a big climb. Three hours and fifteen minutes after starting, they stood on the summit. They nonchalantly strolled into camp in time for a late lunch. So shocked was I by this feat that I neglected to buy champagne.

Speed climbing rarely got this competitive, but those who moved fast, avoided bivouacs, and climbed like demons became part of the picture in the years to come, engendering many discussions and letters to the editors of climbing magazines. For instance, Tom Higgins, a brilliant young climber from Southern California, gave *Summit* readers a thoughtful insight: "Perhaps Yosemite climbing is half idealism, half track meet." This brought a response from Glacier Point Apron expert Bill Amborn in the following issue: "Competition...results in excellence and competence in climbers because of the high standards it imposes. Excellence in climbing is important because it means a greater margin of safety and a better knowledge of one's limitations."

Although speed climbing upset a few people because it gave the appearance of being competitive (though in fact it was simply an evolutionary process), the action was at least local, involving familiar faces. Such minor irritations vanished on March 31, 1962. Outsiders had not only invaded *our* Valley, but they had, on this day, sullied El Cap with fixed ropes. Ed Cooper, a well-known mountaineer from Seattle, had decided he could be a first-rate rockclimber as well. Influenced by articles and publicity about El Cap routes, he and Canadian Jim Baldwin had climbed, in 1961, a 1,000-foot wall on the Squamish Chief, a titanic chunk of granite not far north of Vancouver. They had fixed ropes up this monolith, taken months to finish—while courting the media—and had been feted by the local townspeople upon their conquest. Shades of the Nose! Heady with their victory, the pair moved south toward mecca the following spring, never having climbed in Yosemite but eager for the experience. "There was on El Capitan," Cooper haughtily wrote, "one line left, the direct southwest face, logically left unclimbed to the last." Confident of his talents, Cooper nevertheless succumbed at first view, as we all had once, to the overpowering size of El Cap: "We felt small and inconsequential...doubt gnawed at the back of our minds."

Doubt gnawed at us also, once we saw the pair laying siege to the cliff left of the Salathé Wall route. We well remembered the impeccable style of this latter route, once the lower third had been fixed. This tactic, we felt, had been a necessary experiment; but after this success, no longer would fixed ropes be necessary, even on El Cap. Cooper, a highly intelligent man, as well as reserved and headstrong, remained aloof upon his arrival. By contrast, Baldwin, a gruff and earthy fellow, fit into the Camp 4 scene at once; yet he, too, sidestepped our questions about the propriety of fixing ropes. "You bastards are just envious," he sneered. "Just because you didn't see the route doesn't mean we can't have it!"

Most new routes on El Cap during the sixties contained a grandiose "Wall" in their names, and the route Cooper and Baldwin discovered soon became known as the Dihedral Wall, after the enormous, curving dihedrals that distinguish the lower half of the 2,400-foot-high route. Blank sections separated some of these dihedrals; bolts would be needed. We Valley regulars didn't worry so much about that; we simply didn't relish the idea of yet another drawn-out siege route, especially by people who had never climbed in the Valley. We naively thought that Harding's climb of the Leaning Tower would have been the last example of this technique.

On a less noble level we also didn't think much of Pacific Northwest climbers coming in and going against our "rules." The Northwest had a reputation for producing highly conservative mountaineer types, people who climbed dreary volcanos and rotten crags, people who actually believed in taking the "Ten Essentials" with them. We could just see Cooper up on the wall, plodding along gamely with his compass and flashlight and hard hat. (Harding's list of ten would have included wine and perhaps a copy of *Playboy*.) Had it not been for Baldwin—ribald, full of life, and a quality drinking companion—we Camp 4 residents would have been even more pissed off with the project. Baldwin, with his darting eyes, full beard, and sensuous lips, looked and acted like a satyr, and the sensational sto-

Jim Baldwin, 1962 (Photo: Glen Denny)

ries he told about his sexual escapades—obviously true because they rarely redounded to his credit—caused us to reconsider our ideas about "conservative Northwest climbers."

During April and May the pair spent about ten days fixing their ropes higher and higher, making less than 100 feet a day. Then, while returning on May 15 from the high point, Baldwin had a bad scare. His prusik knots somehow slipped while he was descending a diagonal fixed line, and he slid at high speed some eighty feet to the bottom of the rope, one wisely fixed to an anchor below. This anchor stopped him, of course, but his hands had been badly ropeburned; he was through for the spring. Cooper grabbed me one morning shortly thereafter and talked me into going up for a few days. I knew I was a hypocrite for accepting, but I couldn't resist seeing what the big wall was like. I hunched in slings on a dead-vertical wall, 800 feet above the ground, without moving an inch, from noon one day till dawn the next as Cooper bolted. As daylight arrived Cooper remained expressionless as I started downward with hardly an explanation or a goodbye. I wasn't meant for siege climbing. Ethics aside, my tolerance for sitting in slings at one spot for half a day at a time was nil. The total upward progress of the previous day had been thirty feet, all achieved by bolts.

By the time summer rolled around, the ropes stretched to the 900-foot level, but the rangers once again enforced a summertime ban. Cooper, briefly dabbling in a career as a stockbroker, returned to New York. Baldwin, perennially short of cash, returned to work at odd jobs in his hometown, Prince Rupert, a fishing and logging community near the British Columbia–Alaska border.

Before 1962, relationships among climbers had been remarkably friendly, with little friction and enormous mutual respect. Subtly, this began to change, and part of the reason was an influx of a new group of irreverent climbers. Baldwin and Cooper were one such pair. Art Gran, a thirty-year-old engineer, was another. This voluble fellow, a superb climber on his home turf, New York's Shawangunks, stormed into Yosemite full of wit and arrogance. With his accent and constantly gesturing arms, he was a true character, but one not liked equally by all. Brash and forward, he climbed just well enough not to be considered a buffoon. Gran thought some of us had an overly proprietary interest in the Valley, as did Eric Beck, a college dropout just turned nineteen that spring. He, too, hadn't grown up in the shadow of the great climbers, as many of the rest of us had, and this meant he was free to make fun of the big boys, who, after all, were mortal.

Robbins, the biggest star of all, made an attractive target. Often aloof, he spoke in carefully chosen words, rarely laughed, and took life seriously. I hadn't thought much of this, but when Baldwin, Gran, Beck, Kor, and others parodied Robbins, I saw their point at once. I joined in, a perfect example of peer influence. From this time on, a kind of polarity existed in Camp 4, subtle but ever-present.

Robbins and Frost climbed a new route on Sentinel's north face early in May, and a phrase later written by Robbins in his account of the climb in *Summit* provided a splendid opportunity for derision. The dawn view of El Cap from a bivouac ledge high on the route had been sublime, and Robbins waxed eloquent: "How lovely and wondrous it seemed! I reflected on how easy it was to become anesthetized to the simple and grand things of nature, which really are the best—better even than Mozart."

Other climbers' speech soon became peppered with similar constructions. "How was such-and-such a route?" we'd ask Kor. "Better than Fats Domino!" he would shriek. An unpublished first-ascent article written in 1963 by Steve Thompson and Jeff Dozier contains the phrase "better than Tchaikovsky, but not as good as Brahms." The Sentinel climb, naturally, soon became known as the "Mozart Wall." Robbins, undaunted by such teasing, would write many other controversial passages in the future, though he was also one of the most lively and competent writers of this period.

While the events mentioned above were taking place, life in Camp 4 went along just about as it always had. Basically, we all had our own agendas. I remember getting many letters, most often written in winter, about plans for the coming season. "Let's do Half Dome before it gets too hot." "I hear the east face of the Higher Rock might go." "We'll be the perfect team for the Salathé." A certain subtle hierarchy developed. The agenda of one set of people might be patterned on the agenda done a year or two earlier by a better group. Half Dome's great face, for instance, formed an ideal indicator. Pratt could have done it as early as 1959 but waited till 1960—until he was "ready." I could have done it in 1961 but waited two more years before I felt "ready." So great was the reputation of the big walls—and so timid were most of us—that such procrastination was inevitable. At any given time during this period, at least three sets of climbers strove toward their utterly separate agendas.

Sentinel's north face and the Arrow Chimney, both still the stuff of legend in 1962, became the first big climbs for many. Kor, for instance, climbed Sentinel on his second trip to the Valley, in April 1962; he and Jack Turner did the route in a respectable eleven hours. A month later Kor and Bob Culp, Colorado's second-best climber, raced up the Arrow Chimney in a day, staggering back into Camp 4 at two the next morning. Two days later, obviously in love with Sentinel, Kor repeated the route, this time with Mort Hempel, and this time in only seven and a half hours. Then the Coloradan did Half Dome's face with Bob Kamps.

Kor obviously enjoyed a marvelous two months in the Valley in the spring of 1962; yet one is struck by his lack of first ascents during this period. Most of us—even Kor—plodded along a few years behind the

Robbins-Frost-Pratt group, doing the classics and enjoying them. The time would come, we felt, when we ourselves could do firsts on the great cliffs. Meanwhile, we would work hard and dream.

A few excellent routes were established in the spring and summer of 1962. Chouinard and I climbed the long and difficult Direct North Buttress of Middle Cathedral Rock, a now-classic route of great beauty. During our only bivouac a storm moved in, a rarity for mid-June. Hail and rain and wind struck at midnight; naturally we were unprepared, and we spent the entire next day in a light rain, squirming up chimneys that vomited water. Chouinard did a grand job in some of these slimy slots. When we placed our soaked down jackets on a scale in the grocery store upon our return, they weighed seven pounds each!

That same spring, filled with hubris, Chouinard and I attempted the Salathé Wall, which had not yet been repeated. As we were packing for this venture, Robbins told someone (who within hours reported it to us) that we'd never get past the fifth pitch, which involved bold free climbing, provisionally rated 5.10, just above some long reaches between rurps and bolts. "Yvon's too short; Steve's too chickenshit," he said without mincing words. Furious about this admittedly brilliant line, we stormed up this section in minutes. It happened to be my pitch, and I was elated. "Fuck you, Robbins!" I screamed to the heavens. (A week later Robbins referred to this pitch as only 5.9, which was probably correct.)

We climbed extremely fast and efficiently on the first day, but our crude haul bag began to fall apart, with new holes and tears appearing after every pitch; even the stitches on the main straps unraveled. So in the morning we retreated from Heart Ledge. A legend has sprung up about the manner of this retreat: that I decided matters by hurling the offending haul bag off the cliff. True, I wished to go down. True, I sweet-talked Chouinard into this decision. But only after we had agreed to flee did I grab the bag and hurl it into the void—before Chouinard could change his mind.

Chouinard was hot that year, knowing he was to be called up by the army in October. In late August he and TM Herbert put up yet another route on the north face of Sentinel, a moderate route destined to be climbed often. The Chouinard-Herbert route had a memorable pitch, one soon described by Chouinard: "I could tell at once we were in trouble. The overhang was formed by layers of flakes three to five inches thick, which resounded with hollow Afro-Cuban sounds under hammer blows. To nail these would be madness, for if one broke and fell, it would shoot down and guillotine the belayer." Short on bolts, the pair retreated. A few days later they went back up, bypassed the feature—now called the Afro-Cuban Flakes—and reached the top.

A remote feature next attracted Chouinard: Quarter Dome, a cliff known to no tourists and few climbers. Located several miles up Tenaya Canyon, and invisible from standard Valley viewpoints, this 1,500-foot wall had never been attempted. In early September, Chouinard and Frost spent a little more than two days on this climb, one distinguished by its striking location and great stretches of easy nailing. Chouinard raved about the climb in a letter from his Alabama army post a few months later: "The rock is the best in Yosemite and probably the best in the world I guess. No glacier polish, no dirt, no shit, ants, or bushes. It is probably the most enjoyable nailup ever done in the history of humanity. Recommend it. *Anyone* could do this climb given enough time and provided that they don't get lost, which is impossible not to do."

Soon after the climb of Quarter Dome, Frost and Robbins made the second ascent—and first continuous ascent—of the Harding-Pratt route on the east face of the Washington Column. Taking about two days for the overhanging route, the pair bypassed bolt after bolt, chopping twenty-five out of the original twenty-seven. How was this possible? Harding, depending on fixed ropes over a one-year period, had placed many bolts simply to safeguard the anchor stations. Also, the Chouinard-Frost bongs, by now available in half-inch increments, meant that the wide cracks that Harding had bypassed with bolts could now be nailed. Still, the superb free-climbing skills of both Robbins and Frost allowed them to jam up cracks where Harding had been stymied.

Frost and Robbins, flushed with this success, waited a few weeks before embarking on a much bigger project, the first continuous ascent of the Salathé Wall. This proved to be the most inspiring climb of 1962, a lesson to us all. The pair knew the route could—and would—be done in one continuous effort, without fixed ropes. Wanting this plum badly, Robbins and Frost roared up the wall in four and a half October days. Wind and rain raked the cliff during their fourth bivouac, but by the time they repeated Pratt's great summit pitch the air was cold and sparkling clear. For the first time ever, El Cap had been climbed directly from ground to top by a rope of two.

Cooper had returned in the late summer of 1962 and was joined on the Dihedral Wall in September by Glen Denny; Baldwin would not be available for another month. By this time Denny, who worked in the Valley as a bartender, had become an excellent aid climber. With ten first ascents to his credit he was far more experienced on steep rock than were the two Northwesterners, and Cooper welcomed his presence.

But uneasiness still reigned in Camp 4 about the methods being used on the climb. The climbs of the previous few months had amply demonstrated that a change was in the air: a new route on El Cap could be done without sieging—by honed climbers. Even with the addition of Denny, the Northwest team could not be called truly expert. Some of us even discussed going up Cooper's fixed ropes and finishing the route in good style while he was gone. To my knowledge, no one was very serious about this, though emotions ran strong. Cooper, however, took the rumors at face value:

Ed Cooper, 1962 (Photo: Glen Denny)

"Another party," he wrote later, "intended to complete the climb we had started. The mountains remain noble, but those who climb them do not always remain so.... Perhaps the spirit of competition which exists in the Valley brings out weaknesses in some."

The Dihedral Wall was proving to be a difficult climb. Continuously difficult aid cracks ran upward for hundreds of feet. Sling belays were used on seventeen of the first nineteen pitches: the route had virtually no ledges in the first 2,500 feet. In addition, much of the route leaned to one side or the other, a condition that makes for strenuous nailing. And blank sections meant bolting. Because of all these problems, one can argue that the Dihedral Wall was a more challenging climb, from a logistical point of view, than either the Nose or the Salathé. Could Robbins, Frost, and Pratt have done the first ascent in one continuous push? I think the answer is yes—in a ten- or twelve-day effort. Should Cooper have given up and relinquished the wall to better climbers? No, I believe: he had discovered the route and was doing a competent, if slow, job.

The final push was done in admirable style. Baldwin had returned and the trio climbed the last 1,000 feet in six and a half days, without trailing fixed ropes. On Thanksgiving Day they bivouacked on a startling ledge christened immediately after the holiday. Ten feet wide in places,

Thanksgiving Ledge stretched hundreds of feet across the sheer wall, and the men romped unroped along this "sidewalk" constantly, marveling at their horizontal motion.

Like Harding, Cooper was not adverse to publicity. Glen Denny wrote me four days after they reached the top, his anger leaping from the page: "The summit was dead. Cooper had contacted the world of sensationalism and the goddamn thing ruined the summit. And so the uncomprehending newsmen were there and it was terrible. I walked away from the summit down the trail last, and sad.... Ed, I guess, feels differently.... I'm sorry that climbing for him includes a need to let everyone know about it.... I am not opposed to seeing my name in print as such, but not to sell some bastard's rag to a totally ignorant audience. I regret that the fine thing the summit could have been was ruined by such a foul thing—the very antithesis of the moment."

Robbins was also upset; he wasn't fond of Cooper, once describing him as "like Harding, but darker and more somber, without Harding's liveliness." More importantly, though, Robbins was bothered by the post–Salathé Wall siege mentality. Three weeks later, knowing I was writing a guidebook to Valley climbing, he advised me to list "first continuous ascents" as well as the actual first ascents. "Notwithstanding my questionable purity in advocating this, I still put it strongly forth because it will help combat the fixed rope mania which I think is working to lower the spirit of adventure in American rockclimbing."

Since weekenders weren't really aware of what was going on in Yosemite—especially concerning the new ethics discussed by our small group of Valley residents—it's hardly surprising that a controversy involving weekenders soon erupted. My old friend and climbing partner Al Macdonald decided he'd attempt El Cap's southeast face, the frightfully steep wall to the right of the Nose. He and a friend went up to the base and nailed fifty feet or so up a crack. Shortly thereafter, in the bar one night in early January 1963, Macdonald set forth his bold plan to an astonished group. "It might take a few years," he crowed, "but what the heck! We got the time and we'll come up every weekend. Roper, you gotta come along!"

"Al," I said gently, "this may not be the best idea. You work fifty weeks a year. You got a family. Sure, you have the enthusiasm, but you're not all that good and fast on aid. Why this route, anyway?"

"Hey, man, it's a great place. It's huge! There's a route there, all right. We've named it Odyssey. And it's almost as blank as the Tower!"

"That's not the point, dad." I was getting miffed by this time, though I tried to be tactful to my old buddy. "Look, the thing is this: you guys aren't ready for such a huge climb. Even Royal might think twice about this one. It'll take you years and years, even if you manage to get up it. You'll be bolting all the time, too. It'll take you *ten* years!"

Macdonald, one of the more spirited youths of the era, felt that on a first ascent he could do whatever he wanted. If he had to use bolts where others might place rurps, so what? If he made but fifty feet a weekend, so what? Unaware of our evolving set of ethics regarding fixed-rope climbing, Macdonald could hardly have foreseen the commotion that soon arose—some of it excessively vitriolic.

Glen Denny had been silent at the bar, lulled by the booze and the camaraderie, but his rage erupted two weeks later in an eleven-page letter bursting with passion—and hyperbole. "I'm really pissed off!" he began. "Al's party is not only inferior but flatly incompetent to do any route on El Cap.... His self-generated reputation has him high on an incredible overhanging lead placing psychic pins. Yet he has never in his life placed such pins.... This maniac must be stopped before he rapes El Cap."

Macdonald radiated friendship and enthusiasm. Words welled spontaneously from his mouth; his eyes sparkled as he made his plans for the future. It was fun listening to him ramble. Denny, more incensed than the rest of us, came down hard on him, perhaps too hard: "The split between the actual long, hard climbing in the Valley and Al's ability and experience is so complete that it constitutes a split between himself and reality—a kind of climbing schizophrenia.... How can a sane person figure he'll make El Cap by ineptly bolting what is potentially one of the hardest piton climbs in the world? How can he be so out of touch with standards *and not care?*"

Robbins and Macdonald had a brief spat by mail during the same period. Having looked at the southeast face and decided it could—and should—be done in modern, nonsiege style, Robbins wrote Macdonald that he'd probably remove any fixed ropes from El Cap if Macdonald began a siege climb. Macdonald then criticized Robbins for his "self-important attitude" and told him he would inform the rangers if he, Royal, dared remove the lines. A month-long exchange of letters ended icily, but politely, with Macdonald backing down, fearing the rangers would ban El Cap climbing altogether if word got out regarding the contretemps. This was a gallant act on Macdonald's part: he quietly relinquished his plans for the good of the active climbing community. Soured by this experience, Macdonald soon turned to river-running and long-distance bicycling, activities that presumably had fewer "rules."

Regarding the big walls, Denny eloquently stated a view held by many of us who lived in Camp 4: "The climbs on El Cap should be the particular expression of climbing that Yosemite contributes to the climbing world: amazing virtuosity in pure technical rockclimbing of the greatest difficulty and magnitude.... In order to legitimately aspire to such a great route one must ruthlessly pursue the ultimate in difficulty to do the route justice."

I had thought of Denny as a Curry Company employee, a Harding porter, a Cooper porter, a bolter. During our correspondence of the winter of 1962–63, I came to realize he had experienced an epiphany. He had

Glen Denny, 1964 (Photo: Glen Denny Collection)

seen that all climbs are not for all people, and that publicity was suspect. From this time onward, Denny was part of the small cadre of climbers dedicated to raising the standards of Yosemite climbing. I hasten to add that we were hardly single-minded about such matters: most Camp 4 climbers were neither intellectuals nor humorless automatons. We had great fun climbing up the walls, and we were certainly all too human, as the next chapter will demonstrate.

CHAPTER 7

The Salamanders: 1961–1964

I wouldn't go over there if I were you. They steal from the store and they smell and they wear rags and even piss right outside their tents. I tell you, it's like a leper colony, that place.

> —Yosemite Lodge bellman trying to dissuade a potential girlfriend from visiting Camp 4 (overheard in 1962 by the author, who saw the woman in camp the next day)

B y 1963 Camp 4 was well established as the Valley's climbing center; no one even thought about staying in the other campgrounds. In the springtime climbers occupied perhaps ten of the fifty-odd camp tables, day in and day out. Many of the other sites stood vacant during the week, but on weekends other climbers arrived, as did tourists, and the camp overflowed with humanity. Needless to say, resentment built up between the tourists and the rock jocks, especially on the weekends. The climbers, claiming squatters' rights, regarded the tourists as transient, shallow people, more interested in playing ball than appreciating the natural scene. We would watch with disgust as families carefully raked away pine needles from their sites and then built elaborate plastic fences around them. We sneered at such citified people: the word "tourist" was a dirty word indeed.

The tourists, appalled by our wretched sites—strewn with equipment, down-spouting sleeping bags, and makeshift shelters— tried not to stare at us but usually failed. Our bodies stunk and we wore our ragged clothing like a badge of honor. We enjoyed boisterous parties that lasted till midnight, and our language rang with obscenities. On more than one occasion the head of a family, usually a seething middle-aged man, stalked over to remind us that women were present. We would stare at these people as if they were aliens—and go right back to what we were doing.

Rangers, fetched by irate campers late at night, paid us many a visit, warning us to knock it off. After they departed we raved and ranted for a few further minutes, to show that we didn't bow to authority, then slunk off to our individual sites.

Some of our wild behavior was derivative, for we had been heavily influenced by stories of the Vulgarians, a renegade group of young, antisocial males who climbed in the Shawangunks, that fabulous climbing area eighty miles north of New York City. Vulgarians had pissed onto parked cars from the roofs of restaurants; overturned Volkswagen bugs; removed sacred fixed pitons from the trade routes of the Gunks; and partied loudly till dawn. They hated authority, rebelling against it at every chance. Much of their behavior was directed toward the Appies—members of the staid Appalachian Mountain Club, the same ones who had placed the sacred fixed pitons and owned the VW bugs. These older, more conservative climbers tried to set rules about who was to climb at the Gunks. The Vulgarians, most of them bright college students in the city, rebelled in a big way: the Appies suffered humiliation after humiliation until they finally ceased to be a force in Gunk climbing. The Vulgarians later became mythologized for their free and crude behavior, but there are two sides to the story. A recent letter to the editor of a climbing magazine represented an Appie version: "The Vulgarians were filthy animals with *nothing* to redeem their reprehensible behavior."

By 1960 a few Vulgarians—Art Gran, Dave Craft, and Claude Suhl—had visited Yosemite, regaling us with outlandish tales, even though they seemed to be on their best behavior. They were intimidated by the Valley's

A typical Camp 4 climbers' site, about 1968 (Photo: Glen Denny)

smooth cracks, so unlike Gunk climbing, and none of them ever became a driving force in Yosemite climbing.

The Camp 4 tourists were our Appies. We scorned them, for they represented the values of our parents, our duplicitous politicians, and our society. We mocked the material possessions the tourists toted: fancy ice chests, circus tents, and three-burner stoves. Our scornful behavior, of course, was neither constant nor obvious; the two groups lived peacefully, side by side, for weeks at a time. And a few tourists were marvelous people, though I recall only one by name: Harry Tee. Harry was a stout fellow who carried a huge beer belly and a permanent downturned mouth. His shoulders and back sprouted black hair; he'd always walk around with his shirt off, and from a distance you'd swear a bear was loose in the campground. Harry brought his family to Camp 4 year after year, staying for a week or two in July. Friendly despite his crusty demeanor, he asked us hundreds of questions about climbing, fed us dinner on occasion, and once, when Pratt and I were standing forlornly outside the camp's entrance, hitchhiking back to the Bay Area, walked over and handed us a ten-dollar bill. "Pay me back next year, you guys."

Harry often set up a telescope in the center of Camp 4, aiming it at Sentinel or the Lost Arrow when he knew climbers were up there. A crowd quickly gathered around him, and hairy Harry beamed as he explained the function of pitons and ropes. I would guess that Harry was the most knowledgeable nonclimber in California during the sixties, and he informed hundreds of park visitors about the realities of rock climbing. I can still hear him saying, "No, they don't actually use grappling hooks. You see, they...."

When we weren't climbing, we had to contend with three groups: tourists, the Yosemite Park and Curry Company, and the park rangers. The tourists were the least of our problems, but the other two caused us no end of trouble, most of it of our own making. The Curry Company, the only park concessionaire Yosemite had ever had, tended to be autocratic, so it was the climbers' chief villain for many, many years. Each day, it seemed, brought new problems. The conflict stemmed from one simple fact: climbers, being impecunious, dirty, poorly dressed, and often loud, were not exactly welcome on company property, which, after all, was a commercial enterprise designed to make life pleasant for paying customers. The concessionaire couldn't legally keep us off its property, for Yosemite Lodge, with its lounge, cafeteria, coffee shop, gift shop, and bar, was open to the general public. As long as we behaved ourselves, they couldn't ask us to leave, however much they wished to.

After climbing, or during rainy periods—which sometimes lasted three or four days—climbers almost lived in the lodge, only 350 yards from Camp 4. The complex of several buildings, erected in 1956 only 100 feet from the site of the 1915 lodge, boasted state-of-the art facilities. The gleaming ivory restrooms, in particular, contained miracles: hot water and electric hand-dryers, an unbeatable combination for the quick washing and drying of underwear and socks. (Camp 4 was primitive by comparison, with no hot water and decrepit toilets. Still, both the East Head and the West Head, as we called the two Camp 4 restrooms, were heated, and sometimes we'd sleep in them during foul weather. Stanford climber Nick Clinch, in 1950, was one of the first to discover and use the john for a shelter. "Not too smelly in winter," he later told me.)

The lodge's coffee shop was another favorite place. We'd flirt with waitresses, some of whom would give us a nice break when they made out the check. We'd know the best items to order: a butterflied frankfurter in a hamburger bun tasted far better than a regular hamburger and, at fifty cents, was a dime cheaper. Hours would fly by at a table in the coffee shop, with climbers coming and going.

My most vivid memory of these idle hours concerns the origins of the first Yosemite guidebook. Since the old High Sierra guide had only a few decent routes listed, it was nearly worthless; few even owned the book. Pratt and I were celebrated for our memories, and we kept records of climbs; hence, we were in great demand. Scores of route descriptions ended up on napkins and scraps of paper, and people would always ask us, "When are you guys going to write a guide?" After enough of this sort of prodding, I decided to approach the Sierra Club. Dave Brower, executive director of the Club by this time, loved the idea, and since Pratt soon was drafted, I became the sole author. I began keeping ultra-detailed notebooks in 1962; the Red Guide, as it was called because of its cover, appeared in July 1964. With 195 brand-new routes listed, the guide was welcomed by all.

The lodge's lounge, however, was where we spent most of our spare time during evenings or bad weather, reading, talking, or restlessly peering out the enormous, rain-splattered windows. Several nights each week the Curry Company showed movies (they had only three or four) about the Valley, and sometimes we climbers were the only ones present. During such slow nights we often recited the dialogue in unison. Some of this prose is still etched in my mind. One movie, a good one, featured Ansel Adams. His opening sentences, spoken in a somber, resonant voice, were memorable: "I have pointed my camera ten thousand times at the wildness and splendor that surround me. Nowhere does the earth speak to us so eloquently or with such force." Another movie, a bad one, spoke of "the shy forest creatures," such as bears.

Many lodge employees disliked us. We sat around doing nothing, to all appearances. To them we were simply bums, unkempt kids who not only didn't work but scorned even the concept. They barely knew that we actually *did* work in the winter, at odd jobs. Many lodge workers, especially the older ones with menial jobs, labored all year and bought huge, finned cars to show how far up in the world they had come. The few of us who owned cars had rattletraps perfectly in keeping with our clothes and haircuts. We were aliens. They were aliens.

A gear sortout in Camp 4, May 1963. Left to right: Steve Roper, Mark Powell, Layton Kor, Bev Powell, and Chris Fredericks. Mark Powell holds one of the first jumars to appear in the Valley. (Photo: Glen Denny)

We could be cruel to some of these employees, especially the ones who we felt treated us unfairly. One surly janitor who often ordered, not asked, us to get our feet off the couches had a phobia about germs and, when taking a break in the cafeteria, would drink his coffee left-handed, lips pressed directly next to the mug's handle, figuring no germs could possibly exist in that virgin section of china. It took us a while to figure out what he was up to, but when we did, we'd station ourselves directly in his line of sight and drink our coffee the exact same way, slobbering and slurping loudly.

148

Eric Beck, one of the more interesting characters of the early sixties, was once caught shoplifting a tube of glue (to repair his glasses) by the lodge's manager and expelled from the lodge for six months. He moped around camp for a day, becoming so morose that several of us got together and came up with a plan. If we cleaned him up, shaved him, dressed him well, removed his glasses, and dyed his hair, Beck would look like a different person. It was worth trying, at least. A blinking Beck, wearing a sports coat and with his dark hair glowing copper-red and burnished into a pompadour, duly appeared that night in the coffee shop and settled his bill with the very manager who had caught him. "Thank you, sir. Come again," the man said. Beck soon got rid of the sports coat but remained beardless. Avoiding his climbing friends whenever the manager was present, he went to the lodge just as often as he once had.

Although one could cough up fifty cents to shower at the lodge, we quickly learned to frequent the outlying restrooms sprinkled among the cabins, which were rustic enough not to have any of their own. No problem, for these restrooms, rustic themselves, were always unlocked. In the course of modernizing the facilities, however, the company later installed locks on every single restroom; you needed a room key to enter. Although we soon acquired keys from friendly employees, this was risky business, and many times I huddled in the shower stall, heart thumping, waiting for a janitor to depart.

Some of the employees thought we were bohemian heroes, and they did favors for us whenever possible. These usually had something to do with food. The phrase "bones tonight," for instance, passed down to us by employees, made us salivate instantly. The cafeteria occasionally served prime rib, and a few dozen pounds of the bones, festooned with great chunks of meat because of careless trimming, were kept in the kitchen, available only if one asked for them. On such nights we made sure to arrive just when the cafeteria opened, for the bones would soon be gone. For seventy-five cents we got a plate that would make a vegetarian sick.

Busboys brought food to us on occasion, either using their discounts to save us money or offering scavenged food from other tables. Beck, the least inhibited of all of us, took this one step further: he would stalk the cafeteria like a ferret, pausing meaningfully at tables where the patrons looked ready to leave. They were hardly out the door before Beck would be wolfing soggy pancake fragments and complaining that the tourists had consumed *all* the bacon.

We taught several employees how to climb, or at least how to follow us on our adventures. One busboy, Jim Sims, expressed a great interest in what we were doing, so Chuck Pratt took him, without thinking of the consequences, on the worst possible type of climb for a beginner. The Leaning Tower Traverse, not particularly difficult, consisted of a long and highly exposed traverse, which meant the follower wouldn't have a nice, safe upward belay. It was also necessary to clamber over gigantic sharp flakes, many of which looked ready to part company with the cliff. Sims recalled the experience for me recently: "Midway along the route I came around a corner and saw the rope stretching across this horrible gap. It just hung there, all the way over to Chuck, who must have been sixty feet away. I looked down and almost threw up—the ground was straight down, about 500 feet! A that moment a lot of things were going on in my mind, like, why am I here in this abnormal place? This was my first climb, and besides dealing with philosophical problems, I was struggling with my first taste of exposure. Furthermore, I couldn't figure out how Chuck had gotten to where he was. I had been blindly following the rope, but I realized that going one more foot in that direction would result in a fatal sixty-foot pendulum." Sims then saw shattered ledges traversing the concave face. Pratt, of course, should have protected his partner with some occasional pitons or runners around flakes—standard operating procedure on a traverse—but it had been so easy for him that he'd forgotten. A shaking Sims managed to wriggle across ledges toward Pratt, but then, ten feet from his belayer, he got stuck. "I asked Chuck if I just shouldn't let go and jump. With a quickness and conviction that I've never seen in Chuck since, he assured me that this wasn't such a good idea."

Sims, either a true adventurer or a masochist, didn't quit climbing. A few weeks later I dragged him up a fierce jamcrack, where he struggled and whimpered so much that I thought he'd either die wedged in the crack or kill me later. He came back for more. On his third climb something went wrong with his rappel (we had neglected to teach him the niceties of descending), and he came close to plunging to his death. Sims kept climbing sporadically for the next thirty years, always scared, always thrilled, always game for more.

Head busboy Dave Cook was another sucker for punishment. With his Charles Atlas physique, much more impressive than any of ours, he should have been a good climber. But, as we were learning, climbing was basically a mental exercise, and Cook had his share of problems. A stubborn fellow, he distrusted equipment and standard techniques such as rappelling: he preferred to descend the rope hand-over-hand down steep walls. Cook was strong enough to get away with this, but the sight of him swinging down a cliff like a huge ape appalled us. He also never learned how to tie a bowline properly, and his waist knot sometimes assumed massive proportions as he secured the equivalent of a granny knot with numerous half-hitches. "I would have been just as embarrassed to have someone tie my waist knot as asking someone to zip up my pants," Cook told me recently.

One day Beck persuaded Cook to accompany him on a new route on the north face of Sentinel. Cook had never been on such an imposing wall, and had, in fact, rarely done direct-aid climbing, obviously necessary on this fearfully steep wall. By the end of the first day, Cook, a tired and trembling basket case, told Beck that he couldn't and wouldn't continue the next day. Beck simply grinned and said, "Yes, you will. We're going on."

Cook awoke on the bivouac ledge at dawn, looked up at the sinister wall, and decided to be firm. "I became so desperate that I considered throwing Eric off the ledge. I thought I could get down and then lie about what had happened. To my addled brain, this was plausible. Then I came to my senses and woke Eric up and told him that either he had to retreat or I'd throw him off. We went down, and I didn't climb again for a quarter of a century."

■

Mountaineer Mike Borghoff was another climber who had trouble on the cliffs, even though he had far more experience than either Sims or Cook. Borghoff failed on numerous big climbs, yet he always returned to the Valley he loved. An intelligent nonconformist, he was among the first to perceive that what was happening in Yosemite—the surge in climbing standards by a bunch of bohemians—was special. He wrote several eloquent articles for *Summit,* and his letters to me were full of wisdom and bon mots. A few samples: "Excluding Royal Robbins—who is in a brilliant class all by himself, a Stirling Moss, an index of perfection—Valley climbers are brooding misfits who know only too well what awaits them down in the San Joaquin Valley and beyond." And "You can grunt and heave, sweat and strain, wear yourself out, and unless you simply forget about it and step up, you won't even get off the ground." And "It's so good and wonderful and so other-earth-other-sky transcendentally *different* in Yosemite that I could spend a dozen karmic cycles there and not exhaust the place."

That climbers had stayed in Camp 4 since the end of World War II wasn't exactly a secret, but the first written mention of the site as a climbers' camp occurs in an article by Borghoff, "Of Salamanders and Bongbongs," in the June 1962 issue of *Summit.* (Camp 4 soon became known worldwide, but it is still often wrongly referred to as Camp Four or Camp IV.)

In his article Borghoff cleverly used the amphibian metaphor to describe Camp 4 climbers: "Yosemite salamanders are usually innocuous and quite unprepossessing until seen firsthand upon their native element, flickering up holdless cracks with maddening ease." Borghoff was impressed not only with the climbers, but with the famous boulders of Camp 4, which he felt had been put there "to assure a visiting climber's complete psychological annihilation before he ties on to a rope." The salamanders, of course, having lived in Camp 4 for months, had mastered many of the short little routes—but by no means as easily as Borghoff implied.

Two of Camp 4's boulders loomed above all the others. Columbia Boulder, the biggest, stood near the center of the camp, and it had no easy routes. We practiced on this thirty-foot-high giant constantly, making only one or two routes with consistency. One route, the Robbins' Pullup, especially intrigued us. Robbins had done the route back in the mid-fifties but

Mick Burke (top) *and Steve Roper* (pointing) *offer advice to Mike Covington as he tries a Camp 4 boulder problem, 1968. (Photo: Steve Roper Collection)*

had been unable to repeat it, and no one else had either. The fifteen-foot problem overhung crazily on its lower part; a lieback/pinch-grip pullup was the only real hold to start out with, but it would obviously take superhuman strength to make the move. One day in 1960 we all were standing around in the beautiful late-afternoon light, biding our time on the boulders before either cooking or heading for the lodge. A fellow named Harry Daley, an occasional partner of Robbins, strode over to the problem. We giggled behind his back, for Daley was hardly the strongest among us. He placed his hands up on the pinch-grip and tentatively plastered a foot on a microhold. So far, so good. We'd all gone this far. We smiled condescendingly. Then, incredibly, he pulled up and lunged for an edge far above. He gripped this and levitated upward. He'd made it! We stood with mouths open before bursting into a cheer. Then, even more incredibly, three or four of us scampered up the problem as if we'd been doing it for years. A psychological barrier had been broken. Robbins heard about our feats within hours and strode over and did it on his first try. (The route is gone now, exfoliated by campfires.)

The other famous rock was the high and wide Wine Traverse Boulder, in the upper region of the camp. It owed its name to an exploit done in the mid-fifties by Warren Harding or Bob Swift—no one can remember which. High on rotgut wine, one of the two claimed he could do a tricky upward traverse even while carrying a glass of wine in one hand. Or was it a jug? No one can remember which. The person made the climb. Or did he?

Other, smaller, boulders were named in honor of a climber who did a particularly hard route, hence the Pratt Boulder and the Kor Boulder, still called this today. Many of us, but not all, took bouldering seriously, attempting routes until fingertips shredded. I dreaded the boulders as much as Borghoff did, mainly because I couldn't get up the hard routes either. I simply didn't have the physical or mental capacity to suffer so much for so little reward.

The interplay of climbers was fascinating. Though little personal enmity existed—I can remember no fistfights—Camp 4 was split into subtle factions and cliques. The Southern California climbers—Robbins, Frost, Daley—tended to stay in one part of the camp, often climbed together, and often went to the lodge together. We Northerners regarded them as too clean, too polite, too square for our tastes. We thought they tried too hard to be intellectuals. I recall my early climbing partner Krehe Ritter exclaiming, "Royal used 'pusillanimous' completely wrong the other day, and he barely admitted it even when I straightened him out!" I nodded sagely, having no idea whatsoever what the word meant. Robbins strove always to learn new words, new ideas—and of course he made some mistakes along the way. Perhaps, as a high-school dropout (he later got his diploma through night-school courses), he felt he had to catch up with his climbing peers, many of whom had several years of college under their belts. While Robbins attempted to improve his mind, many of the rest of us tried hard to purge our brains of "book" knowledge.

Robbins was not an especially popular figure around the camp. He tended to be aloof and arrogant, keeping to himself or else surrounded by a coterie of admirers who we considered "yes men." No one, of course, had a bad word to say about his climbing, which was impeccable. But Robbins didn't laugh much, nor did he join in the general anarchy of the climbers' camp.

It's not as if barbarians occupied one part of Camp 4 and pseudo-intellectuals the other. Nevertheless, a division existed, one obvious even to outsiders: Robbins and his cohorts definitely behaved themselves better than did our little group. They put on clean clothes to go to the lodge; they didn't swear in public; and they didn't steal showers. They rarely got into trouble with the Curry Company or the rangers; on the contrary, Robbins sometimes bailed us out of trouble by his conciliatory manner.

The relations between climbers and rangers were often excellent, and we climbed together on many occasions. But the Curry Company always pressured rangers to "control" climbers. The easiest way to do this was to have them enforce the camp time-limit rule: one could stay in the Valley only two weeks—two weeks total per year. This rule was difficult to enforce, since rangers couldn't know exactly when a given individual had first showed up. A questioned climber would immediately lie about when he had arrived: "Oh, I guess it was about four days ago, sir." But when the same unshaven faces appeared month after month in the coffee shop, this was prima facie evidence that something was amiss. Then the rangers were forced to act. Told to leave, we'd either lie low (camping in the boulders well behind Camp 4 and avoiding the lodge), go to Tuolumne Meadows or Tahquitz for a while, or head back to the Bay Area for a week. We'd return quietly and the process would begin anew because, once again, no records were kept, so we could always claim that this was our first trip of the year. Especially annoying to us was that the enforcement often began in late May, just as we were getting into shape for something big. Of course, this was also prime tourist season, a time when Camp 4 swarmed with people.

In 1959 and 1960 the rangers had totally ignored us; in the latter year Pratt had stayed in Camp 4 continuously from June 1 to October 15. As more climbers started living full-time in the Valley, the rangers began hounding us so much that by late June each year we began to spread out across the West. Pratt and I, for example, took a thirty-five-day trip in the summer of 1961 entirely by freight train and hitchhiking, stopping at Devil's Tower, Wyoming, and the Needles of South Dakota. Chouinard usually migrated to Canada or Wyoming. Robbins and Frost visited the Alps, the Tetons, or Canada. Others, such as TM Herbert, actually *worked* in the summer in order to get money for the fall season.

———————————————————————■———————————————————————

Because we were thoughtless and immature, we sometimes got into minor trouble. One winter morning, while Pratt, Al Macdonald, and I danced up some cliff, a sudden storm pounced. Stupidly, we had left our sleeping bags out in the open, back in Camp 4. The question soon arose: where to sleep that stormy night with wet bags and no tents? "How about the chapel?" Macdonald suggested after dinner. "Hey, great idea, man!" I replied. All went well until midnight, when we awoke, freezing to death. "I'll turn the heat on," someone said. Hours later, still shivering, we cranked the dial up to the maximum. Finally it warmed up and we drifted off. Not long after dawn the three of us awoke in a side aisle of the now-sweltering building to hear people milling about. Then we spotted a woeful sight: all around the chapel dozens of candles, placed directly above heating ducts, lay drooped over like Salvador Dali creations. Torn between laughing and crying, we cowered as best we could, waiting for the Sunday churchgoers to leave. More came in. Finally, as we feigned sleep, a man came up and said quietly, "Maybe you better leave now, boys." Mustering what little dignity we still possessed, we strode quickly out into the snowstorm. Someone must have recognized us and reported the incident, for rangers that afternoon strongly advised the three of us to chat about the melted candles with the multidenominational pastors. We did. The Protestant minister ranted and raved about our "lack of sensitivity in a place of worship," but Father James Murphy, the Catholic priest, forgave us instantly and then wanted to know all about Mallory and Irvine on Everest. Later, Macdonald sent a twelve-dollar check to Father Murphy, who wrote back: "This new demonstration of your sincerity brings into higher relief the daring and sturdy characteristics one usually predicts of dedicated mountain climbers. Permit us to return herewith your check: it may be useful in forwarding your adventures and good luck with them."

More serious offenses concerned shoplifting. We hoarded our money so as to stay longer in Yosemite, and the temptation to supplement our supplies by thievery was strong. Our rationale was simple if badly flawed: the Curry Company gouged the public and we would fight back, Robin Hood doing his thing to give to the poor—and we were the poor. We prided ourselves on our honesty back in Camp 4: no one ever lied or stole. But so angry were we at our imagined enemy that shoplifting seemed justified. One day Frank Sacherer took me aside and said, "Roper, I'm out of money. Show me how you do it." We went to the store, where I placed a beautiful marbled steak in the bottom of a paper bag, filled the bag with potatoes, and strolled casually to the checkstand. "See how easy that was," I whispered to Sacherer. "That steak will cost us about thirty cents!" But the bag tipped while on the scale and the potatoes rolled out. The checker's eyes widened as he glanced into the bag. Shy Sacherer, the honor student and future physics genius, turned beet red. "That'll be five-seventy-five," the man said in a monotone as he rang up the newly weighed potatoes and the steak. "And don't show up here again," he hissed. We didn't for a full week— and certainly never again tried that particular gambit.

An even more humiliating moment concerned Irving Smith, the youth who had died on the Lost Arrow in 1960. A year later, while exploring the base of the Arrow Chimney to look it over, I found a large piece of skull, which I stupidly brought back to the coffee shop to show off. Ranger Wayne Merry took me aside the next day, after receiving complaints from waitresses, and sternly told me to take it back to the base and bury it, which of course I did.

Yes, we were puerile youths. We had been taught the correct values at home, yet we rebelled against everything. We thought we didn't need to follow society's rules. We knew more than anyone else; no one was going to tell *us* how to act!

The bears that visited Camp 4 actually caused us more grief than either the rangers, the tourists, or the Curry Company. Many of these beasts roamed the Valley, originally attracted by the garbage dump near Camp Curry. When the dump was shut down, the bears, denied their daily fix, became brazen. Being black bears, and not huge, they posed little real threat to people, yet they ate our food, ripped our tents, and broke into cars. Mike Borghoff put it perfectly: the ursines were "fat, tourist-fed, insolent, monstrously facile at stealing food, contemptuously impervious to indignation, rage, terrified screams, outraged threats, or supplication."

Almost every night a commotion arose in some part of the camp. Often it was a tourist's ice chest that the bears violated, which gave young Jeff Foott an idea. Once, in the dead of night, he removed a few succulent morsels from a random, tableside ice chest, gouged some deep marks in the dirt with a piton, made some grunting noises, and then fled to his campsite. In the morning, as he enjoyed his new bacon, Foott watched a collection of tourists pointing at the "claw marks" on the ground. "It was huge; I saw him," he heard someone wail. "Why don't the rangers *do* something?" Foott justified his thievery on two grounds: maybe the rangers *would* do something about the real bears, and the tourists would have a dramatic story to tell when they got home—well worth the price of a pound of bacon.

Pratt had names for some of the distinctive bears that called Camp 4 home: Beauregard, Spartacus, Caligula, Lancelot, and the looming El Cid. These animals were clever enough—or satiated enough—not to make forays every night; sometimes they would lie low for a week and then catch us badly off guard, destroying our possessions. To this problem we addressed ourselves often, plotting and scheming. Sometimes we would tree a poor bear and, with well-directed rocks, force it to stay up for hours, peeing and panicked. This did little good and we really didn't enjoy the torture. One evening TM Herbert had endured enough. He sat patiently atop the Wine Traverse Boulder cradling a huge rock, waiting for El Cid, who often ambled by this particular boulder at dusk. Sure enough, along came the creature and down crashed the stone onto Cid's skull. A perfect knockout strike! A small "click" resulted; El Cid looked around, shook his massive head twice, and then waddled into camp to see what was cooking.

One fellow retaliated even more harshly. We never knew his name, for he wasn't a climber. We called him the Empire Builder because of his manifest drive and energy. One day Dave Cook came across this lad up in the talus behind Camp 4. "He was skinning a bear," Cook told me recently. "I was terrified at first, because the corpse resembled a naked man quartered between two trees. He'd created a deadfall trap over some big talus blocks and the bear had fallen in. He used the skin for something and jerked the meat. If this wasn't astonishing enough behavior in a national park, the next day he made doughnuts, using bear fat for grease! Surely, by now, he's created an empire somewhere in the world."

Eventually the rangers acted, trapping the worst offenders (the bears, not the people) and removing them to the highcountry. Some of these poor beasts, hooked on people food, migrated to hot San Joaquin Valley towns, where they met sad fates. By the end of the sixties few bear incidents occurred and no familiar bears remained. No one bothered to name the stragglers.

During 1962 and 1963 a small group of newcomers settled into Camp 4, a group that had lots of trouble with motivation. In fact, we invented the phrase "mind problems" to describe some of these people's attitudes. Fear had always played a part in Valley climbing, of course, and many of us came back from first-ascent attempts with tails between legs. We'd generally recover and try again the next day, when the omens were better. The newcomers, meanwhile, languished in camp, semiparalyzed. People such as Cook, who had quit his Yosemite Lodge job to join us, and Beck, who had quit college in early 1962, went out and played around on moderate one-pitch routes. Carl Huff, Jim Harper, Joe Oliger, Don Telshaw, and others talked about big climbs but rarely did any. A group self-named the Podunks consisted of UC Berkeley students John Morton, Jeff Dozier, Bill Peppin, Chris Fredericks, and Steve Thompson; they all were good climbers but they also avoided the big or hard climbs. A fellow named Jim Bridwell showed up and displayed uncommon talents, but he, too, laid low during the early and mid-sixties, rarely attempting the bigger climbs.

Working on my guidebook at the time and thus interested in the direction Yosemite climbing was headed, I felt this aimlessness was a sad sign: we were supposed to go out and climb every day and aspire to the great walls. This was our "job." I had done 260 routes (including repeats) by this time; most of these scoundrels, I knew, might reach that total by the next century. Where, I wanted to know, was the new generation headed? In my introduction to the Red Guide, I attacked the newcomers harshly: "Occasionally there is a group that seems to live in torment in Camp 4. Climbing only when they 'feel like it,' which if they're feeling good is once a week or so, they suffer from, among other things, 'mind problems,' a euphemism for fear and uncertainty. One cannot help wonder what reasons compel these people to remain in Camp 4.... These climbers give the impression that they are waiting, patiently waiting, for some unlikely and ill-defined miracle to transform them...."

Of course, I could have been talking about myself; many of us, including the more active ones, were lost souls waiting for something to happen.

Perhaps my words shocked some of these people into action—although a more likely scenario is that their beginnerhood came to an end—for Beck, Bridwell, and Fredericks soon established excellent routes. (Bridwell's record, not particularly distinguished during the sixties, soon blossomed: he became one of the most noted Yosemite wall rats of the seventies.) John Morton later told me that "the Podunks' undistinguished Yosemite apprenticeship nevertheless served us well in Europe in 1965." Thompson became the first American ever to lead the famous Cenotaph Corner in Wales; Morton and Peppin soon thereafter did a big Dolomite route in the Lavaredo Group, as did Thompson and Dozier. Morton says, "We found these Dolomite routes to be Grade IV's, well within our powers. And it was satisfying to beat the times in the guidebook."

———————————————————■———————————————————

At this same time women came into our lives. Many of us had been painfully shy, with a poor track record in the dating game. Thanks to climbing, however, our self-esteem had shot up, allowing us to begin seeking out female companionship. Some of us got married and unmarried abruptly. Chouinard, for instance, wrote me in late 1962: "After Dec. 29 sex is no longer one of my major problems. I can scratch that number out...." A year or two later the marriage was kaput. Robbins, too, had tried matrimony, in 1957; it lasted but a few months. Herbert and I married best friends, two waitresses in the lodge's coffee shop. His marriage lasted longer than mine did. Others, such as Foott, Pratt, and Beck, shunned marriage and began a series of endless affairs, ongoing to this day. The vast majority of Yosemite climbers in the fifties and sixties either got divorced or never married. The climbing way of life, not exactly a bed of roses for men, proved intolerable to girlfriends and wives. The men set the agenda: Valley in the spring; Tetons and Canada in the summer; desert or Yosemite in the fall; menial work in the winter; start all over again in the spring. Many of the women were fascinated by this way of life—for a while. Then they sensed it was going nowhere.

Wives and girlfriends tried climbing, of course, but they usually did it because their men were doing it—not for any particular love of the sport. The only wife who really got into climbing was Bev Powell; she and Mark did many routes together, and she led many tough pitches. This marriage lasted decades, in part because of the shared adventures; but divorce, even here, came at last.

Two other strong climbers were both named Janie. Janie Dean made an ascent of the Arrow Tip in 1957 with Mark Powell; she did several other hard Valley routes also. Stronger still was Janie Taylor, in 1961 the girlfriend of Robbins. A bright person, and a talented musician, she excelled at rock climbing, though she didn't lead much. In August she and Robbins did two long and sustained first ascents in the Tetons, feats that established Taylor as the most accomplished female climber in the land.

The relationship soon ended, however, and she never again did another equivalent route.

Robbins soon fell in love with a young lady who worked summers in the Ahwahnee Hotel. Elizabeth Burkner, soon known to all as Liz, had grown up in the Central Valley town of Modesto, where the couple would one day take up permanent residence. Married in November 1963, they did many routes together in the next few years, culminating in their ascent of the northwest face of Half Dome in 1967, ten years to the month after the first ascent. Liz, an excellent if nonaggressive climber, thus became the first woman to climb a Yosemite Grade VI.

In the early sixties we didn't want women to be climbing partners necessarily; we wanted sex partners. An enormous amount of our time was spent scheming for this eventuality, but we certainly talked more than we acted. Mike Borghoff once described the sex-starved days of Camp 4: "When I first hit Yosemite in 1957, I was a mountain trooper from Colorado, as straight as a lodgepole sapling and celibate to boot. Fortunately, two derelicts then in garbage-can residence soon put me straighter with vicious amounts of Red Mountain wine. When not busy laying the groundwork for the Golden Age (that's about all they were laying), it seemed to my neophyte eye they stayed drunk. Why not? Even many years later women were unknown to that distant world.... The only thing down at Camp 4 in the Elder Days was dogshit and Tri-Delts surrounded by their betrailered parents, about as accessible as the Crab Nebula. So we had beatoff contests on the bivouac ledges, drenched our sleeping bags in semen, got drunk and indulged in towering fireside smut."

The mores of the fifties still pervaded society in the early sixties, and many women fought hard to protect their dignity, sometimes with Victorian fervor. I remember one prim Valley waitress who, after several "dates" (in parked cars), placed my hand on her clothed bosom. "That breast," she sighed with perfect enunciation, "is yours, and yours alone, to hold." Wanting clothes-ripping frenzies, not a Jane Austen heroine, I got out of that relationship immediately. One by one, however, the Valley climbers lost their virginity. I personally arranged for the deflowering of Eric Beck, a deed he appreciates to this day.

Penny Carr was the woman most often around from 1962 to 1966; she climbed on every spring weekend and sometimes spent weeks in the Valley, living on and off with Glen Denny. A smart, pensive woman, she climbed well and made many friends. Carr fretted constantly about the meaning of life and love—and positively hated the unfairness of our society. In addition, her direction was unclear: she didn't know whether to be a climbing bum or a student. She went to Stanford for a few years, dropped out, lived in Yosemite, and then returned to school at Berkeley. One day in 1963 Carr cornered me in the lodge and asked me to take her up to Sickle Ledge—the first four pitches of the Nose and a climb in its own right. "When we get there," she said, "I'm going to untie and jump off."

Stunned, but not taking her seriously, I argued glibly that a death on my record would look bad; I declined her offer. Three years later, in early May 1966, Carr showed how serious she had been: she hooked up a hose to her Plymouth's tailpipe and died of carbon monoxide poisoning. Pratt saw the account of the suicide in the *San Francisco Chronicle* and ran through Camp 4 announcing the grim news. The phrase "If only I had...." went through all our minds at once. It was a sad moment, and we miss her still. Dave Cook remembers the day that he, a city boy, first tried to make a campfire. He laid a big pile of newspapers flat on the ground, put some sticks over them, and lit the paper. Carr watched this show for a while, then came over, fanned the smoke from her eyes, and said gently, "Dave, you should crumple the paper first." "Every time I light a fire," Cook told me recently, "I think of Penny."

On our nonclimbing days we engaged in other activities. We bouldered; we had contests on the cliffs behind the campground to see who was the fastest nailer; we wandered around the Valley on foot, going aimlessly from camp to ranger station to lodge. We often walked the mile over to the modern supermarket, which had opened in May 1959. We tried to seduce women; we fought bears and tyrants in positions of power. We dealt with the skunks and furtive ringtailed cats that lived in back of the campground and nightly snuffled around our food and heads, badly panicking us when we awoke.

We learned to juggle, thanks to Pratt, who before he had become a climber had mastered the art, thinking a circus lay in his future. He could juggle three balls in one hand; five in both. None of us had the patience or skill to go beyond three with two hands, but all of us can still perform this trick years later. Pratt had also mastered the unicycle, which he occasionally rode around camp while juggling three balls. Few of us dared to try riding the contraption.

Other diversions occupied our nonclimbing time. John Evans, a climber from the Midwest, was fascinated by snakes, so he'd sometimes head to the base of El Cap, a favorite haunt of rattlesnakes, and bring back one in a burlap bag to study for a few days before releasing it. Some of us were uneasy knowing a viper was in camp, even one securely tied up. Beck didn't like snakes in the least and stayed far away, but Pratt went out of his way to be nice to them. Once, up at the base of a route, he had an opportunity to dispatch a huge rattler but declined. Asked why he hadn't caved its head in, Pratt exclaimed, "What, and have every rattler in the Valley looking for me?"

When it rained, we had a more intellectual activity. Chouinard, who migrated to Yosemite whenever he could get away from his forge, had a little black book in which he entered words of wisdom from philosophers, famous authors, poets, and well-known climbers. Chouinard was obsessed with pain and suffering and heroics, and many of his entries dealt with such subjects. His book was always available to us at the lodge, to read from or to add to. The aphorism I remember most vividly came from Dostoyevsky: "Only through suffering can we find ourselves." Another, from Nietzsche, stated: "What doesn't kill me makes me stronger." One from Céline bespoke of arrogance: "I piss on you all from a considerable height."

Sometimes when I was bored with my fellow climbers I'd hike to the base of a popular climb and comb the talus for dropped pitons, in hope of finding a real gem. Word of this got out, and Herb Swedlund, perhaps to pay me back for chopping his bolts on his Lower Yosemite Fall route, played an excellent trick on me. "Roper," he exclaimed one day in the autumn of 1962, "I saw a bunch of Salathé pitons outside the Narrows." I knew he had just come back from Sentinel's north face, and I knew that the blacksmith's pitons might well lie outside the horrible slot, a place where perhaps no one had ever gone again. I asked a few more questions, then the next morning quietly packed up a monster load of four ropes, several quarts of water, food, and a hammer. For four hours I labored up brush- and talus-filled gullies to the top of Sentinel, a 3,000-foot pull. Carefully, ever so carefully, I rappelled 450 feet into the dank Great Chimney, fixing ropes as I went. My anxiety turned to rage as I swung in midair at the Narrows, finding not a single piton. I turned toward Camp 4 far, far below and, hoping Swedlund was watching the fiasco with binoculars, flipped him the finger twenty times, my screams and curses echoing through the chimney. Then I started prusiking up the endless lifeline to the top, a lifeline that suddenly looked as thin as clothesline. Soon I began seeing standard fixed pitons here and there, and I removed these with gusto. And lo and behold, once I pulled out an original Chouinard, one of his 1959 hand-forged jobs. So the day was not a total loss. I thanked Swedlund profusely that night so as not to give him any pleasure.

Since we had so much respect for one another, we often made fun of people's foibles. Limericks were a popular and harmless medium, and the ones noted below are representative. They may not have perfect structure, but to us they were funny and/or insightful. Chouinard, for instance, was a rigorous Catholic in the earlier years, going to Mass every Sunday at the Valley chapel. He also scorned the face of Half Dome since he wanted El Cap so badly, but then he and I were defeated on the Salathé Wall, much to the amusement of Beck, who immediately limned the following:

Chouinard is a man not too tall.
On Sundays he won't climb at all.
Rather stay home than do shit climbs like Half Dome,
Yet he got turned off the Salathé Wall.

After Jim Bridwell suffered a humiliating defeat, the bard Beck turned this into:

There was a climber named Bridwell.
On Grade I's he did well.
But on a Grade VI, he got into a fix
And rappelled to the talus and hid well.

Steve Thompson and Jeff Dozier together invented this self-explanatory one about Chris Fredericks, nicknamed Christ because of his incredible resemblance to the traditional blond, blue-eyed representation of Jesus:

Since Christ became ardently sexual,
His climbing has been most ineffectual.
Sublimation, he found, could be gotten around
With things more directly erectile.

After Eric Beck took a fall on Middle Cathedral, he had steel pins inserted into his broken arm, which Berkeley climber Galen Rowell immediately picked up on:

A climber named Beck was wrecked
Low on the North Buttress Direct.
Alas poor Eric; he's now part ferric,
And his season, we're afraid, is fekked.

Nonclimbers could amuse us, too. A total stranger named Frank Parckel sent me a letter in 1963 after Kor, Denny, and I had done the Nose of El Cap. This fellow, not particularly well versed in the arts of punctuation and spelling, raved, in part: "You Pricks should have your heads examined.... GREAT ACHIEVMENT great work you climbed a hill like a few stupid beatnecks, if you idiots would shave and look presentable, but you are 3 big slobs.... You can now rest on your laurels as the 3 pigs that climbed up a stone steep grade. Get your heads examined."

Each climber's attitude toward humor was different, naturally. Not given to crude levity, Robbins preferred puns, a minority of which proved tolerable. For instance, he named a slab climb Slab Happy Pinnacle and a difficult route on it, involving a dihedral, the Dihardral. A later climb, done using only nuts for protection, became Nutcracker Sweet.

Herbert kept us in stitches whenever he was around. We smiled when we saw him approach, knowing we'd be on the floor holding our stomachs in a few minutes. His bivouac stories became legendary. In the old days we rarely carried sleeping bags on climbs; we simply stopped on a ledge, put on a sweater and a down jacket, then curled up and waited for dawn. When Galen Rowell pulled a sleeping bag from his pack at dusk on the west face of Sentinel, Herbert was mock outraged. "You wimp! You camper! You can't count this as a real bivouac, you know. I'll tell everyone about this. We'll hound you out of the Valley!" He even woke the soundly sleeping Rowell in the middle of the night to reaffirm his views. On another bivouac Herbert actually slept soundly for a few hours, so he woke up his snoring companions to tell them the good news. One of his partners, Don Lauria, later reported that the "crux of the climb" came with Herbert's midnight tirade: "Is everybody awake? I've actually been sleeping. This is the first time I've ever slept on a bivouac. Damn it, wake up and listen to me. I've been sleeping. This is incredible."

Other brands of humor were more introspective. Pratt and Chouinard, five-foot-six and five-foot-four, respectively, constantly blamed their stature for any lack of success with women; their self-deprecating stories about their setbacks kept us in stitches. One day Chouinard announced that he might as well slice his pecker off for all the good it did him. He sulked for a few moments and then brightened when someone said, "What are you

Yvon Chouinard watches as Chuck Pratt tries on a haul bag, about 1968. (Photo: Glen Denny)

going to piss with, idiot?" Pratt's reason for climbing was succinct: "Too short for basketball." Once, after a Bay Area date, Pratt realized he'd left his jacket in the young woman's house. He returned shortly, rang the doorbell, and heard the woman say to her roommate, "I bet it's that little shrimp come for his coat." He turned and ran, jumped into his car, bought some beer, drove to the nearby Pacific, and tried to subdue the surf with his fists. The following day, depressed, hung over, and vowing never again to pursue the traditional dating game, he lay on his sofa listening to all nine Mahler symphonies in succession.

Although life in Camp 4 provided an ever-changing kaleidoscope of climbing, laughter, and lodge lounging, it would be wrong to assume that we did this year-round. All of us worked during the wintertime. Robbins taught skiing at Sugar Bowl, a small ski resort near Lake Tahoe, for four winters in succession. Later he taught climbing and skiing in Switzerland. Pratt often worked as a clerk or "ski-rental boy" at Berkeley's Ski Hut, which Allen Steck managed. I put in a decade's worth of winters there also, as the rental boy and, later, as the ski repairman. Steck's boss didn't pay too well, but if I showed up on November 1 of each year, the job was mine. It was understood that I would leave on April 1, rain or shine.

Chris Fredericks spent one winter deep inside a molybdenum mine, high in the Colorado mountains. Pratt once endured a gloomy winter in Los Angeles, installing toilets in trailer homes, an edifying experience. Some of us worked for a month or so in the early spring or late fall as flunkies in Yosemite; one fall I was the Ahwahnee Hotel's chief daytime pot-washer, a position of great importance. Joe Fitschen became an accomplished waiter at the lodge's bar, serving climbers Black Russians and Brandy Alexanders with aplomb.

Others worked at steady jobs. Harding spent most of his professional life as a highway surveyor. Before he became allied with Chouinard in the piton business, Frost was an aerospace engineer in Southern California. Chouinard toiled at his forge in Burbank, each year turning out volumes of improved equipment. Herbert kept going back to college in order to get his teaching credential; several others, such as Beck and Foott, also became professional students, quitting and then re-enrolling constantly as their values and moods shifted.

The military also figured prominently in our lives, and many of these college maneuvers were simply ploys to remain free of the draft. The slightly older group—Robbins, Herbert, Chouinard, Fitschen, Pratt, and myself—were all drafted and served two miserable years (interestingly, none of us became officers). Chouinard, at least, tried hard to get out. Just before he thought his physical was imminent, he drank a massive quantity of soy sauce to force his blood pressure up to a horrific level, but an unforeseen delay ruined his plan: his system had "desalted" itself by the time the cuff was applied.

The younger group, hearing our stories of the army's mind-numbing routines, fought hard to remain free—and invariably succeeded. After the Vietnam War began to heat up, many college students—and every climber— wished to avoid the dreaded "Robert McNamara Scholarship." One climber studied under a climber-psychiatrist for a week, memorizing subterfuges to employ during his psychological exam. This ploy worked, as did the following ones, with the participants best left unnamed. One climber answered yes to the question "Are you a homosexual?" Then he scratched crude slash marks through the yes box and put a huge "NO!!" next to the scrawl. One asthmatic climber sprayed some insect dope down his throat just before his physical, and another young chap placed a shotgun parallel to his ears and fired off a whole box of shells just prior to his medical screening. By the time I finally met the latter fellow he was still hard of hearing.

Steve Komito, a Colorado climber subject to the draft, quivered at the prospect but maintained his sense of humor, writing me in 1964: "I shall not give myself up willingly. I shall employ every trick of treachery known to my ancestors in ages yore. I shall not marry for that would be like removing my penis to avoid venereal disease. No, I shall flee to the farthest corners of the earth. I shall rack my body and vilify my soul so as to be unfit." One month later he got married. Eight months later he wrote me: "It's a very good life and I'm also draft exempt."

With jobs and the army to worry about each winter, it was truly a relief to get back to Camp 4 each spring and begin our training regimen. Only climbing mattered, and we devoted ourselves to the task at hand.

CHAPTER 8

A Way of Life:
1963–1964

*I feel that my enemy is anyone who would, given the power to
do so, restrict individual liberty, and this includes all officials,
law officers, army sergeants, communists, Catholics, and the House
Un-American Activities Committee. Of course I'm prejudiced, but
I cannot imagine a sport other than climbing which offers such a
complete and fulfilling expression of individuality. And I will not
give it up nor even slow down, not for man, nor woman, nor wife,
nor God.*

—Chuck Pratt, 1965

Yosemite climbers had written relatively little about their achievements,
but this changed radically in 1963, thanks in large part to Yvon
Chouinard. Drafted by the army in October 1962, he had plenty of time to
think about what had been taking place in the Valley during the previous
few years. He knew that few people outside California realized what was
happening on the big walls. The Europeans remained oblivious, and the
non-Vulgarian East Coast climbers, mountaineers not rockclimbers, concentrated on Canada and the Himalaya. Indeed, Yosemite had hardly ever
been mentioned in the venerable *American Alpine Journal*. The sole exception was a lengthy article by Cal Tech student Bill Shand in the 1944
issue, in which he described five or six routes in detail. Overall, however,
the western United States was terra incognita to the Boston–New York
crowd. For instance, in the first three issues of the decade, 1960 to 1962,
places such as the Himalaya and Mount McKinley utterly dominated the
journal. Only six of thirty-nine feature articles concerned the West, and
these were mostly historical pieces, such as "Naming America's Mountains: The Cascades." Not one dealt with California. In the lengthy "Climbs
and Expeditions" section in the back of the journal, Yosemite fared slightly
better. I had been approached by the *AAJ* in early 1962 and asked to write

a few words about what was happening in the Valley. I sent them several desultory comments; one became the first-ever mention in print of the Salathé Wall climb—a dull, four-sentence account.

The American Alpine Club also tended to ignore young climbers; it was truly an "old-boy network" of Ivy Leaguers back then. Dick Leonard, that pivotal figure of early Valley climbing, realized this truth before most people. In 1972 he wrote: "I resigned from the AAC *twice!* This was because I felt that the club was not willing to accept the younger climbers and work effectively with them."

Not all the leaders of the AAC were so shortsighted. Ad Carter, the editor of the *AAJ* and a noted mountaineer from the 1930s, got in touch with Chouinard after seeing a Sunday supplement article written by him. He asked for an article but, as Carter told me recently, "Chouinard wrote back saying that the last thing in the world he wanted was to contribute to a journal for old fogies." But AAC president Carl Fuller wouldn't take no for an answer; he soon flew out to California to talk with the local climbers. "Carl completely won them over, and soon I no longer had trouble in getting them to write about the marvelous stuff they were doing."

The newly persuaded Chouinard gathered four articles about the Valley for the 1963 journal, including an overview he had written. Private Chouinard wrote me in December 1962 from the Redstone Arsenal, in Alabama: "I have finally finished my article; it is 5,000 words long and is completely biased and prejudiced.... I also sent 15 of the best photos I could get my hands on. That ought to really shake 'em up in Europe."

"Modern Yosemite Climbing," Chouinard's seminal piece, appeared as the lead article and opened boldly: "Yosemite climbing is the least known and understood and yet one of the most important schools of rock climbing in the world today. Its philosophies, equipment and techniques have been developed almost independently of the rest of the climbing world."

Eloquent and informative, Chouinard's piece covered every possible aspect of Yosemite climbing, including safety, weather, and aid techniques. He expounded upon ethics and was the first to write about the Valley climbers' definition of "free climbing": "[It] means that artificial aid of *any* sort is not used...." He was here referring to the Continental (not British) habit of hanging on to pitons, or stepping on them, and calling this "free"; Alpine climbers thought that artificial climbing meant only that one stood in stirrups attached to pitons. In other words, a French climber, for example, might hang on to a carabiner at a tough spot and still call the route "free." Such ambiguity led immediately to problems with the rating system; more importantly, it really was an ethical question, as Chouinard implied: "free" should mean using only natural holds for upward progress. A finger stuck temporarily through a carabiner was the same as a stirrup attached to a piton: it was artificial climbing.

After extolling the virtues of Valley climbing for six pages, Chouinard, perhaps fearing he was overdoing it, got personal: "I have always abhorred the tremendous heat, the dirt-filled cracks, the ant-covered foul-smelling trees and bushes which cover the cliffs, the filth and noise of Camp 4...and worst of all, the multitude of tourists...." Later he stated, "If at times I hate the place, it is probably because I love it so. It is a strange, passionate love that I feel for this Valley. More than just a climbing area, it is a way of life."

Bundled with Chouinard's piece were three more Yosemite articles: Ad Carter was bending over backward to highlight the Valley. The first was another Chouinard piece, an account of his and TM Herbert's new route on Sentinel. Then came two El Cap pieces: Robbins's excellent account of the Salathé Wall, describing both the first ascent and the first continuous ascent, and Ed Cooper's story of the first ascent of the Dihedral Wall. Twenty-eight photos, mostly of climbers standing in aid slings, accompanied the four articles.

Each of the four articles was well written and informative, capturing the essence of the Valley's walls. We Camp 4 residents were extremely pleased with the issue: Yosemite was on the map at last, and now we had a forum for our writing. I remember showing the journal to my parents to prove that what I was doing was socially responsible—I was taking part in the American climbing renaissance. My father, who had started me climbing and knew something about it, glowed with pride, though he wanted me to go back to college. My mother simply wondered why I didn't go back to college.

Interestingly, the last sentences of the three climbing articles were similar. It is difficult indeed to close out a climbing account: one has to say *something* about the meaning of it all. Chouinard was overjoyed on the top of Sentinel, "...happy that for a few hours we had been free and happy to take some of this freedom back with us." Robbins chimed in with: "We were feeling spiritually very rich indeed as we hiked down...." Cooper ended his account with "It was the greatest day of our lives."

Chouinard's statement about Valley climbing being "a way of life" struck many of us as an absolute truth. By 1963 people such as Robbins, Chouinard, Pratt, Beck, and myself had lived in the Valley for months at a time. We felt as if we truly belonged in the Valley; it was our spiritual home. Away from the cities and responsibilities, we lived simply, feeling at peace with ourselves and the world. We thought that climbing made us better people, and perhaps it did. Humbled often by the walls, we had to look deeply into ourselves to find out what made us tick. We learned to confront fear, and years later we all would agree that facing dangers on the cliffs, fighting to maintain equanimity, helped us get through difficult times. We acquired confidence; we felt good about ourselves. In short, climbing was good for the soul, a calming influence on our reckless natures. Indeed, it was a way of life.

The weather during the spring of 1963 was the worst in our collective memory; we sat around the lodge for days at a time, never getting into shape, and cursing the gods. Layton Kor paced constantly, for he sensed this was to be his great year. He wanted a new route on El Cap so badly that this was all he could talk about. Chouinard and I had, in early 1961, spotted a potential route up the west buttress, at the far left margin of the southwest face. We had managed one pitch but then, intimidated by the sweeping wall above, retreated. Kor grabbed Beck one day in April 1963 and they went up a few more pitches, leaving fixed ropes because of the bad weather. In retrospect, this was a route that certainly didn't require fixed ropes, and thus a setback in the evolution of Valley climbing. Had anyone else left these fixed lines, we would have been outraged, but Kor said they were necessary and we believed him. Over several weeks Kor and Beck pushed their ropes up, between storms, to the 800-foot level. Beck at this time was a timid fellow and not terribly experienced; never had he been up on a truly big wall. His sleep suffered, and one day in late April he could take it no longer. "Roper," he exclaimed, his always gaunt face now cadaverous with worry, "I want to quit. I'm scared. I don't know what to do."

I saw an opportunity and slyly suggested I take his place. Beck pon-

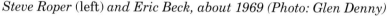

Steve Roper (left) *and Eric Beck, about 1969 (Photo: Glen Denny)*

dered this for a few minutes, realizing his chances for glory would forever be gone if he quit. Then it was his turn to become sly: "What'll you give me if I let you go up."

We played a cat-and-mouse game for a while, finally reaching an agreement. "I'll give you ten bucks," I said. "And a bong—any size you want." The deal was done. Kor hardly blinked when I informed him I was his new partner. He didn't really care who he went with; he simply wanted to get to the top.

That night, while Beck slept blissfully for ten hours, it was my turn to face a night impacted by demons. The wall—huge, steep, and unknown—dominated every waking thought; I dwelled on the possible ways I would die. I saw frayed ropes snapping and imagined long leader falls onto sharp flakes. Dawn came far too soon, and I sullenly trudged up to the base of the wall as the excited Kor whistled "Bolero" over and over.

We worked on the route two or three times during the next week, getting the ropes up to 1,200 feet. Every five o'clock alarm-clock buzzer was traumatic. Dark was evil; partial light was barely acceptable; but sunrise was a joy, a time when my fears began evaporating. Early on May 15, Kor and I cast loose from our umbilical cord and spent three sparkling days forging our way to the rim. Had I written an article about it, I guess I would have ended it with "It was the grandest time of my life." The route, the fourth on El Cap, marked the sixth time the monolith had been climbed. No one greeted us as we unroped: this was the first time a new El Cap route had been accomplished without summit fanfare. We reveled in the silence of the cold spring morning, with the High Sierra peaks so close we felt we could touch them.

Two pieces of equipment appeared in the spring of 1963, as did one major controversy. One innovation was relatively minor: a kernmantle rope from Europe, made from the synthetic nylon fiber called perlon, appeared in great quantities and within the year dominated the market. Kernmantle ropes, with a tightly woven sheath covering an inner core, had been invented in the mid-fifties, but they had only occasionally been used in the United States. (Chouinard had been given one by the legendary East Coast climber Hans Kraus in 1957.) The kernmantle rope had numerous advantages over the traditional three-twist nylon ropes: it was stronger, didn't kink as often, and didn't stretch when one applied weight to it, which made pendulums and other rope tricks a little easier. (Perlon *did* stretch, and stretch nicely, but only when great stress was applied.) In addition, the sheath could sustain minor damage without affecting the "guts" of the rope.

Amazing though perlon was, it didn't change Yosemite climbing the way the jumar ascender did. Invented in the 1950s by two Swiss—Jusi and Marti, hence the compound name—to be used by cavers, the "handle," as it was also called, arrived in early May. Designed to replace the prusik knot, the jumar fulfilled this role marvelously. Tiny metal teeth on a movable cam gripped the rope tightly when one stood in the attached foot sling. Yet, when unweighted, the device slid up the rope with the merest lifting motion. The "handle" part of the gadget also afforded an excellent grip. One could now ascend a rope perhaps five times as fast as with prusik knots, without the hassle of gnarled knots and barked knuckles.

One might wonder why jumars were necessary, given that siege climbing was losing favor. For one thing, on a multiday climb the climbers often fixed a rope or two above a bivouac ledge so as to make use of all the available daylight before returning to the ledge. Thus, in the morning, they had to ascend a few hundred feet to the high point. Using jumars, this chore was trivial. But jumars were best suited for another task, a labor-saving technique invented by Robbins. On an aid pitch the second man, responsible for removing the pitons, formerly hung in slings from a piton to remove the next lower one; this meant awkward reaches downward at times. It also meant that the belayer, far above, had to be attentive, manipulating the rope up and down. The new technique worked beautifully. The leader, finishing a pitch, would simply tie the rope off to his anchors and relax while the second man attached two jumars to the rope and moved upward, choosing the perfect level to work on a pin. Since the jumars could be removed easily from the rope, unlike prusik knots, one simply jumared up to a pin and then clipped the jumars, one at a time, onto the rope above it. Meanwhile, up above, the leader remained free to haul the bag, sort iron, or marvel at the sights.

The jumar had only one disadvantage: it cost ten dollars, about thirty times the price of a prusik loop—and two were necessary. Twenty dollars meant two weeks in the Valley; still, virtually every top climber soon owned a pair. With this superb invention, the walls of Yosemite shrunk a little further.

The big controversy of 1963 concerned the rating system. Flawed in many ways, the decimal system was nevertheless well established in the Valley by this time. Indeed, it had spread eastward to Colorado, the Shawangunks, and many other areas. But Leigh Ortenburger, a Bay Area mathematician and Teton guidebook author, had just invented a more logical system, one he called the National Climbing Classification System, or NCCS. Writing a blizzard of letters to climbers around the country, and publishing articles in *Summit,* Ortenburger tried to get his untried and theoretical system accepted. He was persuasive; many climbers vacillated. Robbins, for instance, wrote Orrin Bonney, author of a guide to Wyoming's Wind River Range, on February 23: "I now think that it would be best to stick to the decimal system.... Ortenburger's plan is lately meeting considerable resistance here in California." But three weeks later he wrote a letter to the editor of *Summit:* "I think Ortenburger's plan should be adopted and incorporated into all American guidebooks."

A highly intelligent man, Ortenburger realized he faced an uphill battle: "Since it is a characteristic of climbers to be independent," he wrote in one letter, "perhaps [my] appeal will have a more negative than positive effect." A mountaineer, not a rock man, Ortenburger had rarely climbed in the Valley, and many of the Camp 4 residents were upset. I was just finishing the Valley guidebook, one totally committed to the decimal system. Two other guidebook authors, Bonney and Art Gran (who'd written about the Shawangunks) joined me to fight the infidel, and within a year we three came out with books primarily using the decimal system.

As a slight compromise, Gran, Bonney, and I all mentioned the existence of the NCCS, but the system soon faded into obscurity, except in the Tetons, where it lasted some years because of its inclusion in Ortenburger's 1965 guide. Dave Brower, executive director of the Sierra Club, and publisher of both Ortenburger's guide and mine, was caught in the middle of the crossfire. After the decisions were handed down on June 9, 1963, by the club's Executive Committee—decimal system for my book, NCCS for Ortenburger's—Brower had the last word. In the June 1963 *Sierra Club Bulletin,* after a lengthy discussion of the matter, he wrote: "We are sure there will be those who will feel much the same as did the famed John Salathé, when he pleaded: 'Vy can't ve chust climb!'"

While this fray was continuing in various locales around the country, ten or fifteen climbers paced through Yosemite Lodge, waiting out the constant storms. On May 9, a restless Robbins snuck off, to where no one knew. Liz Burkner, his girlfriend, muttered something about him having business elsewhere, but we thought it odd that he didn't take her along. Only on the fourth day of his absence did she reveal the truth: he was about to top out on Harding's 1961 route on the Leaning Tower, not repeated since the first ascent. The storm raged on, but this meant nothing up on the overhang, the driest hunk of rock in the Valley. Robbins had patiently worked his way up, replacing dozens of bolts, the ones that Harding had chopped out. One can argue that soloing a predominately aid climb, provided proper self-belay techniques are used, is not an especially difficult task. Still, solo climbing was in its infancy in 1963; no one in the country had ever soloed a big wall. Robbins spent three nights on the cliff as the wind howled and the clouds drifted by. Adding to the adventure was the fact that retreat was impossible; the wall overhung far too radically to rappel. With no umbilical cord to the ground, as Harding and party had enjoyed, the commitment was extreme: Robbins pulled off the finest feat of 1963.

Robbins wasn't the only person on a roll that spring; Kor was hot, too. He, Denny, and I climbed the Nose in three and a half days in late May, a speedy time not dreamed of by anyone, let alone us. This route, like so many done by competent Camp 4 residents, proved uneventful, although at six feet tall I was, for once, by far the shortest person on a climb. How I cursed those long reaches between pitons! The only significant story of this climb concerns a single bolt. Leading Boot Flake, I noticed a bolt halfway up the pitch, on the main wall. It had a "modern" hanger, which I knew wasn't Harding's—Robbins, I knew, had put this in on the second ascent. The wide crack, which I was nailing, didn't seem dangerously expanding, so I didn't touch the bolt. I called down to Kor to chop it on his way up, which he did. Many years later, I kidded Robbins about his "transgression," which he had long since forgotten. I hadn't, for it was the sole time I had one-upped the master. "How could I have done it?" he exclaimed. "I remember now: I was afraid the whole flake would come off. What a shameful act! I wonder how many others there are?"

Just five days after we finished the Nose, while I lay basking on the banks of the Merced River, Kor and Denny set off on what was to be a strenuous new route on Sentinel's north face, an effort requiring two bivouacs.

In mid-June, Robbins accomplished a fine new route with Dick McCracken, but this was sullied somewhat by controversy. Ed Cooper, flushed with his success on El Cap the previous November, had returned to attempt a direct route up Half Dome's great face, the central section that no one had yet touched. His partner for this venture was newcomer Galen Rowell, someone I knew well, for he and I had gone through the Berkeley school system together since diaperhood. A mineral collector and hiker since the mid-1950s, Rowell showed instant talent as a rockclimber. Strong as a bull, he attacked cracks—like a mad bull. "Attacked" is the right word: though he blustered and whimpered and thrashed, he always got up eventually. Displaying an ill-disguised ego at times, Rowell could also be abrasive. Mike Borghoff, always perceptive, once climbed Yosemite Point Buttress with Rowell and wrote me a nutshell impression of his partner: "Beneath his flagrant and shameless exhibitionism, he is really quite decent, and very honest. Not to mention capable."

Cooper and Rowell formed a perfect team in one sense: they were both driven young men, determined to succeed whatever the cost. (Later, they both succeeded spectacularly in the world of photography.) What they lacked, however, was a sense of current Yosemite tradition: as weekenders they, like Al Macdonald earlier in 1963, had no idea that the times were changing.

Cooper and Rowell carried many ropes to the base of the wall, climbed a few pitches, placed five bolts, and then came down, typical behavior in those days, when first ascents usually involved several failures before success. They left their ropes in place, and a few days later they made another desultory attempt, again leaving fixed ropes dangling to the ground.

Robbins had spied a direct route up the dome earlier, and now he tried to talk Kor into going up and bypassing the Cooper-Rowell ropes. Kor balked, feeling this gambit wouldn't be ethical as long as someone had

Galen Rowell, about 1965 (Photo: Glen Denny)

laid claim to the route. Robbins then turned to McCracken, that calm and talented climber who had been my main partner three years earlier. McCracken had no qualms at all, agreeing with the sentiment Robbins later expressed in an article about the climb: "Fixed ropes encourage sloppy climbing, for the lack of a time limit provides no incentive to climb well." Years later Robbins told me that "the idea that a fixed rope signals owner-ship is flawed. Anyone can throw a couple of ropes at a prize and then claim it."

Not touching the fixed ropes, the pair quickly reached Cooper's high point. Then, for three and a half stormy days, the pair toiled up the 2,000-foot wall, placing 295 pitons. Difficult nailing characterized the Direct Northwest Face route: one pitch required six rurps, a knife blade, and four "fifi-hook" placements. The latter device was a small metal hook that the leader could drape over a tiny flake or nubbin and hope it stayed put while he moved up the attached sling. By such sterling aid climbing, the pair had to place only ten bolts. Cooper and Rowell would have undoubt-edly placed dozens and taken weeks on the route. Still, the incident dis-turbed many people, for it marked the first "theft" of a Valley route.

Cooper next attacked the big face to the right of Upper Yosemite Fall, enlisting Glen Denny and Jim Baldwin as his companions. When these two found out that Cooper had contacted the media, they quit the project. Cooper grabbed a fellow Northwest climber, Eric Bjørnstad, and they went up two pitches. Not liking the look of the wall above, they retreated, leaving no fixed ropes. Cooper, not at all pleased with the events of June 1963, soon left the Valley and quit serious rock climbing forever.

Robbins and McCracken, only a week after they finished Half Dome, did the Upper Yosemite Fall route, soon to be known as the Misty Wall. The waterfall, nearly 1,400 feet high and swollen by snow melt, roared nearby, and the wind occasionally blew the icy water onto the climbers. At noon on day three they finally reached the lip of the waterfall. Robbins, always curious about "the meaning of life," asked a question in his article in the *American Alpine Journal:* "What significance had our little adventure?" His reply: "None. Knowing this, we took it for what it was: a stimulating experience which awakened our minds and spirits to a lust for life and a keener awareness of beauty."

Robbins and Kor soon left the Valley for Colorado, where they did the Diamond on Longs Peak, the route pioneered three years earlier by Dave Rearick and Bob Kamps. Days later they made a first ascent of their own, just to the right of the original route. Then they were off to the Northwest Territories of Canada, where, with McCracken and the excellent eastern climber Jim McCarthy, they made a fine first ascent of the southeast face of remote Mount Proboscis. Thus, in a matter of some sixty days Kor had climbed, among many other lesser routes, El Cap twice, Sentinel's face once, the Diamond twice, and the face of a great Canadian peak. Not a bad two months! During the same period, Robbins had soloed the Tower, done two big new Valley routes, and accomplished the same three big out-of-state routes. McCarthy, in his article on Proboscis, called Robbins "one of the finest American technical climbers." And Kor was "one of the most astonishing climbers anywhere." If anything, these were understatements.

Several dozen minor climbs were also established in 1963, and these tended to fall into two categories: short, steep climbs and out-of-the-way climbs. In the former category, specialists in difficult aid climbing or in pure crack climbing did many routes on the slab-pinnacles at the base of El Cap. Glacier Point Apron specialists also became prominent, a subject to be discussed later.

The master of the "out-of-the-way" category was a fellow from Berkeley named Les Wilson, nicknamed Man Mountain because of his lumberjack's physique. Always a weekender, and never technically brilliant, he possessed a great love for offbeat adventure. He and his buddies, most often Max Heinritz, Andrzej Ehrenfeucht, and Leif Patterson, sought out long, hidden chimneys or steep gullies, often in the unexplored Ribbon Fall area, just west of El Cap. Not for this threesome were climbs like Sentinel or Half Dome; they shunned the standard routes, preferring only first ascents. They rarely were seen in Camp 4 since they were constantly bivouacking in some dank slot. Man Mountain and his coterie were not

Charlie Raymond leads Moby Dick, a 5.9 crack climb at the base of El Capitan. (Photo: Glen Denny)

speed climbers; the longer they took on a route the better they enjoyed themselves. Wilson managed an amazing fourteen first ascents during a four-year stretch in the early sixties, seven in 1962 alone. Heinritz, a German, and Ehrenfeucht, a Pole, were the first foreign climbers to accomplish major Valley first ascents. (A subtle distinction could be made regarding the definition of "foreigners": these two men lived in the States and had climbed either little or nothing in their home countries. Yosemite was their home ground. Soon, however, accomplished European climbers were to make special trips to the Valley—and these were the first true foreign visitors.)

Jeff Foott made one of the more novel first ascents of 1963: Patio Pinnacle. In August he spotted a tiny ledge—a "Yosemite pinnacle"—on the broad expanse of Glacier Point Apron. He described his unique adventure for me recently. "I knew no one had ever done a solo first ascent in the Valley, and this seemed like something to do. Robbins had just done the Tower solo and this impressed me. So I grabbed some bolts, strapped on my Zillertals [a soft Austrian klettershoe favored by many], climbed up an approach chimney, and then set off across these smooth friction slabs. I had rigged up a self-belay with a jumar and a prusik knot, so it wasn't too

Jeff Foott, 1967 (Photo: Steve Roper)

dangerous, I guess. I put in about five bolts for protection and a few pitons behind small flakes. It took me most of the day. I told a couple of girls where I was going and told 'em to come look for me if I didn't get back by dark."

After three complex pitches of free climbing (rated 5.9 for many years, but now thought to be 5.8), he finally reached his goal, the tiny "summit" ledge. His fingers, cramped from all the clinging and drilling, curled up horribly as he tried to drill the holes for his rappel bolts. He spent an hour at the task, having to shake his arms out every few hammer hits. "Robbins repeated the climb a few months later," Foott recalled. "I hardly knew him, but one day as I walked by the coffee shop, he jumped up from his hamburger and rushed out to pump my hand. 'What possessed you to do Patio alone?' he wanted to know. I had no real answer."

Most climbers, naturally, weren't out soloing or making first ascents. The standard big climbs received lots of traffic in 1963: the face of Half Dome was climbed four times; the direct north buttress of Middle Cathedral became an instant classic and was done twice; the Chouinard-Herbert route on Sentinel saw three parties. Yosemite Point Buttress, by the eleventh anniversary of its first ascent, had seen about forty ascents.

One might legitimately wonder how we kept track of these ascents. The answer is easy: the Camp 4 climbers were all known to one another, and information was bandied about on a daily basis. As far as outsiders were concerned, they invariably stayed for weeks in Camp 4 before setting out on the big walls, so we knew of these ascents also. Though much of this information was passed along orally, I kept a crude diary throughout these years, listing my own climbs and significant others. Robbins later recorded all the big ascents in *Summit*, after he became the magazine's climbing editor late in 1964. Registers in tin cans on certain spires or ledges also provided reliable information; I remember as a teenager being extremely pleased to have made the ninety-sixth ascent of the Higher Spire in 1958; this was a big number, to be sure, but it was also under 100, a magic figure.

The army finally nabbed me, and five days after John Kennedy was killed—news of which I first heard in the lodge's lounge on my last Yosemite day for two years—I rode off in a bus toward basic training. I was not exactly sorry to leave the Valley: for one thing, November was the traditional time to start work elsewhere. Also, I had become a little tired of the lifestyle, as we didn't call it back then. I seemed to be going nowhere. Time for a change. I remember thinking that if I *really* loved climbing, I would return to the pleasant confines of the Valley after two years and never again leave. On the other hand, if I found something else to do with my life, then I'd not return. It was truly a turning point in my life, and I welcomed it.

During the next two years I received more mail than I had in my entire life up till then. I had begged my friends to keep me informed about Valley happenings—and they did, especially Beck and Robbins. This news, welcome though it was, caused me great restlessness as I eked out my time in Georgia and Vietnam. The bastards were climbing without me—I'd never catch up!

The year 1964 started off well. Robbins, in fine form, spent much of the spring on El Cap. After making an attempt on the wall to the right of the Nose (a story to be related later), Robbins managed two El Cap routes in three weeks; both were second ascents—and both were first continuous ascents. During the first week of June, he and Frost climbed the Dihedral Wall in five days, an excellent time for the second ascent of such a big wall. Robbins wrote me about this climb two months later: "There is a lot of hard nailing on the bastard, but it is not an enjoyable route.... It is also not an esthetic route. In short it has nothing to recommend it except pure difficulty, but there is plenty of that." The pair had an unpleasant experience low on the route, and Robbins lit into Ed Cooper, the leader of the first ascent: "That SOB Cooper had removed the nuts from almost all the first 35 bolts. We had heard that most of the hangers on the route had been removed, but it came as quite a surprise to find the nuts gone also. And we had only six with us!… It's strange that Cooper should fill a page of the *American Alpine Journal* with 'interesting facts' and yet fail to mention this most important bit of information." Robbins questioned Cooper's integrity once again, in the 1965 *American Alpine Journal*: "We removed 13 bolts, but still used 87, which indicates a hundred bolts placed rather than the 75–85 reported in Cooper's article."

A week after finishing the Dihedral Wall, Robbins grabbed Chuck Pratt and, after two defeats, they roared up the west buttress of El Cap in three and a half days. Robbins possessed El Cap that spring: in the space of thirty-one days he had spent ten nights bivouacking on the monolith, on three separate routes.

My other friends were climbing also, but with less success. And sometimes with dire results. After doing several admirable warm-up climbs, Eric Beck and Tom Frost set off on May 14 for the direct north buttress of Middle Cathedral. Full of hubris, Beck began nailing an expanding flake, five pitches up and about forty feet above Frost. A pin popped and Beck plummeted, ripping out his only other piton. He described the eighty-foot fall to me in a letter several days later: "As I fell I apparently hit Frost's anchor and ripped the pack off. I saw the pack falling next to me and thought I'd pulled out Tom's anchor, which was a short, thin knife blade that I knew was no good." Thinking both of them were headed for the talus, Beck figured he was dead—but then he suddenly stopped. Frost, bracing himself with his feet, had somehow managed to hold the huge fall. Beck's arm was shattered, but with the help of Frost he made it to the ground a few hours later.

As springtime came to a close, a far more consequential accident occurred. My good friend Jim Baldwin had returned for his third Valley season, and on June 19 he and the solid midwestern climber John Evans started up the east face of the Washington Column. Baldwin was uneasy, as recorded in a June 18 entry in Evans's diary: "Baldwin has really got cold feet about doing a Grade VI, but finally agreed to start tomorrow noon."

Just after roping up on the nineteenth, Baldwin exclaimed, "I sure wish I could work up some enthusiasm for this climb!" Higher, while leading an aid crack and overdriving the iron "like a fiend," he looked down at his partner and said, "Would you hate me for the rest of my life if I chickened out?" Evans asked what the trouble was, and Baldwin replied, "It's just that this chicky-doll has me all screwed up." Baldwin continued slowly upward, but darkness descended and so did the two men, intending to bivouac in the forest and head back up the next morning. But Baldwin somehow slipped off the end of his rappel rope and plunged several hundred feet into the talus.

That such an experienced climber could die in such a mundane fashion was shocking; that such a lively and gregarious person was lost forever was devastating. Baldwin had been desperately unhappy in the months preceding his death; his future was seemingly in shambles. His great passion of 1963, a self-assured woman named Hope, someone I had introduced him to, had married another man, feeling Baldwin would never settle down to be a proper father to her young girl. She was right, and Baldwin knew this. Late in 1963 he had fallen desperately in love with another woman, Helen, the "chicky-doll." But she ignored him much of the time, tumbling lovers in her bedroom even while he lay wide-eyed on the nearby living room sofa. He wrote me two months before his death: "I am wretched, lost, defeated.... I will write when this thing is worked out. I am too mixed up now."

I'll always wonder if Baldwin's personal problems weighed on him so heavily that he wasn't able to concentrate on routine tasks such as rappelling. I hadn't known about his strong reluctance to climb that fateful afternoon, so when I recently saw John Evans's diary entries of June 1964, I choked up reading the intimate details of those final hours. I was also unsettled by the fact that the diary I held in my hands, its spine broken and dented, had been taken on the climb by Evans. It had been in the haul bag accompanying Baldwin on his fall.

Numbed by the accident, Evans nevertheless had a commitment to keep in just a few days: he, Chuck Pratt, Allen Steck, and Dick Long had agreed to attempt the vertiginous unclimbed wall just to the right of Ribbon Fall. That Evans was able to complete this fine route says something about his solid character and also about the prevailing macho ethos: the death of a partner was not enough to keep one from going up on a huge and unknown wall a mere five days later.

Although the three-day Ribbon East Portal climb, completed on June 27 by Evans, Pratt, Steck, and Long, was hardly a significant step upward in the evolution of Valley climbing, it is interesting for several reasons. First, it marked the first time someone from the new generation (Pratt) had accomplished a hard route with someone from an earlier generation (Steck). By 1964 Steck had been relatively inactive for eleven years. Restless at age thirty-eight, a little bored with his Ski Hut job, and with his youngest child seven, Steck felt it was time to rejoin the action.

The Ribbon climb also marked the emergence of a witty new writer: Pratt. His first major piece, a long note about the route in the 1965 *American Alpine Journal,* was brilliant. If Chouinard's writing was dramatic and prophetic, and if Robbins's writing was somber and philosophical, then Pratt's took a brand-new direction: wry humor. For the first time a writer showed that the big climbs could be fun, at least in retrospect. Starting out with a reference to the four-man group, an unusually large size for a first ascent, Pratt declaimed: "Hoping to succeed by sheer weight of numbers...." He continued: "Each was famed for his ability to live on the granite walls like a rat." And later: "As if to show contempt for the difficulties, we deliberately made the ascent as hard as possible. We began by throwing rocks at our new nylon rope. After several tries, Evans succeeded in striking and cutting the rope...." In the same vein, he talked about the summit day: "The only difficulty encountered on the last day was Long, who tried several times to strike his companions with rocks from above."

The team spent three days on this near-vertical 1,500-foot-high cliff, and they apparently had a good time the whole way up. At one point, however, Pratt had a momentary attack of angst, an incident later reported by Steck. Pratt "suddenly proclaimed with excessive emphasis to no one in particular: 'I could climb for a million years and still not know why I do it...Why?...Why?' he cried, beating his fists against the wall, 'am I here?'"

The concept of the "first free ascent" had been around for a long time. In 1941, for instance, Dick Leonard had referred to a climb of the Higher Spire: "[Three men] eliminated artificial aid at the rope traverse chimney.... These are splendid accomplishments and leave only 10 feet of artificial aid...." Aid climbing was always thought of as a last resort, used only when the rock was holdless. Free climbing was *real* climbing. Yet in the twenty seasons between Yosemite's first "first free ascent" (in 1944, when the Higher Spire was finally freed by Chuck Wilts and Spencer Austin) and 1963, only twenty-two aid routes had been free-climbed. But 1964 marks an amazing resurgence of first free ascents: twelve were accomplished in just three or four months. Frank Sacherer, my companion on my big ice slide of 1961 and on Sentinel's north face the same year, had a starring role in eleven of the twelve.

The Summer of Sacherer remains one of the brightest periods in Valley history. Talented and fearless, the twenty-four-year-old Sacherer consciously set out to eliminate aid from previously done routes. He didn't choose routes that had a mere one or two aid points to eliminate; he usually sought out Grade IV or V routes, ones that had dozens of aid points. His goal was not simply to get to the top: he wanted to get to the top without using aid. Sacherer actually kept a "hit list" of climbs that might go free and once showed it to Tom Higgins. This proved to be a mistake, for Higgins grabbed Kamps and they freed one of the hit-list climbs, the Powell-Reed route on Middle Cathedral Rock, something Sacherer especially coveted. This was the only non-Sacherer first free ascent of the year!

Sacherer's summer list of first free ascents is awesome. Here's a partial accounting. The Salathé-Nelson route on the southwest face of Half Dome, with Bob Kamps and Andy Lichtman. The Arrow Chimney to the notch, an unbelievable feat done with Pratt (dozens of aid points were eliminated). The east buttress of El Cap, with Wally Reed, a route that I had recently done with fourteen aid pitons. The intimidating northeast buttress of Higher Cathedral Rock, with Jeff Dozier. The north buttress of Middle Cathedral, with Jim Bridwell. The right side of the frightening slab called the Hourglass, done with Tom Gerughty. The off-width crack at

Frank Sacherer, 1965 (Photo: Glen Denny)

the top of the left side of Reed Pinnacle, with Dick Erb and Larry Marshik. Bridalveil East, with John Morton. On most of these climbs Sacherer led the hard pitches, the ones where the aid was eliminated. (Two exceptions: Kamps and Pratt were equal in ability to Sacherer and led their share; these three can perhaps be called the finest free climbers of the Golden Age.)

It is clear from the above list that Sacherer's partners changed constantly. It may be that this revolving-door situation was a coincidence; after all, climbers came and went. Yet it seems likely that Sacherer's personality had something to do with it. He tended toward arrogance and recklessness, for one thing. We all predicted he'd die by age thirty, joking about who would be with him when he took the big ride. Layton Kor wrote me in late 1964 that "I am still scared to climb with him." Chouinard also was concerned: "He always climbed on the verge of falling over backwards— using no more energy than was necessary to progress and rarely bothering to stop and place protection.... Apparently his belayers have been so completely gripped they were unable to use a camera. I have not been able to find a single photograph of Sacherer on a lead!"

Sacherer's temper was legendary. High on the Bridalveil East climb, John Morton dropped a piton. "Frank was livid," Morton told me years later, "and for a moment could barely contain himself. He soon cooled down, but I was still not off the hook until I had conducted a search at the base when we got back down. Fortunately, I had memorized the exact spot where it had landed and fetched it to Frank promptly." Sacherer also scorned people who weren't on time, and on several occasions he drove out of Camp 4 alone precisely at five on a Sunday afternoon, the appointed hour to leave for the journey back to San Francisco. His stranded passengers didn't exactly appreciate this tactic, even though they were at fault for missing the deadline.

Sacherer also radiated intensity—and his intensity was not tempered with a smile, as with Robbins or Kor. His was an *intense* intensity. If he laughed at all, his face would settle into a tight grimace within seconds. He was intense at college also. His wife recently told me about an incident at the University of San Francisco, the Jesuit-run school where he did his undergraduate work (and where he graduated first in his class). Sacherer, a strict Catholic by upbringing, began to have doubts at college. During a final in a theology class he listed the five proofs of the existence of God, according to Thomas Aquinas, but then proceeded to refute these according to the laws of physics. He got a C on the final and a B in the course: this was the only college course in which he didn't receive an A.

Sacherer could be intolerable at times; his wife said that he was "famous for impatience and bouts of temper." I can certainly attest to this. One fall day in 1962 Sacherer suggested that we do the Crack of Doom, Pratt's superb crack route of a year earlier. Everyone except Sacherer was leery of this climb—even Robbins and Kor had shunned it. I elicited a promise that he'd lead the 5.10 pitch at the top, and off we went. He led the short and strenuous first pitch brilliantly. On the second pitch, an overhanging, totally unprotected, and severely flared slot, I soon found myself sixty feet above Sacherer. I made the mistake of looking down at the naked rope arcing down to my partner and realized that if I popped I'd plummet straight down 120 feet into the forest. I immediately began wiggling downward, scared out of my mind. My friend, the one I'd been so patient with when he started climbing in Berkeley only two years earlier, screamed, "What the hell are you doing?"

"I can't do it," I announced. "I'm coming down."

"Stay up there, you chickenshit," he shrieked.

I ignored him, fear of death overcoming fear of Sacherer. I slithered, barely in control, down the tight, black depths of the slot and arrived at the belay ledge quivering and with my ass on fire from the too-quick descent. I dropped my pants and craned my neck to see the extent of the abrasions. Sacherer stared at me silently, as if I were a worm. "Rest a minute and get back up there," he finally said in a monotone.

"Fuck you, Frank," I snarled. "*You* do it!" He refused to go up, muttering something about saving himself for the 5.10, so down we rappelled. On the drive back to Camp 4 Sacherer made small talk as if nothing had happened. Then, as we turned into the entrance, his face tightened: "Tell them it was your fault."

"Of course," I said. "It was."

A knot of people strode up to Sacherer's car as we parked, eager to hear if the fabled Crack of Doom had been conquered. Sacherer gave me a meaningful look and I dutifully confessed. Following my humiliation—a minor one, really, since I simply told everyone I didn't want to die that particular day—Sacherer offered me a Coke.

A slight, wiry fellow, Sacherer didn't seem capable of doing the crack climbs he did in 1964 and 1965, but marvelous technique and a reckless disregard for falling overcame any lack of upper-body strength. Oddly enough, he wasn't particularly good on low-angled climbs. Robbins once told me that Sacherer, after expressing contempt for "mere friction climbing," had fallen seven times on an ascent of the 5.9 right side of Goodrich Pinnacle, on Glacier Point Apron.

Over five seasons Sacherer made thirty-three first ascents or first free ascents, becoming, during the period covered in this book, the third-most-prolific first ascender, after Pratt and Robbins, both of whom spent three times as long in the Valley. (For the record, here are the top five first ascenders through 1970: Pratt, with forty-three; Robbins, with thirty-seven; Sacherer, with thirty-three; Harding, with thirty; and Kamps, with twenty-eight. Pratt and Harding made a few more first ascents after 1970.)

Sacherer is rightly a legend in Yosemite climbing, an enigmatic figure who stepped into the limelight for a brief period, wrote nothing, climbed little elsewhere in the West, and then faded into obscurity. By 1966 Sacherer had married Jan Baker, a fine Colorado climber he'd met earlier in the Valley. Soon thereafter he got his Ph.D. in theoretical particle physics and dropped out of our lives, as fascinated by physics as he had once been with climbing. He obtained a job as a theoretical physicist at CERN, the European nuclear research center near Geneva, separated from Jan, and began doing severe ice climbs, something he'd told his wife he'd never do. On August 30, 1978, at age thirty-eight, he and his partner both died in a fall near the top of the storm-enshrouded Grandes Jorasses. I can envision Sacherer shaking his fist at his partner—or God, or the lightning—during his last moments.

Several newcomers arrived in the Valley in 1964. One, the famed French climber Lionel Terray, showed up on June 23 and stayed only a few days— but long enough to appreciate the Valley. Allen Steck, fortunate enough to climb with him, wrote me about his experience: "I heard he was quite impressed with El Capitan. He climbed the Arches Terrace route with Leo LeBon and Robbins and then later climbed the standard Arches route with LeBon and myself. He had injured his arm while in Alaska and could not do much involving pullups. He took to the Valley without difficulty, leading quite a bit of the Arches. Like many newcomers to friction, he was not sure of himself on same." Terray never got back to the Valley to improve his friction skills; he was killed the next year in a fall in France at age forty-four.

Other climbers stayed just as briefly, never to return, but not because they came from far away or were soon killed. Tom Cochrane was one such fellow, and we had a few good laughs at his expense. He did a number of hard routes in 1964 but sold his gear and utterly gave up climbing following an October humiliation on Sentinel. Frost, Robbins, Pratt, and Chouinard, involved in making a movie about the Chouinard-Frost route on the west face, had set up fixed ropes over various sections of the route to speed up the project. Cochrane, thinking the *entire* route was fixed, began rappelling down the face just to have a close look at it. To his great surprise and chagrin he came to a spot where the ropes ended. He had no jumars and no slings to get back up, so he had to bivouac and scream for help. The next morning he was rescued by the movie team. Cochrane wrote in the summit register: "Feeling small this morning."

Another newcomer was to stay around far longer. I first heard of this fellow via a letter from Beck: "An artist friend of Pratt's has drawn in excellent manner a lolling indolent wench upon my arm cast. He is Sheridan Anderson, a brilliant drunkard from San Bernardino with no particular talent for climbing." In these two sentences Beck captured the man perfectly. Sheridan drank massive quantities of beer, climbed poorly, and was

Chuck Pratt (left) *and Sheridan Anderson, about 1971 (Photo: Jim Stuart / Ascent Collection)*

an excellent cartoonist. He saw the whimsical side of climbing instantly and soon began publishing his wry cartoons. His debut was grand: the front cover of *Summit*'s October 1964 issue featured five drawings, one of which showed two climbers standing amid a pile of skulls at the base of a climb. "This looks like a tricky little problem!" says one fellow, looking up at the fearsome wall above. Later, Sheridan made a calendar for *Summit* readers, featuring the months in *alphabetical* order. For many years his rakish figure was a fixture in Camp 4 in the springtime, and his satirical cartoons, often featuring a stern Robbins in a Superman-style cape, delighted climbers worldwide.

Sheridan came up with outlandish ideas occasionally. For instance, in August 1965 he decided to celebrate, of all things, the Matterhorn's first-ascent centenary with festivities in Camp 4. Rangers had to break up the party in the wee hours after complaints from tourists, but before the group disbanded, Sheridan made the rangers themselves sign an oversized post-card, the back of which he had decorated with numerous sketches. The next day he mailed the card to the mayor of Zermatt, who must have been surprised at this outpouring of emotion from the New World.

Sheridan abandoned the climbing scene in the early 1970s, worked as a billboard painter in San Francisco for many years, and then moved to Oregon, where he perfected his already splendid fly-fishing skills. Sadly, in 1984, twenty years almost to the month after he had first walked into Camp 4, Sheridan died, having abused and neglected his body for all his adult life. He was only forty-eight.

One might think that only Robbins, Pratt, and a few outsiders inhabited Camp 4 during the late spring of 1964. Denny headed to the Andes and Frost to Europe. Kor was working in Boulder as a bricklayer. Sacherer, entranced with grad school, climbed only on the occasional weekend. Pratt, out of the army about the same time I went in (I hardly saw him for four years), had begun his comeback slowly, typical of this nonimpulsive man. Chouinard, released from his military obligations in June, came to the Valley tentatively, wondering what sort of shape he was in. Harding had been quiet for several years, working in Sacramento and seemingly uninterested in rock climbing.

One day in July, Harding showed up with a photo of a huge unclimbed wall, one Pratt had trouble recognizing. The south face of Mount Watkins, 2,000 feet high, lay hidden in Tenaya Canyon, invisible from the standard viewpoints. Harding quickly talked Pratt into an attempt; a few days later the pair corralled an eager Chouinard in Camp 4.

The five-day climb of Watkins was notable for several reasons. Three of the most famous Valley cragrats of the sixties—Robbins called them "the great triumvirate of Yosemite Little Men"—climbed together only this one time. Also, the trio used no fixed ropes. Robbins later regarded the climb as symbolic of a new age: the permanent end of Yosemite siege climbing. Finally, Pratt wrote a memorable article for the 1965 *American Alpine Journal*. Employing typical Prattonian understatement and wit, he penned a true classic, full of wisdom, drama, eloquence, and humor. One passage, for instance, described the scene when the trio left their car at Mirror Lake for the long approach. Two curious young women "asked if it were true that Yosemite climbers chafe their hands on the granite to enable them to friction up vertical walls. We assured them that the preposterous myth was true. Then, with perfect timing, Harding yanked a bottle of wine and a six-pack out of the car, explaining that these were our rations for four days."

The wine and beer, of course, were consumed within hours; water would be the preferred liquid en route. Within a few days, however, this began to run out. "We were not prepared for the intense, enervating heat," Pratt wrote. "Those mountaineers who scorn Yosemite... would find an interesting education by spending a few days on a long Valley climb in midsummer. Cold temperatures and icy winds are not the only kinds of adverse weather."

The last two days of the route became a trial of thirst and fatigue. Rationing their water, the men struggled to reach the top. Dehydration set in: Pratt could remove a ring that had been locked onto his finger since high school, and Chouinard could drop his pants without unbuttoning them. Harding, who according to Pratt resembled "the classical conception of Satan," now "took on an even more gaunt and sinister appearance." On the fifth day the heroic Harding, hauling loads up the last section, gave all his remaining water to the two lead climbers. Just before dark on July 22, 1964, Chouinard pulled over the top: the ordeal was over. A great climb done by a great team deserved a great article, and Pratt didn't disappoint us. His "South Face of Mount Watkins" is still considered one of the best-ever Valley stories.

Climber on rippled granite, Rixon's Pinnacle (Photo: Steve Roper)

CHAPTER 9

Pilgrims of the Vertical: 1964–1969

> *Down below there were only ten people who even knew we were up here. Even if we were successful, there would be no crowds of hero worshippers, no newspaper reports. Thank goodness American climbing has not yet progressed to that sorry state.*
>
> —Yvon Chouinard, writing about the Muir Wall, 1966

Rock climbing in the Valley slowed down after the enormous burst of energy displayed by Sacherer, Robbins, and others in 1963 and 1964. A period of consolidation soon set in, and the events related in this chapter thus cover a time span of about five years. This is hardly to say that significant climbs didn't take place; quite the contrary. If these events weren't *quite* as earthshaking as those that preceded them, it's only because the routes of the early sixties had ushered in a unique concept of big-wall climbing. Plenty of big walls still beckoned as of 1964.

The phrase "the last great problem" continually springs to life, phoenixlike, in climbing literature, usually just following the solution to a previous "problem." The trouble with this dramatic idea is that the supply is infinite: like "the tallest redwood," when one is gone, another, by definition, takes its place. This was especially true in the Valley during the early days: the progression of "last problems" from the Higher Spire to the Arrow Chimney to the northwest face of Half Dome to the El Cap Nose was relentless. Ed Cooper continued the tradition by saying that the Dihedral Wall was the line "logically left unclimbed to the last." But, of course, the day after this route was finished, climbers looked elsewhere. And where better than the southeast face of El Cap? No one had ever made a serious attempt on the formation's dead-vertical southeast face, the one with which Al Macdonald had been enamored in early 1963. Surely this 2,000-foot-high cliff was the last great problem! And, yes, temporarily, it was.

The wide, slightly concave cliff was known as the North America Wall because of an enormous section of dark rock (the quartz-free granite called diorite) that closely resembled the shape of our continent. Robbins and Glen Denny had gone up on the NA (pronounced "enn-ay") Wall, as it soon became known, in the fall of 1963, reaching a point 600 feet up. Late the next May the pair, accompanied by Tom Frost, made another foray, spending three nights on the wall and reaching Big Sur Ledge, about halfway up. They rappelled, leaving no fixed ropes, for as Robbins said in reporting this reconnaissance, "The era of siege climbing via fixed ropes is past in Yosemite. This era was inaugurated by Warren Harding on the south buttress of El Capitan. After this historic ascent, the siege technique was perhaps misused.... What fun is there in a game when the odds are a hundred to one in your favor?"

Robbins wanted to finish the NA Wall before others got to it. He wrote me in August 1964: "I know that Galen Rowell, stung by our Half Dome coup, is seriously considering trying to cut us out on EC. He is welcome to do so." But Robbins was being disingenuous here, for he knew that Rowell, proprietor of an auto-repair shop in the Bay Area, would likely not have the time to lay siege to the wall—nor did he have the skills needed to do it in one push. Another possible rival, Ed Cooper, had considered soloing the wall, an idea far ahead of its time, but nothing came of this.

In mid-October, Robbins assembled the finest team ever to climb in the Valley, a group of such competence that success was virtually assured. Robbins, Frost, Pratt, and Chouinard—all in their mid- to late twenties by this time—stood at the peak of their careers. Four men, however competent, on such a wall meant a lot of logistical problems, but Robbins had thought this out carefully. And he had a new idea for the hauling. For years, on multiday routes, we all had hauled our huge duffle bags, filled with water, food, clothes, and extra gear, by one of two Stone Age methods. The leader would sometimes pull a fifty-pound bag hand-over-hand up 140 feet; this was lethal on the hands and the back, and the technique worked only when the leader had a ledge of some sort to stand on to brace his legs. The other technique was painful also: the follower simply dangled the fifty-pound haul bag from his waist, a torture that caused cramped legs and bruised hips.

Robbins had suffered as much as anyone, and in the fall of 1963, on the first-ever serious reconnaissance of the NA Wall, he and Glen Denny had tried a clever new strategy using two jumars, gravity, and leg strength. Finishing a pitch, the leader set up bombproof anchors and then ran the haul line over a pulley and attached a jumar (with an aid sling) to the rope that came down from the pulley. He then simply placed a foot into the aid sling, at calf level, and stood up. His weight did the rest: far below, the haul bag rose a foot or two. A reversed jumar on the other side of the pulley kept the bag from slipping back down again. Then, after sliding the first jumar up a foot or two, the leader repeated the process. He could take a break at any time; he could also change legs to spread the work between both. Meanwhile, of course, the follower was jumaring the main climbing rope, taking out the pitons.

Robbins and Denny perfected the technique, and Robbins and Frost had used it on their June 1964 ascent of El Cap's Dihedral Wall. There, on a five-day route done by two climbers, the old methods would have worked. On the NA Wall, however, the new technique would be a necessity, for the quartet planned on a ten-day continuous ascent. Forty man-days worth of supplies meant about 200 pounds of gear, most of which (132 pounds) was water.

If you assemble the four best rockclimbers in the country—probably the world—and stick them onto a steep, unclimbed Yosemite cliff, you may not have too many stories to tell afterward. On October 31, nine and a half days after starting, the quartet had completed the most difficult rock climb ever done. The exposure had been awesome—much more so than on the Nose or the Salathé—and the nailing difficulties unprecedented. Mightily determined to avoid bolts (only thirty-eight were placed), the team performed aid miracles and made wild pendulums and traverses. The diorite, fractured and lacking structural integrity, belied the fact that Yosemite

Tom Frost leads an aid pitch low on the NA Wall. (Photo: Glen Denny)

usually had the best rock on the planet; loose flakes and strange cracks presented special problems. It had been hot at first; stormy later. Still, all such things were expected, and the team simply dealt with them one step at a time. Just another big climb. Chouinard, who had never climbed El Cap, naturally did well, leading some of the wildest aid pitches.

Robbins wrote me a few weeks later: "The best way to sum it up is to say that there were at least a dozen pitches which on almost any other climb would be the crux pitch. This is the greatest climb I have done, but the Salathé Wall is the best.... Incidentally, Cooper didn't have a chance to do it solo. He would have had to place between 200 and 300 bolts."

Robbins wrote a lengthy piece about the NA Wall for the 1965 *American Alpine Journal,* trying hard to find the meaning of his achievement. Never content simply to report just the raw details of a climb, Robbins prided himself on his philosophical musings, and in this article he left himself open for criticism. Many in Camp 4 hooted when they read such sentences as: "Perhaps if we can learn to face the dangers of the mountains with equanimity, we can also learn to face with a calm spirit the chilling specter of inevitable death." And: "If one could only find meaning to make these hard truths of insignificance and omnipresent death acceptable. Where to find this meaning? Again the search... and we climb on." A few years later, more relaxed about his writing style, Robbins poked fun at himself, beginning an article: "Some people are bothered by thoughts of decay and death. Not me. Rather, I am obsessed."

Robbins worked hard at his writing, getting more polished and talented with each year. (He recently told me that he "sought to write prose worthy of far more worthy predecessors, never thinking I succeeded.") Yet it was hard to pardon him for some of his earlier prose, and a certain cruelness toward him persisted for years. Joe Kelsey, a sardonic climber from the East Coast, once parodied the NA Wall piece—and other Robbins prose—in "The Oceania Wall," a *Summit* article. As Robbins and Ed Cooper (here called Mr. Cask) have a slapstick fight up on a wall, Robbins wonders about the meaning of it all: "As I removed [Cask's] hammer from its holster...I realized that mankind's fate is to have to philosophize about such trivia. If one could only find meaning to make these hard truths of insignificance and the omnipresent Mr. Cask acceptable. Where to find this meandering? Again the search...."

The NA Wall ascent seems to have deeply affected the four climbers; it was as if their entire Valley careers had been geared for this one crowning climb. Frost never again did a major Valley first ascent and soon faded from the scene, going into a ten-year partnership with Chouinard Equipment; climbing often in Peru, the Himalaya, and Alaska; and spending more time with his wife, Dorene, and his newfound religion, Mormonism. Pratt began concentrating on short, superdifficult crack climbs, never again making a first ascent of a Grade VI, though he climbed El Cap several more times by various routes. Robbins lay low temporarily, making only one major Valley first ascent during the next four years. Chouinard, too, soon faded from the scene, to build his business and take up ice climbing; he did only one first ascent of note in the remaining years of his Valley career. But this climb was a big one and he struck soon, capitalizing on the fact that only five routes lay on the two great El Cap faces—plenty of room for another.

The June 1965 first ascent of the Muir Wall by Chouinard and TM Herbert is significant for at least three reasons. Most dramatically, it was the first El Cap route to be done without fixed ropes by a team of two. This was a daring move, for it meant that both men would be working fifteen hours a day, leading, hauling, or cleaning. Bigger teams meant more gear, yes, but also much more rest. For instance, on the NA Wall, the progress of the climbing team was sometimes so slow that the hauling team had nothing to do for an entire day. Big-wall climbing was extremely tiring, what with all the hammering of pitons. One's hands would throb at the end of the day, and barked knuckles would sting all night. A day's rest would cure the former condition and alleviate the latter. One also got a mental rest on a hauling day: let the other blokes do the real work that day!

Second, the new climb also set a precedent for future El Cap routes, for it was the first one to cross an existing route, in this case the Salathé Wall. Since the latter route had wandered across a third of the southwest face—the climbers had searched for, and found, the most bolt-free line—it was inevitable that more direct routes would be done and that they would have to cross the Salathé. The Muir Wall climb set the stage for the dozens of crossed routes to come.

Finally, this was the first El Cap climb ever done without a lengthy reconnaissance beforehand. Two men simply walked up to an unknown wall and climbed to the top. "It is the unknown that frightens brave men," Chouinard wrote later. And the Muir Wall was totally unknown. (The NA Wall, for example, had been explored up to 600 feet before the eventual success, and half the total number of bolts were placed on the reconnaissances, a great saving of time and energy.)

Though he had climbed many of the standard routes in the Valley by 1965, Herbert had not yet been a major player. In his six years of Valley climbing he had done just one significant first ascent: the Chouinard-Herbert route on Sentinel. He preferred shorter routes, especially hard crack climbs, for one thing. For another, he had returned to college a few years earlier and had married recently, which usually meant less climbing. Basically a weekender by 1965, he rarely got into decent enough shape for the big walls, though he was fully capable of this style of climbing—as he soon proved.

Chouinard and Herbert roped up at dawn on June 14, 1965. For the first few days the weather was oppressively hot and their 100 pounds of gear seemed like 200. The hauling was often diagonal, which meant espe-cially frustrating work. "Many a terse word was exchanged," reported Chouinard. On day three, as the fickle weather turned to rain, the duo crossed the Salathé Wall at Mammoth Terraces, a familiar place to both men: each had earlier failed on the Salathé not far above this point.

The fourth bivouac was a nightmare of rain and chill. Herbert became near-hypothermic, and when he spoke he "sounded almost delirious," according to his partner. "We were despondent and for the moment had lost the vision and our courage. Yet we kept any thoughts of retreat to ourselves."

Of the next four days, Chouinard remembers little. The storm had departed, but the two men were tired and chilled. "The artificial climbing blends into the free. The corners, dihedrals, jam-cracks, bulges, are all indistinguishable parts of the great, overhanging wall. The pitches never end...." Earlier in his article in the 1966 *American Alpine Journal*, Chouinard had talked about John Muir and his "profound mystical expe-riences." These, he said, could be explained sometimes by lack of food. Now, high on the wall, Chouinard himself, exhausted and hungry, began to drift into another world. "Nothing felt strange about our vertical world. With the more receptive senses we now appreciated everything around us. Each individual crystal in the granite stood out in bold relief.... For the first time we noticed tiny bugs that were all over the walls, so tiny they were barely noticeable. While belaying, I stared at one for 15 minutes, watching him move and admiring his brilliant red color.... How could one ever be bored with so many good things to see and feel! This unity with our joyous surroundings, this ultra-penetrating perception gave us a feel-ing of contentment that we had not had for years."

Most climbers have occasional days when everything goes so perfectly that nothing interferes with the experience: one's focus is so intense, so one-track, that the hours go by as if they were minutes. The sun goes down and one is stunned by the sight, thinking it noontime. Herbert had such a day near the top. "TM is normally a fairly conservative climber," Chouinard wrote, "but now he was climbing brilliantly. He attacked the most difficult pitch of the climb, an overhanging series of loose flakes, with absolute confidence; he placed pitons behind the gigantic loose blocks that could break off at any moment, never hesitating and never doubting his ability."

Low on food, water, and bolts, the pair struggled to reach the summit. Finally, in the dark, on their eighth day on the wall, they pulled over the summit overhangs, having placed thirty bolts—all but four of their supply.

-- ∎ --

Chouinard's phrase about Herbert's "absolute confidence" could have been said about himself, of course, as well as many other Valley climbers. After Pratt and Sacherer's climbs, the NA Wall, and the Muir Wall, we knew that 5.10 cracks could be climbed and that the big walls could be tamed. We had rarely used the word "impossible," but now even the concept vanished. This is hardly to say that we all jumped on the cracks and walls with new vigor. But we didn't fear the unknown ever again, at least the "big" unknown. The "little" unknowns, of course, remained: Could we protect that off-width up there? Was that wall really blank—or was there a hairline crack?

Layton Kor exemplified this new attitude in the late spring and early summer of 1965. He romped up dozens of routes, including, with Pratt, the face of the Higher Spire and Arches Direct, those two incredible, unrepeated climbs of Robbins. Kor had decided to treat such routes simply as normal difficult climbs, not mythological terrors. He also made ascents of rarely done climbs, such as the north face of Middle Cathedral Rock, the Washington Column's east face, and the Leaning Tower. To top off his campaign he made four first ascents. This six-week eruption of energy, unprecedented in Valley history, was his last such burst. Kor left the Valley in July 1965 and went to Europe the following February to became involved in the winter ascent of the Eiger Direct with his good friend, the noted American mountaineer John Harlin. For weeks, they (and others) struggled mightily to get up this route, but a fixed rope broke high on the route and Harlin fell to his death. Kor was devastated, and although he made the fourth ascent of the Salathé Wall with Galen Rowell in 1967, he soon thereafter gave up climbing.

Others thrived in Camp 4 this spring and summer. Jim Bridwell climbed with friends such as Mark Klemens, brothers Dave and Phil Bircheff, and other youths who kept to themselves, remaining in the background. While these fellows climbed brilliantly on occasion, they belonged to a younger generation, one we "elders," approaching twenty-five, found vulgar and arrogant—just as previous generations had found us! Two letters I received in 1965 demonstrate this subtle contempt. Eric Beck referred offhandedly to "Bridwell and his boys." Mild-mannered Pratt wrote that "Bridwell and his puppets" were climbing "off and on." Bridwell's day would come, but not for a few more years. (He later became not only a Valley legend but also a world-renowned mountaineer, with ultra-bold ascents in Alaska and South America.)

Jeff Foott had become a ranger, and it was strange to see him in uniform and driving a quiet, workable car, so unlike ours. He explained climbing to other rangers and occasionally gave us government steaks that were earmarked for bearbait (by this time the rangers were luring "bad" bears into metal traps and transporting them to the highcountry).

Joe Faint, Chuck Ostin, Gary Colliver, and Chris Jones were also familiar faces in the Valley during this time. Faint was an anomaly in the climbing world: he grew up not in a noted mountain center such as Seattle, Boulder, or the Bay Area, but in West Virginia. Often climbing with Pratt, Chouinard, Chris Fredericks, or Galen Rowell, he stuck around the

Jim Bridwell, 1965 (Photo: Glen Denny)

Valley for about six years, fishing when he wasn't climbing. A quiet and modest man, Faint was good at climbing and expert at fly-fishing.

Chuck Ostin was one of the strangest climbers ever to inhabit Camp 4. Arriving in a white Mercedes (by a factor of ten the most luxurious car in our circle), he would stay in the Valley for a month at a time and then disappear for a year and a half. Then he'd show up on a weekend with several fresh-faced women from Mills College. Then he wouldn't be seen again for months. We all thought he worked for the CIA, since he disappeared so often and seemed to be so well informed on events in Cuba and other outposts. Ultra-polite but also ultra-distant, Ostin was an enigma: we had no idea where he lived or what he did. When pressed, he would mutter something about being an engineer "down south." Though he climbed quite well, he was hardly a natural, and his routefinding skills were minimal. Climbing with him was always an adventure, one often involving pitch-dark descents. One of Ostin's earliest climbs was the Steck-Salathé on Sentinel, which he did in 1961 with Chuck Pratt. Pratt once told me about an incident on this ascent: "I'd led an easy chimney pitch, but Ostin was coming up real slowly. Then the rope stopped moving altogether. I waited about five minutes, yelled a few times, but nothing happened. I couldn't see him, so I tied off the rope and slithered down a few feet to look down into the chimney. There he was, fifty feet below me, wedged tightly into chimney position, scribbling in a little notebook. He was writing a foot-by-foot route description!"

Gary Colliver had been around a long time, doing journeyman climbs for a few years and then graduating to the Nose and the west face of Sentinel, both done in 1965. Though he helped establish six minor new routes, his culminating moment came in 1969, when he climbed the Salathé Wall— the eighth ascent—with Jones.

Chris Jones was an expatriate Englishman, smart and witty. He did many of the traditional big Valley climbs, such as Half Dome and Sentinel; his Valley career culminated in 1969, along with Colliver's, on the Salathé Wall. Jones, fascinated by the history of climbing, went on to write, in the mid-1970s, *Climbing in North America,* the definitive work on the subject.

—— ■ ——

Oddly, the Muir Wall climb was the only Grade VI established in 1965— and not for two full years would another be done. Climbers were turning their attention to free-climbing old aid routes, though many of these were minor, involving the elimination of just a few pitons. One startling exception stood out, however, and it turned out to be one of the last exploits of Frank Sacherer. He and Eric Beck ran up the direct north buttress of Middle Cathedral in one long day, without resorting to aid. This feat shocked me when I heard of it, for Chouinard and I had used an enormous amount of aid on the first ascent, just three years earlier. How, I wondered, could anyone have eliminated every single aid point? The answer was simple: Sacherer and Beck were excellent climbers, better than we were, though admittedly they had an advantage in that the route was a known entity.

Around the same time, Beck and Sacherer accomplished an even more impressive feat, the first-ever one-day ascent of a Yosemite Grade VI. Days after they roared up the west face of Sentinel in fourteen hours, Beck wrote me: "This is the most audacious and spectacularly successful coup I have pulled off. We took one rope, one quart of water, and one can of fruit cocktail.... The first Dogleg Pitch is quite hard; the second is the easiest pitch of the climb. Sacherer led it with no pegs." (This route—as well as some other early big climbs mentioned in this book—was later downgraded to a Grade V by consensus.)

Another developing trend in 1965 concerned difficult crack climbing. Pratt stood head and shoulders above anyone else in this department, establishing routes such as Entrance Exam, Chingando, Twilight Zone, and the left side of the Slack. All these routes involved difficult, off-width jamcracks—and all were either 5.9 or 5.10. It was Pratt's biggest year, with ten first ascents recorded. Chris Fredericks accompanied Pratt on four of these routes; it was his finest year also: he bagged eleven first ascents.

One of the more interesting climbs of the mid-sixties was the first ascent of the Snake Dike, on the southwest face of Half Dome. One Fourth of July weekend, wishing to escape the crowds in the Valley, Beck, Fredericks, and Jim Bridwell hiked up to the dome to look for another route on the broad southwest face. After all, the face was fairly low-angle, and the year before had seen the first free ascent of Salathé's route. Surely another route could be found. To the trio's amazement, they discovered an easy climb that followed a serpentine dike for hundreds of feet. The men encountered one section of 5.7, but much of the climbing was even easier, and they managed the climb in half a day. What makes this climb significant, however, concerns the bolts. Good climbers can romp up 5.6 without worrying much about protection, and the trio did just that. Since the rock was essentially crackless, this meant long runouts between belay spots. Only at these small belay knobs (the route is essentially ledgeless) did the leader set a bolt. When they got to the top, the threesome immediately realized they'd screwed up. Here was a perfect beginners' climb, with marvelous climbing in a prime location. It would obviously become a classic, yet it had no protection and inadequate belay anchors, a poor prospect for beginners. For this reason no one climbed the route again during the remainder of the summer. After I got out of the army, in November 1965, I heard about this fine unprotected route and asked the first ascenders if they'd mind if I went up and stuck bolts in key places. They agreed and I did the climb in 1966, adding four bolts, mainly at belay stations. This was undoubtedly the first time bolts were added to a Valley route with the express permission of the first ascenders. The Snake Dike became instantly popular, and it has now been done thousands of times.

Though no one thought much about the Snake Dike retrofit, bolts were still controversial in the Valley. Bob Kamps wrote a short article in *Summit* about bolt ethics in which he argued for mutual respect: don't place bolts on an established route—but don't remove any either. He spoke of competition and bolt chopping: "It is no longer the bolt that is being removed. It is the person that placed the bolt that is being 'removed'."

A few months later Tom Higgins wrote a long, thoughtful letter to the same magazine. A prophetic and highly intelligent young man, Higgins talked about the ethics of using bolt guns, guide services, and hauling pulleys. He spoke about recent ads in *Summit* that promised "a quick and safe way to maximum adventure." Higgins was one of the first climbers to consider deeply such issues. And he wasn't just some armchair critic: he was already known as one of Southern California's best climbers, a disciple of Kamps. I first heard of Higgins in a letter from Mark Powell: "Higgins is really good, the only one [now at Tahquitz] with the potential to be a great Yosemite climber.... If he has the drive and is not sidetracked by bourgeois attractions, he is a comer and Southern California's first real contribution to the climbing fraternity in years." Higgins later became a star indeed, though he did his best climbs in Tuolumne Meadows, not the

Valley. He never lost his interest in trying to keep climbing "pure" and today still discusses such issues as power drills and preplacing bolts on rappel.

In his role as *Summit*'s rock-climbing editor, Robbins spoke out near the end of 1965: "If we respect the established nature of routes, and refrain from bolt chopping and placing, there will be plenty of climbs for all shades of abilities and tastes—and much less bitterness." Not everyone was enamored of these statements and articles on bolt ethics. A month later, after I had queried *Summit* about a possible article, Helen Kilness, the magazine's co-editor, advised me to go ahead and write, "but, please, not on ethics! I'm afraid we're going to lose all our subscribers if we have anymore of that."

Even though I had chopped bolts in the past, I now took Robbins's phrase "respect the established nature of routes" to heart. When Allen Steck, Dick Long, and I made the third ascent of the Salathé Wall in 1966, I insisted we take no bolts with us. We struggled mightily with difficult pin placements, but we got up. This was my bravest and noblest act as a rockclimber. Later parties, not up to the challenge, desecrated the route with dozens of superfluous bolts, a shameful rape of a beautiful climb.

Big-wall climbing temporarily peaked with the ascents of the North America Wall and the Muir Wall: no more first ascents on El Cap's two major faces were done during the rest of the sixties. At the other end of the spectrum, the free-climbing renaissance begun by Sacherer and Pratt continued at a lesser pace, though some excellent new routes were accomplished free on the first ascent. But the day of "first free ascents" was over: nothing significant was accomplished during the rest of the decade. Two exceptions stood out, since for a few years they were the only 5.11 climbs in the Valley. Serenity Crack, over by the Arches, was freed in 1967 by Tom Higgins and Chris Jones. The normal route on the Slack, at the base of El Cap, involved a short, extremely fierce crack, and this was done without aid, also in 1967, by Pat Ament and Larry Dalke, two superb Colorado climbers. (Both these routes were downgraded in George Meyers's 1976 guidebook, the former to 5.10d and the latter to 5.10c. This subclassification of the upper ratings was invented in the early 1970s by Jim Bridwell. Serenity Crack, according to this new rating system, was the hardest Valley free climb done during the 1960s.)

The late sixties, then, was mostly a period of consolidation, a place for the "pilgrims of the vertical," as Robbins called the Camp 4 climbers, to repeat the "standard" big walls. These walls became less fearful as the second-level tier of climbers managed to get up them. I well remember that in 1966, after Steck, Long, and I got up the Salathé Wall, spending five and a half days making the "first non-Robbins ascent," the feeling of relief in Camp 4 among such people as Beck, Jones, and Colliver was almost palpable. We were good climbers, but certainly not supermen. If we could do it, many others could also. And they did. The big walls saw an enormous amount of traffic between 1966 and 1969: for instance, the Nose was done seventeen times in those four seasons; the north face of Sentinel, sixteen; the west face of Sentinel, ten; and the Salathé Wall, eight.

The pioneers of the early sixties—Robbins, Pratt, Frost, Chouinard, Sacherer, and Kor—still visited the Valley and still did many climbs. The first-ascent lists of all these men tapered off radically, however: the six climbers had done 83 percent of their combined first ascents (an astonishing 171 routes, many, of course, done with one another) by the end of 1966.

These six men didn't go off to rest homes, certainly, but only Pratt and Robbins remained truly active. Pratt did several more El Cap walls and climbed his favorite route, the Steck-Salathé, an astounding nine times in his career. Robbins began managing his father-in-law's paint store in the Central Valley town of Modesto and thus had less time for climbing. In June 1967, however, he made time for yet another El Cap route.

The west face of El Cap is, to use Robbins's phrase, the "plain Jane" face of the monolith; the two main walls—the southwest face and the southeast face—garner all the attention and glory. Hidden around the corner from the southwest face, and easily ignored from the standard Valley viewpoints, the west face is apparently featureless, apparently not too steep. I use "apparently" with the embarrassing consciousness that I have never truly laid eyes on it, let alone my hand. Few have. Robbins thought he should have a look, and, once he did, he thought he saw a route he liked. He went up with TM Herbert and spent four days (and a few hours on their fifth day) wandering back and forth, up and down, and across the slabby expanse. It was a thrilling and adventurous climb, done with but one bolt. "We recommend it," Robbins wrote, "and hope that others will enjoy it as much as we."

Others took the place of the more noted climbers, and foremost among these newcomers was the inimitable team of Jim Madsen and Kim Schmitz. Arriving from the Pacific Northwest in 1966, the two nineteen-year-olds soon gave lie to the feeling many of us had that climbers from up north were far better on snow than on rock. Madsen, an engineering student and football player at the University of Washington, reminded us instantly of Layton Kor, for he was tall, muscular, and constantly in motion. He climbed just about as well as Kor, too, and moved even faster than the Coloradan, if that were possible. Schmitz, shorter and stockier, was a handsome, blue-eyed fellow sporting a gargantuan smile. Both young men were strong and eager, and in September 1966 they made their first big Valley climb together, the third ascent of the Mozart Wall, the Robbins-Frost route on Sentinel. The pair came to our attention the next spring (June 1967)

Kim Schmitz, 1967 (Photo: Steve Roper)

when they ran up the Nose in three days, a commendable time for relatively inexperienced big-wall men.

Neither Madsen nor Schmitz did significant first ascents; two steep, hard, ugly routes on the Washington Column proved to be their finest efforts in this genre. Instead, they were content to repeat the El Cap routes in rapid style. Exceedingly rapid. Their most splendid feat together came in the spring of 1968, when they raced up the Dihedral Wall in two and a half days, a deed that left the Camp 4 regulars speechless. Robbins wrote that "attitudes toward El Capitan will never be the same." Madsen, on a roll that year, even wore out Schmitz. He made the fifth ascent of the Salathé Wall with Loyd Price, a newcomer who worked full-time in the Valley, and then, in August, became the first person ever to climb the Nose twice, when he did it with Coloradan Mike Covington, reaching the top in the early afternoon of their third day, yet another speed record.

Many of these, and other, fleet El Cap ascents were not *quite* as fast as claimed. Robbins put it bluntly: "Most of [these] ascents involved fixing two or three pitches the day before the climb started, giving rise to questions of style and, to some extent, candor. For one thing, it is easier to spread twenty hours of climbing over three days than over two. And some

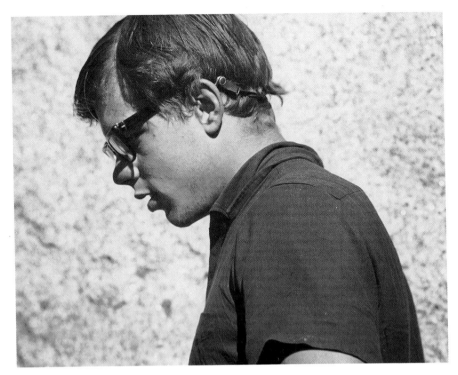

Jim Madsen, 1967 (Photo: Steve Roper)

climbers are extremely liberal in their interpretation of a 'half day': it has a tendency to run up to 5 or 6 P.M." Thus, we'll never know for certain the true times taken on these superb feats.

Madsen was an impulsive fellow, one not given to reflection and calmness. This proved fatal. In mid-October 1968, after a huge storm hit the Valley, Chuck Pratt and Chris Fredericks, high on the Dihedral Wall, holed up in a deep slot, invisible from the ground, to wait out the weather. Madsen, worried that the pair had been immobilized by hypothermia, organized a rescue party as the storm cleared. After he, Schmitz, Price, and several rangers were lifted by helicopter to the top of El Cap, Madsen rappelled over the edge with a forty-five-pound load of ropes and other gear. The men above shortly heard an anguished cry: "Oh, shit!" Then silence. Madsen had fallen 2,500 feet to his death. He had tied a knot in the end of his rope, thinking this would jam into his carabiner-brake setup and hold him while he set up the next rappel. But the knot was too small and slipped through the carabiners.

Pratt and Fredericks, chilled but mobile, continued upward, having heard something big whistle past shortly after sunrise. Soon they discovered signs that a mammal had plummeted down the wall; they hoped that it had been a deer, though when they found shattered eyeglasses on a ledge they knew the worst. Only when they reached the rim did they learn that their friend Madsen had died trying to help them. It was a sad day indeed. Robbins wrote later: "Had [Madsen] lived and climbed, he doubtless would have written an important chapter in the history of American mountaineering, and probably of world mountaineering."

Other accidents marred the late 1960s. An experienced climber from the Stanford Alpine Club named Ernie Milburn was rappelling from a route on the Glacier Point Apron in June 1968 when the anchor sling, frayed by repeated rope pull-downs and weakened by the sunlight, simply broke. He fell 700 feet to his death. All four deaths in the Valley during the 1960s—Irving Smith, Jim Baldwin, Ernie Milburn, and Jim Madsen—involved rappelling, theoretically the safest and most exhilarating part of climbing. (A superstitious climber would do well to avoid rappelling on the nineteenth or twentieth of a month; three of the four deaths occurred on one of those two dates.)

Five other accidents during the mid- and late sixties turned out to be less tragic. A Berkeley climber named Pete Spoecker shattered his leg high on the Steck-Salathé and had to be winched off. This rescue, on June 24, 1965, was the Valley's first major one, and it helped heal some of the age-old strife between climbers and rangers. Four climbers—Glen Denny, John Evans, Jeff Foott, and Chris Fredericks—played a huge role in setting up the rescue. The Camp 4 bums were good for something, it seemed, and from this point onward climbers played a major role in technical rescues.

The other four accidents were serious ones also. Eric Beck badly dislocated his shoulder midway up the south face of Mount Watkins, and he and his partner, Dick Erb, endured an epic retreat, totally by themselves, down the overhanging and diagonal route. "Worst day of my life," Beck told us later. Tom Gerughty, attempting the Nose, was cleaning a diagonal pitch when both jumars somehow became unclipped from the rope. Luckily, he had tied in to the rope's end and fell but 100 feet, badly burning his hands on the rope while attempting to stop. Jim Stanton, one of Bridwell's "boys," took a 180-foot fall on Higher Cathedral Rock, pulling two protection pitons, but since he didn't hit anything major he escaped with only a broken kneecap. I recall that he didn't climb much after this, however. Jim McCarthy, the celebrated eastern climber, broke his arm 700 feet up on the Nose when an aid piton popped. McCarthy, not wishing to overdrive his pitons (a cardinal sin in the Valley), had delicately placed ten aid pitons prior to his accident. Nine zippered during the course of his 100-foot fall.

Second only to Madsen and Schmitz as a remarkable new team were Don Lauria and Dennis Hennek, Southern Californians honed on the routes at Tahquitz. By no means as speedy as Madsen and Schmitz, this pair

Don Lauria, 1968 (Photo: Royal Robbins / Ascent Collection)

nevertheless thrived on big walls; their first major climb together was the third ascent of the Dihedral Wall in September 1967, a five-day effort. In addition to being a rock-solid climber, Lauria proved to be one of the wittiest writers of this era. He described the Dihedral climb as entailing "awkward climbing, difficult piton placement, hanging belays, heavy hauling, hammock bivouacs, scraped knuckles, numb feet, coughing, cramping, torturous sun, threatening clouds, never enough water, rurps, and skyhooks—all the ingredients of a great Yosemite adventure."

I first met Lauria at a campsite below the east side of Half Dome in June 1966; the next day he and new Tahquitz star Mike Cohen were going to do the regular northwest face route, while Pratt and I were going to try the direct northwest face, which had never been repeated. Lauria wrote a hilarious article in *Summit* describing, among many other events, a dawn conversation. Calling Pratt and me, respectively, "Mutt" and "Jeff" so as not to embarrass us in print, he wrote: "I was taken aback when Mutt rolled over in his sleeping bag, and in the affected tone of a cultured dowager, uttered the words every weekend climber wishes he could utter. 'Jeff,' he said, 'we should not feel that we are under any obligation to climb today.' They both convulsed in hysterical laughter." Pratt and I, from our warm sleeping bags, wished Lauria and Cohen good luck as they departed. We were still in our bags, soaking up the sun, when they returned a few hours later, having failed after one pitch.

Lauria later got up the Half Dome route; he was a determined climber. And a year later he and Hennek made the second ascent of the North America Wall in five days.

Hennek and Lauria didn't always climb together. Hennek and Chouinard made the tenth ascent of the Nose in 1967; two years later Hennek made the third ascent of the Muir Wall with Pratt. Thus, in a twenty-four-month span he climbed El Cap four times. Lauria also had a love affair with El Cap: in fifteen months he did it three times.

Neither man—as was the case with Madsen and Schmitz—made significant first ascents in the Valley, a possible indication that the Valley was temporarily "climbed out." The most obvious lines on the big cliffs had been done; it seemed that enormous numbers of bolts would be needed on

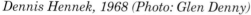

Dennis Hennek, 1968 (Photo: Glen Denny)

the blank walls that adjoined the established routes. No one was yet willing to drill up a devious-looking route.

A fine Southern California climber named Ken Boche (pronounced Booie) got around this dilemma by avoiding the big walls in favor of Glacier Point Apron, where he put up eight new routes, almost all 5.9 and every last one of the small-hold variety. Only fifty degrees in steepness, the Apron is a featureless ocean of granite where one can wander almost at will. Apron climbing requires several talents, ones I personally never mastered. The first prerequisite for the leader of a successful first ascent is to visualize a route on the sea of granite, one that has some sort of finite end, usually a tiny ledge. The plan: start somewhere below this ledge—and end up on it. In between, wander. The leader must remain calm far above the protection, intellectually knowing that even a long fall won't matter much, so smooth is the slope. Routefinding skills are crucial. The way may be clear for thirty feet, but then what? Will this line of holds continue? Will a traverse over to that flake be possible? Where's the next big resting knob? Finally, one must be patient: bolts are often the only form of protection, and they are not easy to put in while standing with cramping feet on a tiny rounded knob.

Boche was a master of this type of small-hold climbing, as were Bill Amborn, Jeff Foott, Joe McKeown, Bob Kamps, and Tom Higgins. Finesse and courage are the operative words for climbing on the Apron. One needs excellent balance, strong toes and ankles, and a will to go on into unknown territory. The leader knows instinctively whether a foot should be placed flat against the rock—a friction hold—or whether it should edge on microflakes or crystals. Apron climbing was indeed a special activity during the sixties, as far removed from the big walls and the crack climbs as the moon.

The type of shoes worn had an effect on Apron climbing also. The climbers of the early sixties had mostly worn either Zillertals or the similar Kronhofers, soft European klettershoes that were comfortable but a little too flexible for standing on narrow edges. By 1965 many Valley climbers wore Spiders, a much sturdier shoe that was good for edging and standing in aid slings, but not so good for frictioning. Robbins helped design an even stiffer shoe in late 1967; this "blue suede shoe," made in France, was excellent for jamcracks, aid climbing, and edging, but, once again, not as nice for friction climbing. Finally, around the same time, an excellent all-round shoe came onto the scene. Made in France, but originally designed by an Englishman named Ellis Brigham, the EB was the first popular climbing shoe to have a smooth sole, a boon to friction climbers. Like the RR, as the Robbins shoe was known, the EB had a rubber rand around its sides and heel, and this made jamcracks a little easier, for the sides of the shoe adhered somewhat to the crack. The EB quickly gained acceptance and became virtually the only shoe used during the 1970s.

As word of the startling Valley climbs and techniques began to spread around the globe, foreigners began visiting Yosemite. The first ever to climb a hard Yosemite route was the well-known Catalán climber José-Manuel Anglada, who, with Robbins and Herbert, climbed the east buttress of El Cap in 1964. (Anglada, watching Robbins and Herbert ingesting huge hunks of cheap salami on this climb, was disgusted. "You guys are true barbarians," he informed them.)

The British were not long in arriving. Two Scots, Jock Lang and Eric Rayson, became the first non-Americans ever to climb a Grade VI Valley route when they did the northwest face of Half Dome with American Dave Dornan in 1965. Robbins, hearing this story, wrote early in 1966 that "It won't be long before [foreigners] will be climbing El Cap." (El Cap's east buttress, done in 1964 by Anglada, has never been considered a true "El Cap route," lying as it does far to the side of the main wall.) It wasn't long at all: Chamonix guides André Gaunt and Jacques Dupont had taught skiing in Yosemite during the winter of 1965–66 and by April came up with the idea of doing the Nose. We snickered behind their backs, since they didn't exactly set the Valley on fire during their brief training regimen before the climb. Yet we underestimated their enthusiasm and drive: they made the fifth ascent in the relatively long time of six days, facing storms in the middle and thirst at the end.

Robbins visited Great Britain in May 1966 and climbed with some of the famous hard men, notably Joe Brown and Tom Patey. He wrote me a month later that "Rockclimbing is a man's sport in England, somewhat like bullfighting." He invited every climber he met to Yosemite, and that fall a few showed up. In October, Mike Kosterlitz climbed one of the Valley testpieces, the west face of Sentinel. Shortly afterward, an English legend showed up in Camp 4. Don Whillans (along with Brown) had been admired from afar by Camp 4 climbers since the early sixties; he was the ultimate British cragsman, author of severe routes on local gritstone outcrops and in the Alps. Short, grumpy, acerbic, Whillans drank, smoked, partied, and climbed—in about that order. But in October he put aside his decadent habits long enough to climb the northwest face of Half Dome with Jim Bridwell and two English comrades. Best known as a crack specialist, he later was shown the various testpieces and fulfilled our image of him: he had little trouble with the Crack of Doom and the Steck-Salathé. Pratt wrote a short note about the British visit for the 1967 *American Alpine Journal:* "The climbing techniques required in Yosemite presented no problem to the British, whose talent and versatility place them at the pinnacle of the sport."

Following Whillans's visit, Pratt told Robbins, "The era of the supremacy of Yosemite climbers has ended." And, in fact, foreign climbers, mostly from the British Isles, flocked to the Valley in the next few years. Dave Bathgate and Ian Howell climbed the face of Half Dome shortly after the Whillans-Bridwell ascent, thus making the first all-foreign ascent.

Mick Burke (later to die near the summit of Everest) climbed the Nose with Rob Wood in June 1968, capturing a grand prize: the first all-British ascent of an El Cap route.

Another English climber, later to become a prominent writer, visited the Valley in August 1968. Ed Drummond, a self-assured fellow, had written Robbins about his grandiose plans for the Valley, which included the North America Wall, as yet unrepeated. Robbins replied, "The brimming self-confidence shown in your letters and elsewhere borders on audacity, and engenders in me irritation." Though Drummond was humiliated by El Cap, he managed to get up the Lost Arrow Chimney—barely. He wrote later, with a graphic touch, "My puffed and bloody knees, ripe from the night, softly exploded in crimson berries on my dirty trouserless legs."

Rounding out the decade, the most famous Scottish climber of the era, Dougal Haston, made the fourth ascent of the south face of Mount Watkins, with American Rick Sylvester, in the spring of 1969.

Canadians were also active in the late sixties. Neil Bennett and Gordon Smaill climbed the Nose in June 1969 for the first all-Canadian ascent. A few months later, Smaill, with Seattle climber Al Givler, did the Salathé Wall. "We marvelled at the free climbing," wrote Smaill later. "Friction, boulder moves, jams and chimneys, but way up there."

As climbing became more and more popular, our thoughts occasionally turned to making money from our sport. Most climbers of the sixties scorned publicity and commercialism, though, hypocritically, we were tempted by "easy money" at times. The Sierra Club once arranged, by mail, for me to guide Joyce Dunsheath, a well-known British mountaineer, up a Tuolumne peak. I had visions of my aristocratic patroness handing me a hundred-dollar bill, even though nothing had been arranged in advance, since we were both too genteel to discuss something as crude as cash. At the end of a long, long day, Dunsheath led me to the rustic Tuolumne café and said, "Steve, that was wonderful; let me buy you a hamburger." That, it turned out, was my fee.

Some of us thought that we might get a free meal, or a few dollars, from showing slides or movies while traveling. My first—and last—effort at this gambit took place in 1967. Returning from a trip to the desert, Pratt and I had been asked by a friend of mine to show movies and slides to two Utah climbing clubs. Pratt's offering was twofold: some North America Wall slides from the first ascent and a movie of a 1964 Sentinel west face climb, filmed mostly by Tom Frost. My offering was a homemade movie, enlivened with dramatic moments, filmed on the Salathé Wall by Steck, Long, and myself in 1966. The two movies were the finest American rock-climbing movies yet made, mainly because they were the only two. My diary shows the following entry for April 14, 1967: "To Provo to show films. Assholes got wrong projector for my film. Pratt shows his, makes

$14. Dejected." The next day we moved up to Salt Lake City: "Seminar at U. of Utah Student Union. Make $14 each. Show NA Wall slides and show off our 'sophisticated equipment.' Show movies again at Student Union. Make $16 each! 140 people." We escaped to the Valley shortly thereafter.

■

Several significant climbs of the mid- and late 1960s cannot be easily categorized, for they were neither first ascents nor typical climbs of the day. In May 1966 Jeff Foott and I managed to climb the regular northwest face route of Half Dome without a bivouac, the longest climbing day of my life. From the first glimmer of daylight to its last hint, we toiled up the twenty-four pitches, placing and removing about 250 pitons. Eric Beck soon came up with another Half Dome first: in July he spent two and a half days alone on the same route.

One of the more dramatic incidents of the time also took place on Half Dome, on the "unknown" back side, the south face. By the fall of 1968 Warren Harding had been relatively quiet for four years; his only major first ascent since Watkins had been on the outside face of the Lost Arrow, from the base; this fine climb, done in excellent style, was accomplished in June 1968 with Pat Callis. Neither had Galen Rowell climbed big new routes in the previous few years, concentrating, as many did, on repeating some of the fierce crack problems for which the Valley was so noted. Harding, however, had spotted a potential route on the enormous, rounded south face of Half Dome, and he convinced Rowell to try it. This route proved to be quite controversial; Harding's stock once again went down a notch in the opinion of many climbers. Typically, the word "bolt" figures in the story. "We decided," Rowell wrote later, "that a route was possible with no more than twenty-five percent bolting." This cavalier figure shocked us: the Salathé Wall, for example, had been about 2 percent bolted; the direct northwest face of Half Dome had been about 4 percent bolted. If this 25 percent figure was acceptable, that could mean a profusion of contrived new routes on El Cap, for instance. Still, we all felt that climbing had no rules. Harding was a renegade, and there wasn't much to say—or do. Luckily he had few imitators.

In early November 1968, when Harding and Rowell were two-thirds of the way up the face, a monstrous storm moved in, plastering the face with snow. Retreat was impossible, and the men quickly became hypothermic. After two days and nights of suffering, the desperate pair radioed for help. As Harding and Rowell prepared for their seventh night on the wall, a helicopter deposited a rescue team on the summit, and Robbins rappelled 700 feet down the face, in the dark, to the two chilled men. By midnight all three had jumared to the summit and were ensconced in warm sleeping bags, sipping brandy in the moonlight. Two years later Harding and Rowell returned, a story to be recounted in the following chapter.

The "biggest non-first ascent" of the second half of the sixties belonged to Robbins. His nine-and-a-half-day solo ascent of El Cap's Muir Wall (its second ascent) in April 1968 stunned the climbing world: the only comparable feat in world alpinism had been a six-day solo first ascent on the Petit Dru, in the Alps, by Walter Bonatti in August 1955.

Why did Robbins put himself through this long ordeal? He tried to answer the question in an article in the *American Alpine Journal:* "But what is this solo nonsense, anyway? Oh, just solo nonsense. Just another way to prove something. A sort of spiritual onanism. The thing about a solo climb is that it is all yours. You are not forced to share it. It's naked. Raw. The fullest expression of the climbing egoist.... I don't know *why* I solo. But I sense it has much to do with the ego, and with proving something." Later he talked about his "unrelenting demon inside": "He always asks for more, more, more. He never gets enough. He is insatiable, gluttonous, ever lusting for more of the peculiar meat upon which he feeds."

Day after day Robbins moved upward in that most boring and tedious of all climbing modes, solo aid climbing. After leading a pitch, he would rappel, on a second rope, back to the pitch's base and then start back up, cleaning as he went. After removing the pitons he was faced with hauling the bag, which by then was hanging on the end of the rappel rope. "I began to hate the climb," he wrote later. "Here I am, what am I doing?" On the sixth or seventh day he became slightly panicked when he thought he might be off route. He had brought only three bolts with him, hardly enough if he had to forge new ground. "Now I shouted at the insensate rock, and into the void at Chouinard and Herbert. Irrationally, I felt they had betrayed me. I was looking for scapegoats, but didn't spare my ego, castigating myself for a blundering fool." One can imagine his relief when at long last he came upon a bolt placed by the first ascenders.

Talking to himself, singing crazily, he moved upward day by day, hating, loathing El Cap. Near the top he placed a rurp that went in but a quarter of an inch. "Moving up on that pin," he wrote, "required a monstrous effort of will very akin to the discipline needed to keep one's mouth shut when riding with a driver in whom one has no confidence and who is driving too fast down a twisty mountain road." Moving above this flimsy device, he had enormous trouble getting something to stick, and when he finally stood up on it, it popped. Incredibly, the rurp below held. But he was so badly psyched out that he had to place a bolt, one of two times in his career he did so on a non-first ascent. (The first had been in 1960, on the Nose, as related earlier.)

By midmorning on his tenth day he reached the summit and was greeted by his wife, Liz, who had hiked up the back side. Robbins had now climbed El Cap eight times, by all seven existing routes, making either the first or second ascents of all seven—a remarkable record, one never to be equaled.

CHAPTER 10

Ringing Down the Curtain: 1970–1971

Harding and Caldwell's epic ascent of the Wall of Early Morning Light was a great adventure which focused our attention on several issues: media exposure, the bolting question, once again, and finally the aesthetic consideration of whether the line was natural. The last point is almost academic since the climb forced many of us to realize what we already knew. The great natural routes in Yosemite have been done. The Wall of Early Morning Light merely rang down the curtain.

—Jim McCarthy, 1971

Who can say when the Golden Age ended? Although it certainly didn't happen overnight, a good case can be made for 1970, when numerous significant events took place, some involving climbing, some not. This was the year that Camp 4 was "renovated," a facelift that led directly to its renaming; Sunnyside Campground, with its "unitized" and numbered sites, was a far cry from the "throw down the sleeping bag anywhere" style of the past. The entire upper half of the campground, the climbers' favorite section, was permanently closed, though I'll admit it was an overtrampled eyesore, indeed worthy of reclamation. A camp fee of three dollars a night was levied, a steep price for many climbers; Robbins regarded this act as the end of the "traditional laissez-faire camping...a tradition long-doomed by population growth, increased leisure, and four-wheeled 'campers.'" (During the summer of 1972 part of Camp 4 became a walk-in campground; later the entire camp was so delineated.)

The rest of Yosemite was changing also. The Valley floor had become a city, complete with smog, crime, jammed parking lots, and even a bank. Two visitation figures for the park best tell this sad story: 250,000 annually when Dick Leonard and his group arrived in 1933; 2,500,000 by 1970. Chris Jones decried one effect of this tenfold population explosion in "The

End of the Mountains," a wistful article in the 1970 *American Alpine Journal*. "Governor Reagan," he wrote, "has announced a statewide computer reservation system, and ironically enough this is defined as progress. To mountaineers this is the antithesis of progress; it is another freedom lost."

Jones also talked about those who were "playing up the heroic and flashy" aspects of mountaineering and warned his readers to "beware...the sensation seeking media and promoters who would turn mountaineering into another vast business." Jones was here alluding in part to the previous year's establishment of a Valley guiding school, which peddled "Go Climb a Rock" T-shirts as well as climbing lessons. Wayne Merry, of El Cap fame, and Loyd Price, a strong climber and a rising star in the Curry Company, ran the concern. We Camp 4 residents detested the idea, feeling that Valley climbing was too precious and too personal to tarnish with commercialism. Even the easterners, at long last tuned in to Valley happenings, were concerned: Jim McCarthy wrote that "climbers associated with some of the climbing schools, whose orientation is purely commercial, should examine their consciences. Those who are truly called to the mountains will come—we need not be evangelists." Ed Leeper, a piton maker who had climbed sporadically in the Valley for more than a decade, also bemoaned the new commercialism: "I think we ought to go out and work hard to restore the unsavory image that climbing and climbers had a few years ago." It was Galen Rowell, however, who put it most bluntly:

> *Why should climbing be free?*
> *Thought the infamous Y.P. & C.*
> *Now Merry and Price ply the world's oldest vice*
> *And share the concessionaire's fee!*

Along with the crowds, the renovated campground, and the climbing school came a marked increase in the number of rockclimbers. The "antiestablishment" era of the late sixties had spawned a vast movement of young people wanting to "return to nature," and backpackers and climbers swarmed into the Sierra Nevada. Some of our discomfort in all this, of course, came from the fact that we weren't doing anything unique any longer. Tourists and hippies were climbing the cliffs, having no idea whatsoever of the amazing history of the Valley or its place in world climbing. They enjoyed themselves on the cliffs, of course, but one of our gripes was that we now had to stand in line to do some of our favorite routes, those which in our youth were done only two or three times a year. Trash on, or at the base of, routes became a problem. Mike Graber, a Valley newcomer just beginning a distinguished mountaineering career, was appalled at the amount of garbage he saw on the northwest face of Half Dome: "I thought climbers were of a different breed."

Not all the problems involved climbers. A riot involving flower children and mounted rangers in Stoneman Meadow, below Glacier Point, on

July 4, 1970, made the front pages of San Francisco newspapers and also caused Camp 4 climbers to reassess their once-serene locale. Did we want the "real" world and its problems brought into Nirvana? Robbins warned his *Summit* readers that "those contemplating a visit to Yosemite might do well to look straight, have the automobile checked over for minor faults, and expect to be searched."

━━━━━━━━━━━━━━━━━━━━━━━━━━━━━━■━━━━━━━━━━━━━━━━━━━━━━━━━━━━━━━

Many significant, positive changes in climbing were happening in the Valley at the same time, naturally. Foremost among these, perhaps, was the arrival of a new piece of equipment that within a few years completely changed the style of American climbing. British climbers had shunned pitons ever since they'd been invented early in the century. Depending on pitons, they felt, was an unsavory modern crutch—a Continental habit not to be emulated. But as climbing got harder and more dangerous, the clever Brits came up with a partial solution to protect themselves from long falls: "artificial chockstones." Beginning around 1926, these hobnailed pioneers gathered stream pebbles en route to a climb and then wedged an appropriately sized one into a crack when the going got tough. By wrapping a sling around the pebble and clipping in a carabiner and the climbing rope, these climbers enjoyed a protection point similar to what a piton offered—but without the stigma of "mechanization." In the late 1950s climbers began using large machine nuts, which had a distinct advantage: one could thread a sling through the hole in the nut ahead of time, thus saving time and energy while on the route. By the mid-1960s English climbers John Brailsford and Trevor Peck had begun manufacturing specialized aluminum "nuts" with holes for slings and also tiny knurled nuts attached onto small but strong wires.

Pitons, of course, were perfectly adequate for protection, and, except in Great Britain, they were the very symbol of the rockclimber worldwide. Nuts would never have taken hold so quickly in America if, at the same time that they were becoming sophisticated in England, another phenomenon had not been taking place in Yosemite and other areas. Every Valley climber was aware by 1967 that the hardened chrome-molybdenum pitons could destroy cracks. With each removal of one of these splendid pitons, a crack was worn down and widened slightly: steel is harder than granite. On trade routes such as Serenity Crack, cracks that had once taken quarter-inch horizontals now took one-inch angles. The scarring of such cracks was visible from hundreds of feet. (One advantage of such scars—the only one—was that they allowed many climbs to be done free, as humans had unintentionally manufactured jamcracks and pockets perfect for fingers and toes.) The mid-sixties were also the beginning of the age of environmental consciousness, and we Camp 4 denizens began noticing the scars and wondering what to do. Were fixed pitons the answer? No, that wasn't the Valley tradition, and people would simply steal them from routes. Bolts? God forbid! What to do? Nuts, which don't damage the rock in the least, came along at the exact right moment.

The first mention of nuts that I can find in an American climbing context occurs in the April 1965 issue of *Summit*. An English climber named Anthony Greenbank, having climbed in Colorado using nuts brought from home, wrote an article about their use. Robbins happened to be in Boulder at the time (the summer of 1964), and he climbed with Greenbank. Using a nut at one point in Eldorado Canyon, Robbins told Greenbank (in words that sound somewhat invented by Greenbank), "You know, these nuts are good. I've actually got one fixed really well; trust the British. How could a little country like that rule the world so long without being extremely clever?" He told the Brit that "nuts are okay, but I think they would take too long on a big climb."

By June 1966, even though he'd climbed twice in England by this time, Robbins hadn't fully embraced nut use for Yosemite. He wrote me: "I think we can learn a lot from the British, and I see a place in the U. S. for the concept that placing a lot of pitons is not good style, and also for the use of nuts at places like Tahquitz, where years of placing and removing pitons have worn the cracks so much as to change the routes." But in 1967 Robbins saw the light, and that year a flurry of articles appeared in *Summit,* of which Robbins was the climbing editor. Most significant was Robbins's "Nuts to You," published in the May issue. The corny title came from an outburst made by Chuck Pratt when Robbins told him he was carrying some nuts along on their next climb. Pratt, a traditionalist, didn't like the idea, obviously, though he finally accepted nuts. In his article, Robbins presented a short history of nut use and admitted he had been slow to jump on the nut bandwagon: "Although I could understand their usefulness in Britain, I then judged that pitons were far more efficient for use in the U. S., and that in Yosemite, in particular, the cracks were not good for holding nuts. I was wrong. I have since realized how I had underestimated these cleverly-conceived gadgets."

One of the reasons that nuts weren't instantly accepted by Valley climbers was that many of the cracks, wedged by frost action, were extremely parallel and thus not conducive to solid nut placements. In fact, the several photos of nut placements in Valley cracks in the May issue of *Summit* are hardly good arguments for nuts: the devices look like they'd pop out immediately. Yet another reason for the relatively slow acceptance of nuts concerned their size and shape. Early nuts were crude and tended to be locked into a certain range, able to fit cracks only from a quarter-inch wide to an inch and a quarter. Also, their crude shapes meant they could be inserted in only one or two ways, thus limiting their usefulness.

Robbins was, by this time, well qualified to write about nuts, or what he nicely termed "silent aids." The previous autumn he and Liz, along with two English climbers, Mike Dent and Victor Cowley, had quietly done a new route near Sentinel Rock using only nuts. First known as Chockstone Gorge, and later as Boulderfield Gorge, the 1,000-foot route was not trivial: it involved 5.9 climbing and a bivouac. Robbins wrote that it "was possibly the hardest climb of its length in the U. S. which has been done without pitons." If a plaque were placed at the base of the route, it would read: "Here, on September 29, 1966, pitonless Valley climbing was born, an event that saved Yosemite cracks from massive destruction."

During the same month that "Nuts to You" appeared, Robbins and his wife made a significant first ascent, again piton-free, near the Lower Brother. This route was to become the most popular Valley climb ever, and rightly so, for it ascends exquisite crack systems for six pitches, with consummate belay ledges and sterling views of the lower Valley. Called Nutcracker Sweet by punster Robbins, the climb's name was quickly shortened to just Nutcracker. This superb 5.8 route is still a mandatory climb for Valley newcomers.

Although Valley regulars used nuts perhaps two-thirds of the time by the end of the sixties, others were slow to adopt the new toys. Some neophytes caught on immediately, however, and proved the worth of the little aluminum trapezoids. One day in May 1970 I arranged to climb with Fritz Wiessner, the legendary seventy-year-old who had come close to reaching the top of K2 in 1939. Fritz casually mentioned he'd like to take along two friends, Toni Hiebeler and Richard Hechtel. Although these names immediately rang a bell—they also were "old" and famous climbers—I winced, not really wanting to be in charge of a group of semistrangers. Fritz sensed my plight and graciously asked if I wanted someone else to help me shepherd them. My roving eye spotted Joe Kelsey, sitting forlornly at his Camp 4 table, spooning his oatmeal. I went over and told him of this golden opportunity, to be able to climb with Fritz of K2, Hiebeler of the Eiger, and Hechtel of the Peuterey Ridge. He hesitated. "Joe," I pleaded, "think memoirs; think stories for your grandchildren. Help me, for Christ's sake!"

He grunted, sensing a trap. "I'm a guide, is that it?" He squirmed some more, studying his gruel carefully. "Besides, it's my rest day."

We conferred. We bickered. I promised return favors. In the end, like the knights of old, Kelsey couldn't refuse an adventure. He issued a single proviso, however: "I don't want any problems. I'll want to lead my rope, okay?" This echoed my sentiment exactly: we couldn't let any of these fellows lead. First of all, they ranged in age from forty to seventy—and they weren't in the best shape. We, on the other hand, were close to thirty, as lean and mean as Dobermans. Second, they little feared the smoothness of Yosemite granite. We did. Third, tradition, an ancient one dating back all of three years, demanded that we do the Nutcracker solely with nuts— and these guys had undoubtedly never even *seen* the things. We had.

"You're right," I agreed. "Someone's going to get hurt unless we take charge. We gotta be firm."

At the base of the route we showed our bundles of chocks to the three

Old World climbers. Hechtel claimed to know about them. "I am a physicist," he stated with authority. "I know the principles involved." But as Kelsey and I watched him fondle the things, squinting at them from all angles, we realized he was as innocent as a newborn in their use.

Kelsey and I looked at each other, and I whispered, redundantly, "You lead the second rope. All the way, for God's sake." He promised.

I set off, using a horn and a single nut for protection on the first pitch, a smooth but straightforward open book. Fritz followed nicely, removing the gear. I wondered if I'd be climbing that well when I was seventy.

So far, so good. The first rope was having great fun and moving efficiently. Kelsey and his two world-famous clients would soon be moving up, enjoying themselves on this already classic route. I smiled to myself, thinking of my sterling executive abilities. I should have been a real guide! The Nutcracker was ours!

Midway through the next lead, a traverse with a perfect view downward to the rope-up spot, I looked down and stopped in midmove: Hechtel was leading the first pitch! Hiebeler belayed while Kelsey stood off to the side, a chagrined look on his face. Hechtel had somehow convinced Kelsey that he was up to the task, and now he was thrusting nuts impotently into the crack above him. Finally he lodged one and yelled down to his partners, "Ya, is good. It stuck good, I sink."

I told myself not to worry, not to yell down my displeasure or proffer advice; it was only 5.6, after all. Soon Hechtel was fifteen feet higher, moving nicely. Seconds later came a great scudding noise, and I saw Hechtel plunging crazily toward the forest. But his nut, the first placement of his life, stayed put! After a thirty-foot tumble he was caught by the rope, bouncing like a yo-yo just above the ground.

Kelsey later told me of his first thoughts during the fall: "Oh, shit! This guy's old. He's going to break both legs!" Our new friend had turned fifty-seven the previous day, and from our perspective, we were climbing with geriatrics.

Hechtel, shaken but unhurt, sported a faraway look. "I wouldn't mention this to my wife, ja?" he finally said to his comrades. His haughtiness had instantly evaporated, even though his scientific hunch about the principles of nut placement had been flawless.

"Well, the rock's especially slippery in that particular area," Kelsey lied tactfully as he quickly tied into the sharp end of the rope. With all feelings soothed, he set off. No one said a word about him leading the rest of the route.

As the Golden Age drew to a close, we Camp 4 cragrats began turning our attention to matters other than climbing. If I have given the impression so far in this book that we paid scant attention to "outside" events, this is generally true. We rarely talked about politics or the "real" world;

we disliked, equally well, government bureaucracies and big business and tried hard to ignore both. But during the mid- and late 1960s three significant events were taking place in the outside world, ones we could hardly ignore: the Civil Rights struggle, the hippie/drug culture, and the Vietnam War. The struggle for equality and black voting rights in the South captured our attention and fomented many discussions, but this action was so far away, so detached from our sheltered middle-class lives, that we didn't relate to what was happening. I was one of the few climbers who took part in the struggle, though it was a brief encounter. In April 1965, as an army private stationed in Georgia, I took part in one of the celebrated Selma, Alabama, marches, striding proudly thirty feet behind Nobel laureates Martin Luther King and Ralph Bunche as they led a march across the Pettus Bridge toward the state capital. I will never forget the sense of solidarity with a just movement, nor will I forget certain Selma townspeople who, upon seeing California plates on my distinctive black VW bus as I parked on the outskirts of town, hissed and hooted at me.

When the army shipped me off to Vietnam in the spring of 1965, I had barely heard of the place. Because I was a clerk, and since I was back long before the action heated up, I had few stories to tell the Camp 4 residents about my experience. But neither did they have many questions. I almost forgot about Southeast Asia during the next few years, though I took part in several peace rallies in San Francisco. Few of the climbers I knew expressed strong opinions about the conflict; none became activists. As related, few of the Camp 4 habitués were drafted after 1963, for one reason or another.

Most of us easily fell in with the hippie lifestyle, for in our own quiet ways we had been rebelling for years against the "establishment." We later considered ourselves pre-hippies, or perhaps post-Beatniks: we didn't have nine-to-five jobs; our hair was long and scraggly; our language poured forth without inhibition; and our morals, as Henry Miller once said about the bohemians of Paris, were of "the reptilian order." We fit right in with the hippies, though we prided ourselves on at least having a sense of direction: climbing.

Though a limited number of us had tried marijuana in the late fifties and early sixties, most of us were innocents even by 1963. But when I returned from Asia, in the late fall of 1965, my friends instantly cajoled me into trying grass. During the time I'd been gone, smoking the weed had become second nature to most climbers. Personally, I wasn't too fond of the stuff and never smoked it on climbs, as many did. Of the more powerful hallucinogens, many of us experimented with LSD, peyote, and mescaline, all cheap and easily obtainable in the Bay Area. Few climbers took more than a half-dozen trips on these drugs; Kim Schmitz and Jim Madsen were exceptions, and the most notorious story about them concerned the monster amount (four times the "therapeutic" dose) of acid they each took high on an El Cap route. They later told us they hardly noticed this trip, so high were they anyway, what with adrenaline and other hormones rushing through their systems.

The saddest case of drug burnout concerned my friend Mort Hempel, a promising youth I'd helped introduce to climbing in 1959. An incredibly bright fellow, he was one of the most natural climbers I'd ever seen. Calm, strong, talented, he was destined for greatness, as a climber and as a person. Hempel took up the guitar and eventually taught himself to play a twelve-string one. At Camp 4 parties he'd entertain us for hours with folk songs. By the time I got out of the army he had become a zombie, the result of LSD. He took relatively few trips—but apparently enough to trigger permanent chemical changes in his brain. His climbing suffered; after 1964 he did virtually nothing. Although Hempel still played and sang for a few more years, he drifted slowly and with much angst into schizophrenia and alcoholism. Antidepressant drugs and abstinence from liquor finally—decades later—got him back onto his feet, though his special talents were lost forever.

It is possible that the relative lack of first ascents in the late sixties was a result of our more laid-back lifestyle, which certainly included smoking lots of dope, a ritual not conducive to dawn starts and hard routes. In the last four years of the decade only ninety-six first ascents were made, in contrast to the previous four years, when 160 were done. But other factors must be considered. For one thing, our group was getting older. With this came other interests, marriages, and obligations. We also had somewhat more money, the result of working longer each year at higher-paying jobs. This often meant that we had better cars, which, in turn, meant more travel. I, for one, discovered the joys of traveling through the fabulous Sonoran desert of Baja California, in those days devoid of people and asphalt. I spent four weeks down there each spring during the late sixties, feeling not at all bad about missing out on part of the spring season in the Valley.

We began drifting away from the Valley, our obsession diminishing year by year. Most of us had accomplished splendid climbs: our dreams had come true. Those of us who had done El Cap routes knew we had achieved the ultimate in Valley climbing. Chouinard, in his pivotal 1963 article in the *American Alpine Journal,* had seen this early, writing that the future of big-wall climbing lay outside the Valley, in the world's great ranges. But few of us really wanted to suffer on remote, icy walls. Tom Frost was one of the few to go the Himalaya more than once; he also became a noted Andes climber. Robbins dabbled in the Alps, Canada, and Alaska, but he never did fearsome mixed climbs such as the Eiger. Neither did Chouinard, though he occasionally climbed in Scotland in the winter and did a few tough Canadian climbs and Alpine routes. Chris Jones, faithful to his Alpine upbringing, was an exception: his awesome routes in Canada are considered classics to this day. But the majority of Camp 4 climbers—Beck, Pratt, Fredericks, Erb, Gerughty, Kelsey, myself, and others—rarely visited the high-mountain world.

Climbing didn't come to a standstill, of course, even though only eighteen first ascents were done in 1969, the lowest annual total since 1958. Nevertheless, five of these eighteen were big ones, and all were accomplished between May and September of 1969. Harding, Rowell, and Faint did the imposing southwest face of Liberty Cap, a climb distinguished by a long, overhanging blank wall, which had to be bolted. Harding and Rowell later forced a rather ugly route up to the top of Glacier Point, following the gray scar of the Firefall, the spectacle that had finally been banned a year earlier. Pratt and Ken Boche completed the Gobi Wall, a nondescript new route up the flat north face of Sentinel. Robbins and Glen Denny climbed a magnificent new line on the Washington Column's south face. This 1,000-foot route, known as the Prow, ascended one of the prettiest Valley cliffs but used a fair number of bolts: thirty-eight, the exact number used on the far more formidable NA Wall five years earlier. When funnyman TM Herbert heard about this, he raved to Robbins in mock disgust, "Hell, you'll set a bad example. Pretty soon we'll have guys bolting up blank walls all over the Valley…. Robbins, you're finished. You're going downhill." Herbert was prescient, not about Robbins going downhill, but about blank walls being bolted. This soon happened on a climb involving none other than Robbins himself, on the fifth and last major new route of 1969.

By far the biggest climb of the late 1960s was Tis-sa-ack, Robbins's third route up the sheer northwest face of Half Dome (he was to establish a fourth, Arcturus, in 1970). Named after a lass of Indian legend—she had been transformed into stone, and her tears had formed the immense black streaks that so dominate the right-hand side of the sliced northwest face—Tis-sa-ack was a controversial climb, leading some to think of Robbins as a hypocrite. Blank sections, visible from the ground, would require bolting. But how much was justified? Robbins had set a fine example up to this point, never establishing a route that required more than 4 percent bolts. He was also, of course, well known for criticizing climbers who simply bolted their way up walls. Tis-sa-ack would obviously require a higher percentage than he was accustomed to. Robbins, obsessed by Half Dome, and knowing others had looked at the wall to the right of the existing two routes, decided that he had to have it. Maybe, he thought, the blank walls wouldn't be that blank.

Robbins, Pratt, and Dennis Hennek made an attempt on the enormous wall in October 1968, retreating after four days with less than half the wall done. A year later, with Hennek injured and Pratt uninterested in returning, Robbins found a partner in Camp 4, the first—and last—time that he sought out a stranger for a big climb. "I could not wait," he wrote, "and joined up with a young Coloradan, hot as a firecracker, hot as a bloody branding iron, a young football player who climbs like a fullback

Dennis Hennek at the top of the Zebra, on Half Dome's Tis-sa-ack route, 1968 (Photo: Glen Denny)

charging a line...." Don Peterson, an excellent climber, was insolent and overconfident, and Robbins, always honest in his writing, stated his displeasure bluntly: "We didn't get on well. I was establishment. Don would be." In another article, he maintained the same theme: "For eight days we would be locked in sullen conflict, each too arrogant to understand the other's weaknesses."

Such antipathy between climbing partners had never before happened on a big route in the Valley. It's not as if personality conflicts had taken place and we'd kept quiet about them—they simply didn't happen. We climbed with friends. Climbs were stressful, sure, and occasional harsh words erupted. But we knew one another, respected one another, mostly liked one another, and thus climbs involved friendly teamwork. Robbins, far too hasty in his choice of partner, suffered daily on Tis-sa-ack. Peterson expressed his feelings constantly, and he was not a happy climber. "This is a lot of shit!" he exclaimed once. Robbins had never experienced such outbursts on a route: "I was shocked and mildly terrified by Peterson's dark passions bubbling repeatedly to the surface."

Robbins's finest article of his career concerned this climb, and it appeared in a relatively new magazine. Allen Steck, Joe Fitschen (who had returned from Europe and was going to grad school in San Francisco), and I had started a climbing magazine called *Ascent* in 1967. Well received by the climbing community, it was a glossy journal sponsored by the Sierra Club and bereft of advertisements. We were highly pleased to publish Robbins's "Tis-sa-ack" in our 1970 issue, for it was a splendid piece of work. Fascinating and original, it was also one of the first climbing accounts to talk openly of conflict. The British were famous for writing with a "stiff upper lip," never deigning to address the controversies and stresses common on expeditions. American writers weren't much better: one would think every aspect of every climb went smoothly—which, of course, usually was the case. In the same year that Robbins's article appeared, mountaineer David Roberts came out with *Deborah: A Wilderness Narrative,* an astute account of personality conflicts on an Alaskan expedition. Perhaps sparked by these two accounts, climbing writers soon developed a let-it-all-hangout genre, but not all who wrote of mountain strife showed as much perception as did Robbins and Roberts.

Tis-sa-ack had required 110 bolts—close to 25 percent of the aid used—a new and disturbing Valley record. Because Robbins was the acknowledged leader of the Camp 4 climbers, he received only minor criticism about this route. For one thing, he hadn't planned in advance—as had Rowell and Harding on the south face of Half Dome—to place such a huge number. Robbins explained to me recently, "I thought we'd find rurp cracks and little flakes scattered about on the blank sections. On every other climb I'd ever done, this had been the case. You can't really tell from the ground what's up there, but there's always something. But Tis-sa-ack really *was* blank. It was the only climb I've ever done where I ran out of bolts."

The Tis-sa-ack bolting-percentage record didn't last long, for Harding and Rowell finished their oft-tried route up the south face of Half Dome in the summer of 1970. By this time Harding had invented bat-hooks, tiny hooks that would jam tightly in shallowly drilled bolt holes. This speeded up progress considerably. Nevertheless, bolts—and the holes drilled for bat-hooks—accounted for 180 out of 470 tool placements, about 38 percent. Harding had carefully arranged press coverage for this climb (even to the point of dropping film canisters to friends on the ground so that photos would be available *during* the climb, not just after), but the support party didn't do an adequate job and the media coverage was minor.

■

Half Dome wasn't the only attraction in 1970: Sentinel Rock was the locale of two marvelous feats. Steve Wunsch and Jim Erickson, excellent climbers from out of state, climbed the Steck-Salathé free in 1970, avoiding the short aid stretch on the Headwall via a devious 5.9 pitch to the left. In the same year Robbins made the first ascent, alone, of In Cold Blood, a route just to the right of the Chouinard-Frost route on the west face. This was by an order of magnitude the most impressive solo first ascent ever done in the States. In his write-up of this climb, Robbins quoted a hack writer who had called solo climbing "insanity." "I love to read such fatuous remarks," wrote Robbins, "coming as they invariably do, from the ignorant."

Two splendid young women climbers appeared in the Valley at the turn of the decade. Easterner Elaine Matthews climbed the west face of Sentinel with Tom Bauman in May 1970. Around the same time, she and Chuck Ostin attempted the Nose, but a blizzard hit the pair six pitches below the top and they had to be rescued. Had the weather been decent, Matthews would have been the first woman to climb El Cap. Unlike previous women climbers, she was not content to follow: she shared leads all the way to Camp VI. Much later, Matthews told me how difficult it was for her to break into the big climbs: "All the Yosemite greats were around in the Valley, but it was very difficult to find partners to climb with at first. Sometimes the only ones I had were hung-over Scots. Being a woman was a drawback. Who would have thought it seemly for a woman to climb El Cap—or even dream of it? When I look back, it seems I was always lacking confidence. On some levels even I doubted my ability to climb the Nose, though I'd had that as a goal for two years."

Nor was Bev Johnson a follower. She swung leads up the northwest face of Half Dome and later became the first woman ever to do the Steck-Salathé on Sentinel; she and Pete Ramin made the fifty-second ascent of the latter route on the same day rioters and horses were trampling Stoneman Meadow. Johnson, giving the lie to the idea that women couldn't get up hard cracks, accomplished several 5.10 routes, including the notorious Crack of Doom. She later climbed the Dihedral Wall solo, the first time a woman climbed El Cap alone.

Meanwhile, a free-climbing renaissance was under way, sparked by what Robbins called "a coterie of yogurt-eating health food faddists." The leader of this group was Jim Bridwell, who had his finest year by far. Of his eight first ascents in 1970, four were rated 5.10, and one, New Dimensions, became the first bona fide 5.11 Valley climb. Bridwell replaced Pratt as the free-climbing master that year and went on to some truly significant first ascents during the 1970s. He easily holds the record for Valley first ascents, having made at least seventy between 1964 and 1986.

Two new routes in 1970 and one repeat climb in February 1971 symbolize the end of the Golden Age. All involved El Capitan, surely a fitting locale for these events. Each climb—to be described in detail below—differed from the other as black differs from white. The climb of the Heart route, a near-secret ascent done in impeccable style, made most Camp 4 residents sit up and cheer. The second climb, the Wall of Early Morning Light (usually called the Dawn Wall), proved to be the opposite, an event involving the media as no other route ever had. The climb caused a rupture in the friendship of the two protagonists and resulted in much breast-beating from pundits and peripheral observers, including Ansel Adams. The final route, the "erasing" of the Dawn Wall, was applauded by some, but this drastic and unprecedented act, so out of character with the spirit of Valley climbing, still symbolizes, to many of us, the end of the special era we all had so enjoyed. The sixties were over—and so was the Golden Age.

Recent Stanford graduate Chuck Kroger and current Stanford senior Scott Davis hadn't planned on doing the Heart route, a fairly obvious line that led up through the enormous and well-named formation on the southwest face of El Cap. Instead, the pair, who together had already climbed three El Cap routes (including the third ascent of the NA Wall), desired an even bigger route: the Dawn Wall, a contrived line just to the right of the Nose. Bridwell, just coming into his own as a big-wall climber, had also spotted this route, along with others. In late March 1970 he and Kim Schmitz had fixed a few ropes on the wall, staking their claim. When the best Valley climbers did this, others respected it—as did Kroger and Davis. They saw the ropes, heard who had placed them, and backed away. Kroger, by far the wittiest climbing writer of the early 1970s, didn't particularly wish "to be torn limb from limb by the barbarians," his tongue-in-cheek word for the Camp 4 regulars. He and Davis looked elsewhere for a new El Cap route.

The Heart looked climbable, so off they went. They fixed ropes for about 300 feet, a common ploy in those days, one not thought of as fixed-roped climbing, but more of a psychological boost, a next-day-for-sure commitment. Indeed, they set off the following morning—and without fanfare. "We did not intend to amuse a thrill-seeking audience of tourists watching from the doorsteps of their mobile homes as they consumed Curry Company hot dogs and beer," Kroger wrote. "Feeling that this 'El Capitan Circus' idea is obscene, we avoided it by asking the rangers not to release our names or details of our climb."

Although Kroger and Davis were highly experienced Yosemite big-wall climbers (Davis had also climbed the famed Bonatti Pillar, in the Alps, in record time in 1968), neither had ever done a major first ascent—and neither had ever placed a bolt. The pair took only six drills, and by the end of their second day, having bolted a fair amount of blank terrain, they discovered that all six were dull. Luckily, they had taken a whetstone and were able to crudely sharpen the drills.

Just above the Heart, disaster almost struck: Kroger was jumaring the rope when it knocked a large flake down onto him. He ducked and the flake tore through his pack as it whistled downward. "It took my breath

Chuck Kroger approaches the top of the Heart, on El Capitan's Heart Route, 1970 (Photo: Scott Davis)

away," Davis recently told me. "It was the size of a suitcase; I watched from above, but of course there was nothing I could do."

Farther up, after the pair had calmed down, they arrived at a light-colored pinnacle attached to the wall. "Since 'White Tower' has a nasty connotation these days," Kroger wrote, "we called it 'Tower to the People.'" Higher yet lay a pitch they named the "A5 Traverse." This was, in reality, rated A2, "but every other big El Cap climb has an 'A5 Traverse,' so we figured we needed one too."

On the seventh day, still some 400 feet below the top, Davis placed their twenty-seventh bolt—the last one they owned. Such an act is not exactly conducive to calmness, as Chouinard and Herbert had found out five years earlier on the Muir Wall. What would happen if another bolt were required? They couldn't go on, and they couldn't retreat, since the route had been replete with traverses and overhangs.

Blessed with the dumb luck of youth, the pair encountered, on the morning of their eighth day, an easy aid dihedral that shot directly to the top: Fat City, they called it. No bolts! No problem! Kroger carefully combed his hair before mantling onto the summit of El Cap, in order that "Royal and everyone else on the summit would like me. Then I stepped onto level ground. No one in sight...[so] we started running around looking behind trees and boulders, screaming, 'All right, you guys, we know you're up here somewhere. Don't play games with us. You can't fool us.'" Kroger, of course, was poking fun at one of the customs of the Golden Age climbers. He had read that after El Cap first ascents the team was invariably greeted on top by bronzed young women toting picnic baskets and magnums of champagne.

Although Kroger and Davis had corresponded regularly with Robbins about their various El Cap routes, a gulf nonetheless existed between the old guard and the new; few Camp 4 regulars deigned to climb with Kroger and Davis, thinking they were just upstarts—despite the fact that they were obviously the two finest young big-wall climbers in the country.

Davis recently gave me his views about this generation gap: "The earlier generation was caught between its desire to maintain its godlike status by standing above the rest of us and seeing their routes wait years for second ascents—and its desire to maintain its status by encouraging big-wall climbing to continue so that they, in retrospect, would be seen as the first in a long line, rather than aberrations in a sport that dead-ended."

Davis, knowing that his various El Cap climbs with Kroger had been done fast and in impeccable style, went on to describe his later feelings of disillusionment: "To us, the earlier generation had been larger than life. They were our heroes and we clung to them, disregarding the mounting evidence that they were mere mortals. Yet, after the Heart route, we bent under the knowledge that our gods had crashed. Now we were adults without heroes in a large and unfriendly world."

Some climbers wish to avoid a circus atmosphere; some crave it. No one can now say that Warren Harding and Dean Caldwell set out purposefully to garner headlines on their Dawn Wall ascent; Harding has denied it, but rarely did he do a climb that failed to make the papers. Whatever, the Dawn Wall route became the most intensive media event ever portrayed in American climbing.

Oregon climber Caldwell had been coming to the Valley for eight years, although he rarely stayed long and rarely got up the big routes. More of a mountaineer than a rockclimber, he had done some fearsome ice climbs in Peru, including the first ascent of the intimidating northeast face of Yerupajá in 1969 with Chris Jones and others. He fell under the spell of the forty-six-year-old Harding in 1970, and they laid plans for a typical Harding epic: carry an enormous amount of equipment—including wine and hundreds of bolts and bat-hooks—and prepare to spend weeks on the wall.

To Harding's credit, he didn't even think of using siege tactics: even he had finally seen the light regarding fixed ropes. He and Caldwell would start at the base and climb one pitch per day until they got to the top. This plan was magnificent, but in the end it was tainted by two factors: the "excessive" bolting and the enormous publicity.

The bolting began on the pair's first day, October 23, 1970, for the Dawn Wall, on its lower part, is remarkably blank. But Harding wanted a superdirect route to the top, and if he had to bolt his way up to the upper crack systems to make a *direttissima,* then so be it. As it turned out, the route required 330 drilled holes, some filled with bolts and many others used for bat-hooks and rivets, another new invention that used shallow holes and thus cut the drilling time. For a 2,800-foot route, the 330 holes meant that more than 40 percent of the route was bolted, a new Yosemite high.

For three weeks the pair worked upward, averaging about 100 feet a day. Incredibly difficult nailing alternated with blank sections. Harding took a fifty-foot fall at one point and went right back up to work. Storms came and went; in early November, when only halfway up the wall, the pair spent 107 straight hours huddling inside their bivouac tents, soaked and shivering. The food began to run out at the same time, and the pair began to ration it.

Harding and Caldwell had a support group at the base, including some who didn't mind contacting the media. Photographers from *Life* magazine appeared on November 7, and a week later gigantic headlines began appearing in California newspapers, a result of a bizarre rescue attempt. Rangers, worried at the team's lack of progress, and knowing they were low on food, heli-lifted an enormous rescue crew to the top of El Cap. The two climbers had not called for a rescue, and luckily an Associated Press

Warren Harding reaches the top of El Capitan's Dawn Wall, 1970 (Photo: Glen Denny)

reporter, Bill Stall, who was a climber, set the record straight within a day: the Park Service had overreacted and even lied about who had instigated the rescue.

Harding was able to communicate his disapproval of all this activity by means of fervid notes he stuck in cans and hurled off the wall. Caldwell shouted his displeasure: "A rescue is unwarranted, unwanted, and will not be accepted." Both messages were heard, and the Park Service backed down, keeping a skeleton crew on the summit in case something went wrong later.

This fiasco, even though correctly reported by Stall, naturally fueled the public's interest in the climb; the front page of the November 14 *San Francisco Chronicle* featured a ten-by-twelve-inch aerial photograph showing two black specks adrift on an immense sea of granite. The caption: "Climbers Hang Tough." One of Harding's spokesmen had submitted a catchy quote to the reporters: "The closer to death Harding gets, the meaner he gets." Helicopters buzzed the cliff, taking pictures, and newsmen scurried to the Valley.

Newspaper accounts appeared daily until the pair topped out around noon on November 18, their twenty-seventh day. Some seventy people, mostly out-of-shape reporters who had hiked up the eight-mile trail to the top of El Cap, greeted the pair. Harding and Caldwell didn't have much to say to the ignorant questions asked them, though one line was eminently quotable: "He smells like a decaying rhinoceros," Harding said, pointing to Caldwell, "but I think I smell like a beached whale." Asked why he climbed, Harding replied, "Because we're insane."

Within days letters to the editor of the *Chronicle* appeared. One eloquent fellow fond of metaphors wrote that the pair's courage was admirable: "It is exactly that of a bull in the arena. Confused and tormented by something far beyond their understanding, they react to the sight of a cliff as the bull to the cape. Not knowing why, they charge." Ansel Adams checked in from Carmel: "The super-spectacular 'engineering' achievement... has little relation to the spirit of mountaineering and appreciation of the natural scene.... I resent the obvious publicity effort associated with this event."

The climb's aftermath utterly destroyed the relationship between Harding and Caldwell. Although Harding had told reporters on the night

Cameramen and reporters besiege Dean Caldwell (in plaid shirt) *and Warren Harding* (to Caldwell's right) *atop the Dawn Wall, 1970. (Photo: Glen Denny)*

Epilogue

I find that rockclimbing is the finest, most healthiest sport in the whole world. It is much healthier than most; look at baseball, where 10,000 sit on their ass to watch a handful of players.

—John Salathé, 1974

In the quarter-century that has fled since Harding and Caldwell reached the summit of El Cap, people have infiltrated the Valley in numbers undreamed of by John Muir. Park visitors topped 4,000,000 in 1993, double the number who came to the park annually at the end of the Golden Age. Nevertheless, one could argue that today the floor of the Valley is basically unchanged from what it was in 1970. The parking problems, the over-crowded restaurants and museums, and the heavily trampled popular trails and campgrounds seem just about the same as they once did: the Valley reached a saturation point years ago. Perhaps the most obvious change from the old days concerns the rhythms of the weeks. We once looked forward to Sunday evenings, when the dust from departing campers would settle, when "our" lodge's lounge would empty. Sunday evenings nowadays might see fewer people, yes, but "fewer" now means "many." The crowds are ever-present.

Similarly, one no longer drives up to the Valley on a Sunday afternoon thinking that private campsites will be available. One may be fortunate and be allowed by the rangers to share a numbered site in Sunnyside with five other climbers, but gone forever are the casual camping attitudes of the past. Climbers by the hundreds now occupy Sunnyside every month (except in the dead of winter), and this has some advantages, to be sure: you'll be able to find a partner, and you'll meet interesting people from all over the world. Still, the solitude, the feeling of doing something unique, the naive excitement, the "sacred" aspects of climbing—all are gone. If we older climbers mourn this, then let us remember that each generation can—and will—enjoy its own special age.

Rockclimbers have flocked to the Valley in even greater proportion than the tourists, and routes have proliferated—sixty exist on El Cap alone.

Fortunately, most climbers have shunned bolting in favor of a whole bag of tricks and skills made possible with new equipment and techniques. These highly competent climbers have accomplished unbelievable feats. A completely new generation came along around 1971 and joined forces with Jim Bridwell and Kim Schmitz, just about the only Camp 4 regulars who thrived in the Valley during the 1970s. This generation, a loosely knit one that included the Stonemasters, a group of wild, honed youths from the Southland, made the Golden Age climbers proud. The names that dominated the Valley in the 1970s include John Bachar, Henry Barber, Werner Braun, Hugh Burton, Mark Chapman, Jim Donini, Jim Dunn, Peter Haan, Ray Jardine, Ron Kauk, Mark Klemens, John Long, George Meyers, Charlie Porter, Bill Price, Tobin Sorenson, Steve Sutton, Billy Westbay, Kevin Worrall, and Steve Wunsch. Some of their marvelous feats stagger the imagination; only a few will be mentioned here. The Steck-Salathé on Sentinel was soloed in 1973, mostly unroped, by Barber, in two and a half hours. On a different time scale, the Salathé Wall was soloed in six days in 1971 by Haan, a short-route specialist who had never before done a big wall. It was inevitable that a new route on El Cap would be done solo, and Dunn did it in 1972, with his climb of Cosmos, the sheer sea of granite just to the right of the Dihedral Wall. The first all-female ascent of El Cap was accomplished in 1973 when Sibylle Hechtel, daughter of Richard Hechtel, climbed the Triple Direct (a combination of three routes: the Salathé, the Muir, and the Nose) with Bev Johnson.

The Nose was climbed in one day, largely free, in 1975, by Bridwell, Westbay, and Long. The east face of the Column was climbed entirely free the same year—and renamed Astroman—by Long, Kauk, and Bachar, an exploit I still have great trouble comprehending, remembering as I do the vast amounts of direct aid I used when Pratt, Beck, and I thrashed up the route eight years earlier. The first-ever free ascent of a big El Cap route came in 1979, when Jardine and Price did the west face without aid.

Such splendid new equipment appeared in the late seventies and early eighties that climbing became "easier," meaning that we old-timers, heading to the cliffs about as often as the pioneers did in the 1930s—that is, infrequently—could do 5.10 routinely. But this equipment, basically Jardine's superb camming devices known as "Friends" (1978) and shoe soles of "sticky rubber" (1981), opened up a whole new realm of possibilities on the Valley's cliffs. Supremely skilled climbers, using the new gear, managed 5.12, 5.13, and, finally, 5.14 climbs.

By the late 1980s and early 1990s, remarkable free ascents became commonplace, as did one-day ascents of El Cap. The Canadian climber Peter Croft became known for his bold but well-thought-out solo climbs; he would sometimes climb the Steck-Salathé before breakfast as a warm-up to harder climbs later in the day. "Enchainments" also become popular: in 1986, Croft and Bachar did the Nose *and* the northwest face of Half Dome in a single long day! Climbing in impeccable style, never courting publicity, ignoring competition climbing, fully capable of downclimbing a route when he didn't feel sharp, Croft became a hero to the old Camp 4 gang, a true "keeper of the flame." We need more climbers like Croft.

The Salathé Wall was climbed free by Todd Skinner and Paul Piana in 1988, a 5.13b effort requiring many weeks and dozens of falls. By then we old-timers knew the Nose would go free soon, but we never dreamed a woman would do it first. In 1993 the superclimber Lynn Hill managed to climb the route without aid, freeing such horrendous pitches as the Great Roof and the final overhang, the one Harding had labored on during that lonely November night thirty-five years earlier. I have barely touched upon the outstanding achievements of the past quarter-century: several books deserve to be written by, and about, the generations following the Golden Age.

Where are the stars of yesteryear? Of the 1930s and 1940s pioneers mentioned in this book, many are no longer with us. But Dave Brower, the most influential American conservationist of the second half of the century, remains active at his work, as does his chief Valley climbing partner, professor emeritus Morgan Harris, who at age seventy-eight daily goes to his office at UC Berkeley to continue his research on cell genetics. Jules Eichorn, that splendid climber of Higher Spire fame, lives in Redwood City, California. His partners on that long-ago adventure, Dick Leonard and Bestor Robinson, both died a few years back. Marjory Farquhar, still feisty at ninety, lives in San Francisco. Ax Nelson, suffering from Parkinsonism, lives in Berkeley.

Most of the 1950s and 1960s group are still alive and climbing, or writing about climbing, or at least thinking about climbing. Some, however, are no longer with us: I have mentioned the deaths of Sheridan Anderson, Jim Baldwin, Penny Carr, Don Goodrich, Jim Madsen, Frank Sacherer, and John Salathé. Don Wilson was killed while rafting an Idaho river; Willi Unsoeld was buried by an avalanche on Mount Rainier in 1979. Bill "Dolt" Feuerer manufactured high-quality equipment during most of the 1960s, but he was a tortured man, despondent about his love-life and his business. He hanged himself at Christmas 1971. Leigh Ortenburger died in the monstrous Oakland Hills fire on October 20, 1991, while visiting his old friend, Al Baxter. Baxter, badly burned, survived. Bev Johnson was killed in a helicopter accident in April 1994.

At least four climbers went on to become professors. Mark Powell teaches geography in southern California. George Sessions, who teaches philosophy at a college near Sacramento, is a deep-ecology pioneer. Wally Reed taught botany, and Joe Fitschen taught English; both are now retired.

Galen Rowell left his auto-repair business in the early seventies and became a renowned photographer specializing in wilderness images. Although he wrote early in 1973 that it was "doubtful that these big routes

[El Cap and the face of Half Dome] will ever be possible without pitons," he himself, along with Doug Robinson and Dennis Hennek, made the first all-nut ascent of Half Dome's face that August. This climb sealed the fate of pitons forever.

Jeff Foott and Ed Cooper also went on to distinguished careers in photography. Foott specializes in wildlife movies and lives in Wyoming; Cooper is well known for his crystal-clear images of the American West.

Many of the old Camp 4 group—among them Glen Denny, Chris Fredericks, Tom Gerughty, Tom Higgins, Al Macdonald, John Morton, Krehe Ritter, Jim Sims, and Les Wilson—ended up in the San Francisco Bay Area, where they work at various professions.

Others live elsewhere but remain close to the cliffs. Bob Kamps, just about ready for Social Security, lives in Los Angeles and climbs 5.11 flawlessly. TM Herbert climbs almost as well and still entertains his partners with the same flair; he lives on the east side of the Sierra, as does Don Lauria. Eric Beck, now a fit fifty-one-year-old marathoner, ended up in San Diego as a programming whiz kid; Dave Cook is a college administrator in Chico, California; and Kim Schmitz makes Wyoming his home. Wayne Merry runs a guide service in the remote northwest corner of British Columbia. Elaine Matthews returned to her old stomping grounds, the Shawangunks, where she manages a climbing gym—and climbs 5.11 overhangs in her spare time. Joe Kelsey guides in Wyoming in the summer and works in the San Francisco Bay Area in winter as a computer programmer. He has written two climbing guides to the Wind River Range of Wyoming. Bob Swift lives in Arizona; Frank Tarver and Scott Davis reside in Seattle. Chuck Kroger lives in Telluride; Dennis Hennek in Hawaii; and John Evans in Evergreen, Colorado. As one can see, very few Camp 4 climbers left the West.

In 1971 Royal Robbins accomplished his last major Valley "first": he guided Johanna Marte, along with her husband, Egon, up the Nose. Marte thus became the first woman ever to get up El Cap, a fine feat, but one tarnished slightly by the fact that she was a nonleading client. A few years later Robbins spent four days alone trying a new route to the right of the NA Wall, but he retreated, his heart not in it. Still residing in Modesto with his wife, Liz, Robbins left the paint store around 1970 and started a successful outdoor clothing business. Later he took up whitewater kayaking, making the first descents of many wild rivers in the Western Hemisphere. His partner on some of these adventures was Yvon Chouinard.

Chouinard and Tom Frost together produced the world's finest mountaineering equipment for a decade; Frost retired in 1975 and now lives in Boulder, Colorado, where he runs a photographic equipment business. Chouinard still operates the original business, now evolved mostly into the Patagonia soft-goods line, but he travels constantly, climbs often, and thinks about retiring.

Layton Kor became a Jehovah's Witness after the death of John Harlin and vanished from the climbing scene for two decades. He recently returned to the rocks again, with much less intensity; he lives on Guam at the moment.

Chuck Pratt guides in the Tetons during the summer and lies indolent on Thailand's beaches in the winter; we all wish he had written more.

Warren Harding still loves his jug of red wine; he now labors on a "climbing soap opera," which apparently will star some highly recognizable characters. He lectures occasionally, still raving about Valley Christians, his stock in trade. At age seventy, he lives in Northern California.

Allen Steck, long since retired from the Ski Hut and from Mountain Travel, which he helped found, climbs whenever he can, and far more proficiently than he once did, though at age sixty-eight he no longer enjoys bivouacs or long approaches. He labors now on his autobiography, having reached 1942 recently.

I gave up big-wall climbing in 1972 and began exploring remote sections of the American West; Yosemite is not the only beautiful place. I later took up flying and had adventures equally as scary and exhilarating as hanging around on El Cap. Though I still do short routes, I find that writing about climbing gives me almost as much pleasure. Almost as much.

The Camp 4 entrance sign, winter 1969 (Photo: Jerry Anderson)

Sources

Listed below are the sources for the quotes that appear in this book, keyed by page. Individual page numbers of these sources are not given; a look at the tables of contents of the various journals will quickly lead the interested reader to the cited article. A distinction is made between an article and a note: the latter, not listed in a journal's table of contents, appears in the California or Yosemite section in the back of a particular journal. Three abbreviations are used below. *AAJ* refers to the annual *American Alpine Journal. SCB* refers to the *Sierra Club Bulletin,* almost always the annual issue, not the monthly number. SR refers to the author.

Epigraphs

6 Borghoff's paean to Yosemite appears in his article in *Summit,* June 1962.

6 Chouinard's view of Valley climbing appears in his first article in the1963 *AAJ.*

Chapter 1

16 The epigraph comes from Robinson's article in the June 1934 *SCB.*

16 Greeley's observations appear in his book *An Overland Journey* (New York: C. M. Saxton, 1860).

16 Muir's "earthly dwelling" comment appears in William Colby's article in the March 1948 *SCB.*

16 Emerson's statement is reported in *A Western Journey with Mr. Emerson,* by J. B. Thayer (Boston: Little, Brown, & Co., 1884).

16 Muir's "overwhelming influence" remark is from his book *My First Summer in the Sierra* (Boston and New York: Houghton Mifflin Co., 1911).

17 Chase's "great cleft" description appears in his book *Yosemite Trails* (New York: Houghton Mifflin Co., 1911).

18 Muir's "harmless scum" and "fifty visitors" comments come from William Colby's article in the March 1948 *SCB.*

22 Leonard's description of the joys of rappelling comes from his article in the February 1940 *SCB.*

23 Leonard's "ineffectual climbing" quote comes from his note in the June 1934 *SCB.*

23 Leonard's "pitons as a direct aid" quote is found in his note in the June 1934 *SCB.*

23 Underhill's assertion about doing climbs unaided comes from his article in the February 1931 *SCB.*

25 Leonard's description of the Flake comes from his note in the February 1935 *SCB.*

25 The evaluation of Dave Brower comes from an unsigned report in Dick Leonard's files; SR has a copy.

26 Meyer's description of Dave Brower comes from his letter to SR, February 23, 1993.

29 Bunn's comment about women comes from his article in the January 1920 *SCB.*

29 Bedayan's remark about women comes from his note in the June 1939 *SCB.*

29 Leonard's statement about Marjory Bridge comes from his note in the February 1935 *SCB.*

29 Lippmann's description of the West Arrowhead Chimney climb comes from his note in the August 1942 *SCB.*

32 Hansen's story about John Salathé on Hunters' Hill comes from his letter to Tom Jukes, dated July 26, 1993.

32 Leonard's "undefined borderline" quote comes from his note in the February 1936 *SCB.*

34 Leonard's two comments about the difficulties of the Lost Arrow appear, respectively, in his notes in the February 1936 *SCB* and the April 1938 *SCB.*

35 Salathé's recollections of his experience on the first pitch of the Arrow were told to Nick Clinch in the early 1950s; Clinch related the story in a letter to SR, February 9, 1994.

36 Thune's comments on the Salathé-Thune attempt come from Thune's unpublished manuscript dated April 21, 1975, a copy of which SR has.

Chapter 2

39 The epigraph comes from Allen Steck's article in the May 1951 *SCB.*

39 Nelson's "unclimbability" quote comes from his article in the March 1948 *SCB.*

40 Leonard's "terrifyingly clear" comment appears in his note in the February 1940 *SCB.*

41 Nelson's view of the fairness of using bolts appears in his article in the March 1948 *SCB.*

41 Nelson's statement about losing weight appears in his article in the March 1948 *SCB.*

42 Nelson's recollection of the "mining" of flakes in the Arrow Chimney comes from his unpublished manuscript dated April 3, 1975, a copy of which is in SR's possession.

42 Nelson's comments on the urge to climb appear in his article in the March 1948 *SCB.*

43 Chase's description of Sentinel Rock comes from his book *Yosemite Trails,* 1911.

45 Most of the quotes on this page and the following ones about the first ascent of the north face of Sentinel appear in Allen Steck's article in the May 1951 *SCB.*

48 The cobra venom story was told to Allen Steck by Dick Leonard on April 1, 1991. Doris Leonard added details in a conversation with SR, March 17, 1994.

48 The outlines of Salathé's life on this and the following pages come from the files of Allen Steck, SR's three personal interviews with him (1963, 1986, 1991), and from city directory files in the San Mateo, California, library.

48 The story of Salathé on the Matterhorn appears in John Thune's unpublished manuscript dated April 21, 1975, a copy of which SR has.

50 Clinch's stories of his halcyon days in the Stanford Alpine Club come from his letter to SR, February 9, 1994.

51 Brower's recollection of the proposed "pole" ascent of the El Cap Tree comes from his note in the December 1952 *SCB.*

51 Steck's commentary about future rock engineers comes from his note in the December 1952 *SCB.*

51 Steck's description of the fog on Yosemite Point Buttress comes from his note in the December 1952 *SCB.*

52 Dunmire's recollections of his accident come from his letter to SR, December 5, 1992.

54 The story of the midnight meeting is related in a letter from Nick Clinch to SR, February 9, 1994.

56 Harding's "brute stupidity" comment comes from an interview that appears in the March 9, 1986, issue of *Image,* the Sunday magazine of the *San Francisco Chronicle.*

57 Tarver's recollections of meeting Harding, climbing Middle Cathedral Rock, and making the Arrow Chimney climb come from his letter to SR, February 2, 1993.

57 Harding's story of paving the Valley floor appears in Bob Swift's article in the April 1955 *SCB.*

58 Wilson's view of bivouacking appears as a note in the June 1957 *SCB.*

59 Powell's warnings about the Arrowhead Arête climb come from his note in the June 1957 *SCB.*

62 Harding's "ambitious dreamer" statement comes from his and Wayne Merry's article in the April 1959 issue of *Argosy* magazine.

62 Sherrick's concerns about publicity come from the November 1958 *SCB.*

Chapter 3

63 The epigraph comes from Wilson's book *The Lore and the Lure of the Yosemite* (San Francisco: Schwabacher-Frey, 1926).

66 Shonle's comments about Warren Harding appear in his letter to SR, February 3, 1993.

66 Harding's comments about tires and wineries appear in an interview in Nicholas O'Connell's book *Beyond Risk* (Seattle: The Mountaineers, 1993).

67 Harding's view of the aesthetics of the El Cap Nose appears in his book *Downward Bound* (Englewood Cliffs, NJ: Prentice Hall, 1975).

71 Harding's description of the traffic jams below El Cap appears in the 1959 *AAJ.*

71 Robbins's explanation of why he declined to join Harding can be found in an interview in *Mountain,* November 1971.

72 Harding's comment about using nylon ropes comes from his article in *Argosy,* April 1959.

73 Harding's dismissal of the Dolt Cart comes from his book *Downward Bound,* 1975.

74 Harding's explanation of why Dolt dropped out of the El Cap climb comes from his book *Downward Bound,* 1975.

76 Harding's story of "conning" climbers appears in the 1959 *AAJ.*

76 Merry's comments about the exposure come from his letter to SR, March 15, 1993.

77 Harding's comment about the ranger enforcement comes from the 1959 *AAJ.*

77 Harding's view of the "monotonous grind" appears in the 1959 *AAJ.*

78 Merry's comment about the naming of the Glowering Spot comes from his letter to SR, March 15, 1993.

79 Calderwood's view of the pressure appears in a story in the *San Francisco Chronicle,* November 12, 1958.

79 Calderwood's comment about his work ethic was made in a phone conversation to SR, April 13, 1993.

80 Harding's comment about Ellen Searby comes from the November 13, 1958 *San Francisco News.*

81 The editorial about global peace appears in the November 13, 1958 *San Francisco News.*

81 The quote about stamina and courage appears in an editorial in the *Oregon Journal,* November 15, 1958.

82 Wirth's statement about stunt climbing is reported in Doug Scott's *Big Wall Climbing,* 1974.

Chapter 4

83 The epigraph comes from Sessions's letter to the editor in *Summit,* April 1958.

85 Powell's comparison of his route on Middle Cathedral Rock to Sentinel comes from his note in the October 1959 *SCB.*

Chapter 5

Chapter 6

134 Amborn's view of competition appears in his letter to the editor in *Summit,* September 1963.

137 Robbins's "Mozart" comment comes from his article in *Summit,* March 1963.

139 Chouinard's description of the Quarter Domes route comes from a letter to SR, December 1962.

140 Cooper's remarks on competition come from his article in the 1963 *AAJ.*

141 Denny's summit impressions appear in a letter to SR, November 29, 1962.

141 Robbins's characterization of Harding comes from an interview in *Mountain,* November 1971.

141 Robbins's views on first continuous ascents appear in a letter to SR, December 22, 1962.

142 Denny's thoughts on Macdonald appear in a letter to SR, January 15, 1963.

Chapter 7

145 The quote about the dark side of the Vulgarians comes from Ted E. Kirchner's letter to the editor in *Climbing,* December 1993.

150 Sims's story of the Leaning Tower Traverse was related in his letter to SR, February 22, 1994.

150 Cook's two stories come from 1993 E-mail communications with SR.

151 Borghoff's comments appear in his letter to SR, August 15, 1963.

151 Borghoff's "salamander" descriptions come from his article in *Summit,* June 1962.

155 Father Murphy's comments come from his letter to Al Macdonald, January 16, 1960.

156 Borghoff's description of the Camp 4 bears comes from his article in *Summit,* June 1962.

156 Cook's story of the Empire Builder comes from an E-mail communication to SR, March 27, 1993.

158 Morton's story of the Alps comes from an E-mail communication to SR, September 23, 1993.

158 Chouinard's comment about sex comes from his letter to SR, December 1962.

159 Borghoff's rave about Tri-Delts comes from an unpublished manuscript in the possession of SR, dated January 31, 1975.

161 The four limericks, with subtle variations, have been passed down orally through the years. The chief custodians: Eric Beck, John Morton, and Jeff Dozier.

162 Parckel's view of climbers appears in his letter to SR, June 1963.

162 Herbert's Sentinel bivouac story was told to SR by Galen Rowell, February 16, 1994.

163 Herbert's "wake up and listen" story is related by Don Lauria in his note in the 1971 *AAJ.*

165 Komito's two comments come from letters to SR, dated, respectively, January 6, 1964 and August 7, 1964.

Chapter 8

166 The epigraph comes from Pratt's letter to SR, March 18, 1965.

167 Leonard's reflections about the AAC come from his letter to Galen Rowell, June 25, 1972.

167 Carter's musings about the California climbers come from his letter to SR, March 1, 1994.

167 Chouinard's views on his article appear in his letter to SR, December 7, 1962.

167 Chouinard's several comments about the Valley come from his article in the 1963 *AAJ.*

171 Robbins's remark about sticking to the decimal system is quoted in a letter from Orrin Bonney to the American Alpine Club Council, May 1, 1963.

171 Robbins's quote about Ortenburger's plan comes from a manifesto, dated March 15, 1963, that he sent to many people, including SR.

172 Ortenburger's view of the independence of climbers appears in his undated (but undoubtedly early 1963) circular mailed to numerous people, including SR.

173 Robbins's remarks about his "transgression" come from a letter to SR, March 7, 1994.

173 Borghoff's view of Galen Rowell appears in his letter to SR, April 19, 1964.

174 Robbins's comment about sloppy climbing comes from his note in *Summit,* April 1964.

174 Robbins's remark about claiming the prize comes from a note to SR, January 13, 1994.

175 Robbins's comment about the stimulating experience comes from his article in the 1964 *AAJ.*

175 McCarthy's evaluation of Robbins and Kor appears in his article in the 1964 *AAJ.*

176 Foott's recollection of his Patio climb comes from a phone interview with SR, October 27, 1993.

178 Robbins's comments about the hangers come from his letter to SR, August 9, 1964.

179 Robbins's view of Ed Cooper's integrity appears as a note in the 1965 *AAJ.*

179 All quotes by John Evans come from his diary entries, June 18 through June 22, 1964.

180 Baldwin's comments on his wretchedness come from his letter to SR, April 18, 1964.

180 Pratt's several witticisms about the Ribbon climb come from his note in the 1965 *AAJ.*

181 Pratt's rave on Ribbon is reported by Allen Steck in his article in the 1967 *Ascent.*

181 Leonard's comment about direct aid on the Higher Spire comes from his note in the February 1941 *SCB.*

182 Kor's trepidation about climbing with Sacherer appears in his letter to SR, December 30, 1964.

182 Chouinard's comments about Sacherer come from his article in the 1970 *AAJ.*

182 Morton's story of the dropped piton comes from an E-mail communication to SR, May 18, 1993.

183 The story of Sacherer's grades is related in a letter from Jan Sacherer to SR, November 7, 1993.

184 Steck's recollection of Terray in Yosemite comes from his letter to SR, July 22, 1964.

185 Beck's view of Sheridan Anderson appears in his letter to SR, May 1964.

186 Robbins's characterization of Pratt, Harding, and Chouinard comes from his note in *Summit,* January/February 1969.

Chapter 9

189 The epigraph comes from Chouinard's article in the 1966 *AAJ.*

190 Robbins's comment on fixed ropes comes from his article in the 1965 *AAJ.*

192 Robbins's view of the difficulties on the NA Wall appears in his letter to SR, December 12, 1964.

192 Robbins's thoughts about the "chilling specter" appear in his article in the 1965 *AAJ.*

192 Robbins's comment about decay and death comes from his article in the 1968 *Ascent.*

192 Robbins's comment on why he writes is from his letter to SR, February 15, 1994.

192 Kelsey's spoof of Robbins comes from his article in *Summit,* April 1970.

194 Chouinard's various descriptions of the Muir Wall climb come from his article in the 1966 *AAJ.*

195 Beck's comment about Jim Bridwell's "boys" comes from his letter to SR, May 1965.

195 Pratt's mention of Jim Bridwell's "puppets" comes from his letter to SR, August 8, 1965.

196 Pratt related the Chuck Ostin/Sentinel story to SR in 1961.

197 Beck's brag about Sentinel comes from his letter to SR, May 19, 1965.

198 Kamps's comment about bolts comes from his article in *Summit,* July/August 1965.

198 Higgins's views of Valley climbing appear in his letter to the editor in *Summit,* September 1965.

198 Powell's view of Higgins appears in his letter to SR, June 18, 1964.

199 Robbins's view of tolerance appears as a note in *Summit,* October 1965.

199 Kilness's plea comes from her letter to SR, December 9, 1965.

199 Robbins's comment on "pilgrims of the vertical" comes from his note in *Summit,* June 1968.

200 Robbins's recommendation of El Cap's west face comes from his article in the 1968 *AAJ.*

201 Robbins's comment about attitudes comes from his note in *Summit,* June 1968.

201 Robbins's views on pre-fixing pitches on El Cap appear in an interview in *Mountain,* January 1973.

203 Robbins's comment about Madsen appears in his note in *Summit,* October 1968.

204 Lauria's witticism about the Dihedral climb comes from his article in *Summit,* September 1968.

204 Lauria's comments on "Mutt and Jeff" appear in his article in *Summit,* September 1966.

207 Robbins's mention of foreigners comes from his note in *Summit,* January/February 1966.

207 Robbins's bullfighting comparison comes from his letter to SR, June 17, 1966.

207 Pratt's view of British talent appears as a note in the 1967 *AAJ.*

207 Pratt's comment about the end of an era is quoted by Royal Robbins in his note in *Summit,* March 1967.

208 Robbins's comment about Ed Drummond's attitude comes from Drummond's article in *Summit,* April 1969.

208 Drummond's description of his knees comes from his article in *Summit,* April 1969.

208 Smaill's comments about the Salathé Wall come from his article in the 1970 *Canadian Alpine Journal.*

209 Rowell's bolting percentage quote comes from his article in *Summit,* May 1969.

210 Robbins's views of soloing appear in his article in the 1969 *AAJ.*

210 Robbins's three comments on his travails on the Muir Wall come from his article in *Summit,* March 1969.

Chapter 10

211 The epigraph comes from McCarthy's article in *Summit,* November/December 1971.

211 Robbins's remark about camping comes from his note in *Summit,* July/August 1970.

212 McCarthy's view of climbing schools appears in his article in *Summit,* November/December 1971.

212 Leeper's view of commercialism appears in his letter to the editor in *Summit,* January/February 1971.

212 Rowell's limerick appears in *Vulgarian Digest,* Fall 1970.

212 Graber's comment about trash comes from his letter to the editor in *Summit,* January/February 1972.

213 Robbins's warning about future visits to the Valley comes from his note in *Summit,* July/August 1970.

214 Robbins's view of nuts is reported by Anthony Greenbank in his article in *Summit,* May/June 1965.

214 Robbins's comment about learning from the British comes from his letter to SR, June 17, 1966.

214 Robbins's disclosure of his underestimation of nuts comes from his article in *Summit,* May 1967.

215 Robbins's description of Boulderfield Gorge comes from his article in *Summit,* May 1967.

219 Herbert's view of Robbins's downfall is reported in Robbins's article in *Summit,* July/August 1970.

219 Robbins's first two characterizations of Don Peterson come from his article in the 1970 *AAJ*. The nree quotes come from his article in the 1970 *Ascent*.
221 Robbins's description of the blankness of Tis-sa-ack comes from a phone interview with SR, January 11, 1994.
222 Robbins's rebuttal about solo climbing comes from his article in the 1971 *AAJ*.
222 Matthew's views on being a woman climber come from her letter to SR, January 21, 1994.
223 Robbins's comment about faddists comes from his note in *Summit,* November 1970.
224 Kroger's comment on the "circus" comes from his article in the 1971 *AAJ*.
224 Davis's description of the falling flake comes from a letter to SR, March 14, 1994.
225 Kroger's comments on the Heart climb come from his article in *Climbing,* January 1971.
225 Davis's views of the earlier generation come from his letter to SR, March 7, 1994.
228 Harding's description of body odor and reason for climbing both come from a story in the *San Francisco Chronicle,* November 19, 1970.
228 The bull image comes from Thomas L. P. Davies's letter to the editor in the *San Francisco Chronicle,* November 19, 1970.
228 Adams's view of the Dawn Wall climb appears in his letter to the editor in the *San Francisco Chronicle,* December 1, 1970.
229 Harding's comments on Caldwell and making money both come from a story in the *San Francisco Chronicle,* November 19, 1970.
229 Harding's undated (but undoubtedly 1971) "To Whom It May Concern" letter is in SR's possession.
229 Robbins's appraisal of Harding comes from his note in *Summit,* December 1970.
229 Robbins's explanation for the "erasure" comes from an interview in *Mountain,* January 1973.
229 Lauria's comment about castration appears in Harding's book *Downward Bound,* 1975.
230 Robbins's view of the Dawn Wall as contrived appears as a note in *Summit,* April 1971.
230 Robbins's comment about hard nailing comes from an interview in *Mountain,* November 1971.
230 Herbert's statement about the Dawn Wall "erasure" comes from his note in the 1971 *AAJ*.
230 Harding's comment about Robbins's motives comes from his letter to the editor in *Mountain,* November 1971.
230 Rowell's views of the future of Valley climbing appear in his article in *Climbing,* May/June 1971.
230 Wilson's observations about the Dawn Wall and Harding come from his editorial in *Mountain,* May 1971.
230 Harding's characterizations of Robbins, Chouinard, and SR come from his book *Downward Bound,* 1975.
230 Robbins's review of *Downward Bound* appears in *Mountain Gazette,* May 1975.

Epilogue

233 The epigraph comes from Salathé's letter to Allen Steck, September 8, 1974.
235 Rowell's doubts about pitonless ascents appear in his book review of the Chouinard catalog in the 1973 *AAJ*.

Index

About the Author

Steve Roper, veteran of more than 400 climbs in Yosemite Valley, including repeats, enjoys the unusual distinction of being both a successful climber and an accomplished writer. With Allen Steck he wrote *Fifty Classic Climbs of North America;* the two have also been co-editors of the highly regarded magazine/book *Ascent* since its inception in 1967. Roper has also written many articles and several guidebooks, including two editions of the *Climber's Guide to Yosemite Valley.*

(Photo: John Morton)

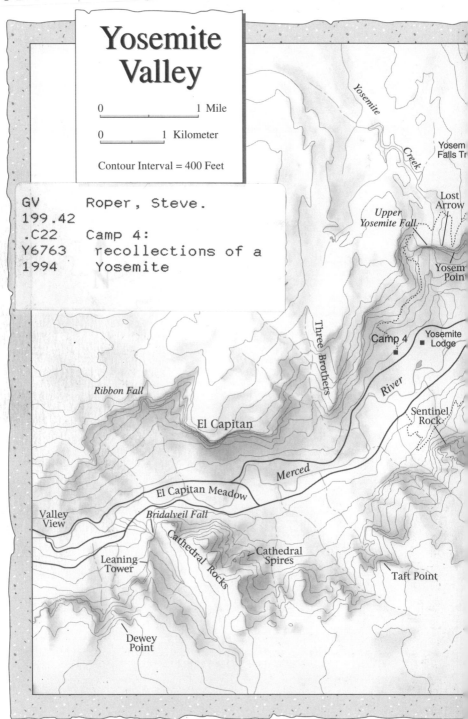

Yosemite Valley

0 ——————— 1 Mile

0 ———————— 1 Kilometer

Contour Interval = 400 Feet

Yosemite Creek

Yosem
Falls Tr

Lost
Arrow

Upper
Yosemite Fall

Yosem
Poin

Three Brothers

Camp 4   Yosemite
          Lodge

Ribbon Fall

River

El Capitan

Sentinel
Rock

Merced

El Capitan Meadow

Valley
View

Bridalveil Fall

Cathedral Rocks

Cathedral
Spires

Leaning
Tower

Taft Point

Dewey
Point

Matt Kania